MW00649137

BEHOLD

I MAKE ALL THINGS NEW

BEHOLD

I MAKE ALL THINGS NEW

How Judaism, Christianity and Islam affirm
the dignity of queer identities and sexualities

Introduced by
DEVDUTT PATTANAIK

Edited by
REV'D J.P. MOKGETHI-HEATH
REV'D LORAINE TULLEKEN

Contributors

Riffat Hassan
Rabbi Jay Michaelson
Rev'd Rowland 'Jide' Macaulay
Imam Ludovic-Muhamed Zahed

HarperCollins *Publishers* India

First published in India by
HarperCollins *Publishers* in 2020
A-75, Sector 57, Noida, Uttar Pradesh 201301, India
www.harpercollins.co.in

2 4 6 8 10 9 7 5 3 1

P-ISBN: 978-93-5357-455-0
E-ISBN: 978-93-5357-456-7

Typeset in 11/16 Garamond
Manipal Technology Limited, Manipal

Printed and bound at
Thomson Press (India) Ltd

'... *and since love is what makes us human and gives us life*
these men and women are callous and cold, cruel and cowardly
though they wear
the masks of sages and madonnas and cherubs;
and they are always ready to strike my eternal heart because
I dare to live and love.'

— Riffat Hassan

Contents

Foreword   ix

Editor's Note   xiii

Definitions   xix

Preface   xxiii

About the Authors and Stakeholders   xxxiii

1. Introduction   1

2. In the Name of God: A Letter to Muslims,
    Jews and Christians   11

3. A Jewish Perspective   63

4. A Christian Perspective   147

5. A Muslim Perspective   203

    Notes   265

    Index   291

Foreword

The Uppsala Festival of Theology is an event that has brought together lay and ordained people from across Sweden and many visitors from around the world. It has grown since its inception eight years ago to be a space for lively and engaging discussion, debate and discourse.

The 2015 event, themed 'Behold, I Make All Things New', included a number of key streams of which 'Human Dignity and Human Sexuality' was one that the Church of Sweden International Department engaged in, and that involved interfaith dialogue between the three Abrahamic faiths.

With a more than 150-year history in international development work, the Church of Sweden has worked in many interfaith environments. It is clear to us that the protection of human dignity through human rights is a critical element of personal, social, national and international development. Interfaith dialogue becomes a crucial tool to explore together how our different faiths approach important aspects of our being human and of living in community.

Within the Church of Sweden, self-awareness and the understanding of human sexuality has been a journey over many decades, and to host an interfaith dialogue on this topic was indeed a privilege. The dialogue at the Festival of Theology generated so much interest that we decided to present and share its outcomes in the form of an anthology. As such it is intended as a contribution to an evolving conversation about human dignity and human sexuality, as well as a model that could be used for interfaith engagement in this area.

As you work through the separate sections of this book you will find, as we so frequently do, that people of different faiths hold much more in common than what divides us. As with every other part of what it means to be human, our sexuality is a beautiful gift from God. The contributors to this current exploration through sacred texts uncover the ways in which sexuality in its diversity is affirmed. They also look to how culture has played a role in moulding the way in which we interpret and apply some of the historical understandings that have been held in the Abrahamic faiths on this topic.

This book does not pretend to be a declaration on human sexuality for Judaism, Christianity and Islam. Rather, it offers readers a window into the complexity of the issues, with the assurance that not everything is black and white. We hope that it will be read by people who are questioning themselves and their own sexuality, as well as by people who seek to find tools to explore human dignity and human sexuality more deeply. Above all, we hope that this book offers the reader the assurance that sexuality is integral to being human, and that our all-loving Creator is a God of mercy, love and compassion. One who creates us in perfection and celebrates who we are.

I offer here my thanks to those who have contributed to this anthology, both through their writings and in other ways. We are very proud that we have been able to produce it collaboratively with the Global Interfaith Network for people of all sexes, sexual orientation, gender identity and expression (GIN-SSOGIE). We are delighted and grateful that they were able to provide us with the crucial resource people to attend the Uppsala Festival of Theology and with those who subsequently contributed to this book.

The opinions expressed in this anthology are those of the authors and do not necessarily reflect the views of the Church of Sweden, the Church of Sweden International Department or GIN-SSOGIE. May it feed your faith, assure you of God's love, and challenge you to think more deeply on issues which touch every human being deeply.

The Reverend Dr Gunilla Hallonsten
Director, International Affairs
Church of Sweden International Department
Trinity Tide 2016

Editor's Note

Patriarchy remains pervasive, more so in the reading and interpretation of our sacred texts. Men are ascribed more value than women – the more 'manly', the more power. The major intersections between patriarchy and sexuality are two-fold. Firstly, the one who is penetrated has less value than the one who penetrates, and this plays out in language within the lesbian, gay, bisexual, transgender and intersex (LGBTI) community, such as 'no fems, straight acting'. Secondly, in the gender fluidity made possible by men and women accepting and adopting the opposite role, they either relinquish or acquire power. This threatens patriarchy and attempts are made to apply heteronormative patriarchal language and models. A good example is: 'So, who's the man and who's the woman?' The lived life experience, the suffering this has caused women as well as LGBTI people, is the point of departure for this book.

Sacred texts have been and continue to be read through the hermeneutical lens of gender hierarchies. Adam was created first. Eve was made to be his helper, not his equal – a simplistic view easily challenged with a deeper reading.

Ad'am, a gender-neutral word in Hebrew, means Earth creature or made from the earth, ad'amah. Likewise, where most translations speak of Eve's creation from Adam's rib, the

Hebrew word for rib – ala – is nowhere to be found in this text from Genesis. Rather, the word tsela, or side, is used. Likewise, Eve is created to be Adam's helpmate. Yet the Hebrew word for helpmate, ezer keegdo, is used about God when God intervenes to save. So, it is possible and very reasonable to see Eve as somebody who stands up to Adam, to be his companion and his equal. In the Hebrew-Christian tradition, man was created first and claims superiority; a gender hierarchy is established. Although the Qur'an describes the creation of man and woman as simultaneous, within Islam too, man has been seen as superior. Yet, in the first Creation story, placed at the beginning of the Hebrew Bible, the human being was created last and in the image of God, as male and female. (Genesis 1:27)

Today there are many interpretations of gender and sexuality. Gender fluidity is one notion. New voices have reverted to more egalitarian interpretations. It is, however, important to be aware that various hermeneutical lenses have competed from the very beginning. Nothing can be said to be orthodox without a close relationship to what is labelled heretic.

In this book we want to encourage a spiritual reading of sacred texts from the Abrahamic faith traditions. This is not against dogma, or sometimes even literal readings, but an attempt to read without patriarchal lenses, to take suffering and experiences seriously. As the Church of Sweden is one of many churches internationally to have taken the decision to marry same-sex couples, this is a natural initiative, which draws on personal experiences of liberation that have opened up deep spirituality, beyond ideologies of the sacred family or hierarchies.

It also draws from the Uppsala Festival of Theology stream on human dignity and human sexuality, developed in collaboration with the Reverend Dr Anna Karin Hammar, and supported by the dioceses of Uppsala, Stockholm, Strängnäs and Västerås. The Global Interfaith Network for people of all sexes, sexual orientation, gender identity and expression (GIN-SSOGIE) identified member-theologians to reflect on their sacred texts, informed by their theological training and their lived experience.

We planned a dialogue ahead of the Festival of Theology that included people who were both affirming of the diversity of human sexuality and those who found this more challenging. Instead of simply 'preaching to the choir' we wanted to achieve meaningful engagement.

To stimulate the dialogue our GIN theologians were asked to prepare resource packs. What followed were three of the most amazing days of my life. With sharp minds and hearts ablaze with passion, we engaged on some of the hidden understandings and histories related to sexual orientation and the Abrahamic faiths.

It soon became clear that we had not just material to stimulate dialogue; it needed to be compiled and published as a book. Anna Karin Hammar again came to the fore, with the idea of approaching a highly respected Muslim scholar who could draw these texts into a seamless whole. What started as a draft statement ended as a thirty-page letter from Professor Riffat Hassan.

Passion was definitely not a missing ingredient!

While I had worked on previous books and training materials, I had never been involved in something this complex. A skilled editor was needed. In 2001, a year after I had tested HIV+, I was introduced to a dynamic priest from the diocese of Johannesburg. At the time Loraine Tulleken was working as Archbishop Njongonkulu Ndu-ngane's public relations and media consultant. Her skill, energy and commitment to equality made a deep impression. With her agreement to shape and jointly edit this book, we finally had all the ingredients for a critical and engaging publication.

The Church of Sweden's publishing team has been remarkable, and the support they offered me, working in the International Department, is deeply appreciated. Always encouraging, always forgiving, they have taken tough deadlines and made them possible. A special word of thanks to them. Of course, none of this would have been remotely possible without the deep commitment to acknowledge and support the human dignity of every person, which is at the core of the Church of Sweden's developmental work. It has allowed us the space and finance for the book.

To the Church, those mentioned above and others too numerous to include, I say a huge thank you. I pray that our combined efforts will lead you, the reader, to cherish every human you encounter, regardless of marginalizing facts. Within them the breath of God has kindled life, and within each of you, that life-giving, life-affirming Spirit calls us to live and love.

The Reverend J.P. Mokgethi-Heath
Policy Advisor on HIV and Theology for the Church of Sweden

Definitions

Presuming that many readers will opt to refer to the information provided for their specific religious belief, we have kept the writings for the Abrahamic faiths separate. But the following definitions apply within the contributions for all three.

Sexual orientation is an individual's enduring romantic, emotional or sexual attraction towards other persons. For example, heterosexual, bisexual and homosexual orientation ranges from exclusively heterosexual to exclusive homosexuality.

Gender identity is one's sense of self as a woman, man or transgender. This may or may not conform to the person's biological sex.

Gender expression is the outward expression of gender by, for example, behaviour, clothing, hairstyle, voice and body language. In this book we predominantly speak of LGBT and LGBTI, but other related acronyms are LGBTIQ, SOGI or SSOGIE.

LGBT and **LGBTI** are people who define themselves as lesbian, gay, bisexual, transgender or intersex. It is a self-referential category.

Lesbian is a woman whose enduring physical, romantic, emotional and/or spiritual attraction is to other women. This does not imply any same-sex sexual expression or activity.

Gay describes people (e.g., gay man, gay people) whose enduring physical, romantic, emotional and/or spiritual attractions are to people of the same sex. In contemporary contexts, lesbian is often a preferred term for women and gay for men. Again, this does not imply any same-sex sexual expression or activity.

Bisexual is an individual who is physically, romantically, emotionally and/or spiritually attracted to both men and women. A bisexual person may be more attracted to one sex than another and this may vary over time. This does not imply physical or sexual expressions with people of both or either gender, neither does it imply multiple relationships.

Trans, transgender, transsexual and **transvestite** are umbrella terms for people whose gender identity or gender expression differs from the sex they were assigned at birth. It may include but is not limited to: transsexuals, cross-dressers and other gender-variant people. Transgender people may identify as female-to-male (FTM) or male-to-female (MTF), and may or may not decide to alter their bodies hormonally or surgically.

Intersex (previously known as **hermaphrodites**) is an individual who has atypical development of physical sex attributes. These may include but are not limited to external genitals that are not easily classified as male or female. Or there may be incomplete development of internal reproductive organs. Some intersex characteristics are recognized at birth. Others are delayed until puberty. The term 'disorders of sexual development' (DSD) often refers to intersex conditions. In the case of LGBTIQ, the 'Q' refers to 'queer' or 'questioning'.

Queer is a political term for all of sexuality outside of heterosexuality. It is often self-selected by those who either object to or prefer a non-gender-specific term such as gay and lesbian. The term has also been used to qualify those who go against normal convention, so it is not necessarily attached to sexual orientation and/or gender identity.

Questioning refers to a state of being unsure of your true sexual identity but being willing to examine what it may be. This does not imply sexual expression or experimentation.

SOGI means sexual orientation and gender identity. For a deeper understanding of SOGI, please refer to the 'Genderbread person'.

SSOGIE is a particular definition used by the Global Interfaith Network (GIN) for people of all sexes, sexual orientation, gender identity and expression.

Preface

*The Reverend Loraine Tulleken and
Reverend J.P. Mokgethi-Heath*

In February 2015, as more than 1,100 participants in the Fourth Uppsala Festival of Theology converged on the university city, there was a warm sense of expectancy, despite a chilling winter temperature of –2°C. Their optimism was well warranted. The biennial event had, since 2008, gone from strength to strength.

Convened by the diocese of Uppsala (Church of Sweden) and held at the University of Uppsala, the festivals are open to people of different faiths and backgrounds. They include theologians, laity, professionals, social activists, parish workers, scientists and others interested in the survival of the earth and issues relating to humanity. In 2015, the festival was jointly sponsored by the dioceses of Stockholm, Strängnäs, Uppsala and Västerås.

For one group of distinguished scholars, eminent theologians, facilitators, activists and delegates, the theme, 'Behold, I Make All Things New', was of particular significance. For the first time, there would be a public panel discussion on 'Human Dignity and Human Sexuality'. It was one of the only two English streams and supported jointly by the Festival of Theology, the Church of Sweden's International Department and the Global Interfaith Network, better known as GIN. The objective was to critically examine what the sacred texts of the Abrahamic faiths – Judaism, Christianity and Islam – say regarding human sexuality; more specifically, how those texts and the religious practices of Jews, Christians and Muslims respond to sexual orientation and gender identity (SOGI).

The stream needed careful preplanning. In the run-up to the festival, theologians in each of the faiths were asked to develop resource packs to stimulate discussion. The format was to be specifically designed to deal with arguments used to discriminate against lesbian, gay, bisexual, transgender or intersex (LGBTI) people in the Abrahamic faith communities: 'it's not in our culture; it's not natural; and it's not scriptural'. The authors were also challenged to offer a new way of looking at human sexuality through the eyes of faith. Those packs and subsequent input are the basis for this anthology.

The first challenge in getting the Human Dignity and Human Sexuality stream accepted for the festival was to approach it from an interfaith perspective. Imam Hashim Jansen was invited to speak to Archbishop Emeritus Anders Wejryd, who was easily convinced of the need to approach the topic from an Abrahamic faith perspective. A team was put together to develop the individual faith responses. The key was to have members of GIN-SSOGIE compile the resource packs, to ensure that they were constructed from individual lived faith experiences for people with diverse SOGIs.

Three writers were invited to Uppsala for the initial discussions and planning. These were Jacq Carver, a Jewish woman from Netherlands; Reverend Jide Macaulay, a Nigerian living and working in the UK; and Imam Hashim Jansen, also working in the Netherlands.

Imam Jansen had indicated from the beginning that he would develop the Islamic resource pack in conjunction with Imam Ludovic Zahed. When he fell ill, Imam Zahed accepted the challenge on his own. Similarly, Jacq Carver suffered a stroke soon after the ILGA (International Lesbian and Gay Association) meeting in October 2014. Rabbi Amichai Lau-Lavie, a member of GIN-SSOGIE, who attended the Festival of Theology, referred the planning committee to renowned author and LGBTI activist Rabbi Jay Michaelson in the USA. He, in turn, generously shared material from his acclaimed book *God vs Gay*.

The festival organizers were acutely aware that though the new stream was exciting and long overdue, there were no guarantees that it would work. Was it realistic to attempt to draw theologians and activists into a reasoned discussion on LGBTI matters? Could the liberals and conservatives emerge from their corners of diversity to listen to each other? Could the three Abrahamic faiths find common ground on issues that have left them bruised and divided within their own ranks? Moreover, was it possible to reach deep into the Torah, the Bible and the Qur'an to find a shared theological thread? What of the Talmud and the Hadith? Did they shed any useful light on interpretation?

Indeed, all this would prove more than possible!

Distinguished theologians and religious leaders from the Abrahamic faiths were invited to participate in a three-day dialogue before the Festival's open panel discussion on 7 February 2015. Notably, the main event would involve people of both heterosexual and homosexual orientation. This was principally to ensure that participants would talk *to* each other, not *about* each other. Moreover, throughout the process the Church of Sweden, despite its predominantly liberal approach, was determined not to impose its perspective on LGBTI issues.

Two eminent people were invited to moderate the session, His Grace, Archbishop Emeritus Anders Wejryd, the World Council of Churches (WCC) European president, and Dr Riffat Hassan, a Pakistani-American professor of Islamic studies.

In his opening address Anders Wejryd stressed the significance of engaging in dialogue because the human rights of sexual minorities around the world are suppressed, and such suppression is often sanctioned by religious communities.

He spoke of how, against the backdrop of strong taboos, sexual minorities often do not know their rights and cannot speak for themselves. Others have not been able to speak for them. 'But,' he assured, 'we now live in a wonderful time when many theologians are going back to the old scriptures, seeking words that speak of the rights of sexual minorities.'

Dr Hassan, with forty years' experience in developing and teaching feminist theology from a Muslim perspective, was also charged with developing a letter that could open doors to dialogue. She put forward two key arguments for engagement;

the first was the nature of God, and the second was that sacred texts had been interpreted by men within a patriarchal setting. For an authentic reading of sacred texts this needed to be acknowledged, and the voices of both women and LGBTI people needed to be heard in terms of their context and understanding. Within this, the clear guideline was that our interpretation of our sacred texts must be authentic to the nature of God.

As she pointed out, 113 of the 114 Surahs, or chapters of the Qur'an, start with the words: *In the Name of God, the Most Merciful and Gracious, the Most Compassionate and the Dispenser of Grace.* Muslims recite this at the beginning of any important event in their daily lives. It is the key nature of God. Any interpretation of, or action leading from an interpretation of, the Qur'an that does not reflect this must be seen as incorrect.

This, she posited, was not unique to Islam. The merciful and compassionate nature of God is also repeated, over and over again, both in the Torah and the New Testament. Of clear importance in the festival engagement was the general understanding of sexuality and marriage that the various Abrahamic faiths hold. Professor Hassan said though there is a very strong affirmation of both topics within Judaism and Islam, this is not the case within Christianity. So, she hypothesized that much of the current negativity about human sexuality has effectively come into Judaism and Islam from Christianity.

Much of this is related to doctrinal teaching by the likes of St Augustine and even the leaders of the Reformation. In early Christianity, celibacy and the monastic life were seen as the highest state of spiritual awareness. Not surprisingly, the father of the Lutheran church, a former Augustinian monk who married a nun, would say, 'No matter what praise I give to marriage, I will not concede that it is no sin.'

The three-day pre-festival discussions were hosted by the Lutheran Diocese of Uppsala. The participants felt that an ongoing dialogue, which included both an interfaith component as well as the voices of all affected, was critical. This was affirmed in the following statement that they all signed:

Uppsala Abrahamic Faith Statement on Human Dignity and Human Sexuality

We, a group of Jewish, Christian and Muslim theologians met during the 4th Uppsala Festival of Theology from the 4th to 8th of February 2015. We believe that God is merciful, compassionate and just and has breathed the divine spirit into us to become stewards of the world, to care for the earth and to care for each other; and has endowed each person with worth and dignity that human judgement cannot set aside.

We engaged in communal worship and spiritual practice to create a bond within our diversity and to open our hearts, minds and spirit and to lead us into life.

We conducted the dialogue in ways that affirmed the values of our common humanity and our faiths.

We created a space that was safe for people to be who they are and share their stories. We found our witnessing of stories of pain and exclusion of lesbian, gay, bisexual, transgendered and intersex people a valuable and necessary experience for next steps of repairing a suffering and broken world.

We felt greatly deepened and enriched by this interfaith dialogue. It created for us a renewed sense of responsibility and accountability, and instilled a sense of urgency to create safe spaces in our communities and in our world. Hence, we call for the dialogue to be continued and expanded within and between our faith communities and the wider society.

The statement was initially signed by: Prof Amina Wadud, Rabbi Amy Klein, Geronimo de Ocampo Desumala III, Reverend Jan Bjarne Sødal, Mr Mirza Aslam Beg, Prof. Riffat Hassan, Reverend Jide Macaulay, Mohamed Farid, Amichai Lau Lavie, Reverend Michael Schuenemeyer, Reverend Audrey Hick, Bishop Stephen Ismail Munga, Archbishop Thabo Makgoba, Archbishop Emeritus Anders Wejryd, Reverend Anna-Karin Hammar and Reverend J.P. Mokgethi-Heath. Most of the seventy participants to the Human Dignity and Human Sexuality stream later affirmed this statement by signing it as well.

The meeting was held under Chatham House rules, allowing opinions to be expressed without fear of retaliation or retribution. What emerged was a deep respect among all participants and a dialogue that shaped the contributions in the plenary session. This, in turn, led to deep and meaningful participation within the particular stream.

Ultimately the Uppsala 2015 Human Dignity and Human Sexuality panel discussion would reveal that human dignity and human sexuality are not mutually exclusive. As Archbishop Emeritus Anders Wejryd concluded, it had emphasized the significance of engaging on this topic: 'In our meeting we had good conversations. We did not always reach the same conclusion, but we acknowledged each other's conclusions.'

The miracle of the entire exercise was the opening of a global door to a new theological approach. It was mutually accepted among conservatives and liberals alike that ours is a God of love and compassion. Off this sound base, the pre-festival dialogue and subsequent public panel discussion quickly evolved from pure theory into the realm of practicality. Within months of the festival, this anthology, aimed at theologians and a broader audience, was commissioned. This could not have happened without the appropriate groundwork.

The resource packs and the preliminary interaction were integral to the historic festival panel discussions. Overall, the outcomes were so encouraging and too important not to share. Within a month of the festival, this anthology had been commissioned for global distribution.

The final piece in the puzzle of putting this together as a book was a letter developed by Prof Riffat Hassan in preparation for the Festival of Theology. It frames this anthology, just as it did the Uppsala discussions. The outcomes of the dialogue also powerfully underpinned the official launch of GIN. There were soon plans for a dialogue in India around the sacred texts of Hinduism, Buddhism, Sikhism and Jainism. Moreover, the Church of Sweden International Department has affirmed its ongoing commitment to supporting future dialogue.

Of course, there is still a long, hard road to travel.

As Anglican Archbishop Thabo Makgoba reported to his constituency, 'I travelled to Sweden, where I took part in the Uppsala Festival of Theology. The main reason I was there was to join an international interfaith panel to discuss human dignity in relation to sexual orientation and gender identity. On the panel, Jewish, Muslim and Christian scholars and practitioners shared rich insights on a deeply challenging issue facing people of faith. The debate resonated with me especially because the Synod of Bishops (Anglican Church of Southern Africa) had just agreed to ask all dioceses to consider in the months ahead a set of draft pastoral guidelines regarding civil unions in our Province.

'Both in our own church, and again in Uppsala, I have said that this is a sensitive issue, which calls for patience and tolerance as we seek to discern God's will for the way ahead. Our Province has shown the Anglican Communion in the past that we can hold together as we work through potentially divisive issues, and I pray that we can set an example to the world again on this matter.'

It should be noted that Africa is home to some of the most conservative legislation in the world including the death penalty for homosexuality. Moreover, though South Africa permits same-sex marriages, Archbishop Makgoba's flock is deeply divided over most LGBT issues.

The main chapters in this anthology are based on the resource packs developed for the festival. It must be noted that the anthology has not been peer-reviewed, as would be the case for an academic publication. The character of the chapters vary; some are more based on personal experiences than others. We pray it will prove a useful resource for faith leaders, theologians, activists, the LGBTI community and many others across a broad spectrum. May it offer courage, comfort and assurances that our God does make all things new.

About the Authors and Stakeholders

Reverend Loraine Tulleken

While others will surely carry the baton for the historic 'Human Dignity and Human Sexuality' stream, that first event was very much the sum of its contributors. Primarily, the Church of Sweden, GIN and the theologians who put an inordinate amount of time, effort and thought into the resource packs. There was also Professor Riffat Hassan who developed the letter on feminist theology.

We need to approach these contributors with healthy suspicion. Who are they? What is their agenda? Can we trust their motives? Can the questioning laity quote them with confidence? An entire book could be written on each of the imminent authors and stakeholders. Historiography, or the study of the writing of history, teaches us that it is impossible to reflect on history without bringing who we are to it. A transparent approach is to declare beforehand who the author is and in which way their own person may influence their writing of history. The same, of course, and probably more so, is true for an anthology like this one. Hopefully, what follows is sufficient to inspire confidence in those who are looking for answers and resources.

The Church of Sweden

On 22 October 2009, the General Synod of the Church of Sweden voted 176–62 in favour of allowing its priests to wed same-sex couples in new gender-neutral church ceremonies, including the use of the term 'marriage'. That same year, Eva Brunne was elected and consecrated as the Church of Sweden Bishop of Stockholm. She was the first openly lesbian bishop in the world and the first bishop of the Lutheran denomination in Sweden to be in a registered same-sex partnership.

The Church does, however, permit priests to decline to marry couples of the same gender, as is the case for heterosexual couples. The only special proviso made for same-sex couples is that every parish has a responsibility to make it possible for them to marry in it, regardless of the opinion of clergy concerned.

A powerful indication of the Church's democratic DNA is that it entitles every member over the age of sixteen to vote on all its decision-making bodies. It is also why the Church declined to exert influence over the outcomes of the Festival of Theology dialogue and panel discussion.

The Church of Sweden was the first major denomination and religion in Sweden to approve same-sex marriage. By comparison the Catholic Church and the Pentecostal Movement – the third and fourth largest Christian denominations in the country – declared themselves 'disappointed' by the decision. The Muslim Association of Sweden had already stated that no imams would marry same-sex couples. The Great Synagogue of Stockholm performed its first gay marriage in 2013, against a backdrop of varying Jewish opinions.

The vote for same-sex marriages also set the Church of Sweden apart from others within the Lutheran World Federation. The issues of same-sex cohabitation and the place of LGBTI people in the Church have been discussed and investigated since 1972. Notably, the Church of Sweden had permitted the blessing of same-sex unions and the ordination of partnered gays and lesbians since 2006.

Describing itself as a folk or people's church, as opposed to a state church regulated by parliament, it embraces the whole country. Parishes and clergy are overseen by bishops. About 70 per cent of the Swedish population are baptised in the Church; about 50 per cent go forward for confirmation in their early teens and are later married by the Church. Close to 90 per cent are buried with a Church of Sweden service.

The Church is so integral to Swedish culture and traditions that it is sometimes said: 'Everybody belongs but not everyone is a believer.'

Thus, the focus is on ministering well beyond active church members and Sweden's geographic boundaries. You will find some forty churches in twenty-five other countries, which minister to students, tourists, seafarers and Swedes living abroad.

The Church has been engaged in international diaconal work, such as long-term development, advocacy and emergency relief, for more than 150 years. It now does this in cooperation with the Lutheran World Federation, the World Council of Churches, and the ACT Alliance (Action by Churches Together). It is also engaged in international missionary work in relationship with churches and ecumenical organizations in Africa, Asia, Latin America and the Middle East. In the ecumenical dialogues, the decision made by the Church of Sweden in relation to same-sex marriage has been a point of discussion. Representatives from the Church have clarified how and why the decision was made, and have given priority to keeping the relationships going, despite differences.

In Sweden about 10,000 volunteers are engaged in spreading information, collecting money and shaping opinion for international church work. Roughly US $30 million is contributed every year for this work.

The festivals

The Church of Sweden's approach to contentious theology is well illustrated by the Reverend Dr Anna Karin Hammar, of the Diocese of Uppsala. In her opening address at the Fourth Uppsala Festival of Theology, she declared theology 'everybody's property', 'a creative action' and 'a form of art for the survival of the earth'. Communication, she added, is about God and cannot be locked in a religious or academic building. Instead, it is carried by humans who experience both the innermost and the outermost of existence.

The vision for the festivals was to wrench theology from the experts and 'encourage each of us to feel: I am a theologian. In my body and in my life, I carry with me important experiences and observations that have something to say about the innermost and the outermost of our existence.'

Reverend Hammar reminded delegates that everyone has something important to add to the understanding and transformation of our world – not least, our bad experiences. God does make all things new. Theology is everybody's property and not an exclusive intellectual understanding.

By addressing theology as a creative action, she pointed to the senses, creative understanding and the meeting of new people. A purely philosophical approach that encourages only rationality could provide only a poor sense of the suffering, the beauty and the challenges in this world. God is present in the entire Creation and all our senses are needed as a response to this presence. Even if we look upon ourselves as laypersons and barefoot theologians, our experience is on a level with that of great theologians.

She posited that theology needs a certain amount of creativity when ancient texts are confronted with new situations. Because religious traditions focus on sacred texts they are both rich and vulnerable. When construing the traditions without regard to past context or the present, dogmatism and fanaticism might cause our hearts to harden. 'The gift of creativity might allow new things, a new future to come out of the old.'

Her suggestion was that, as co-creators, we humans are called to be part of the renewal in this world. When individuals gather, new lines of thought appear. 'Out of the meeting between people comes living theology. That is why we wanted to make the Theology Festival a meeting point for different traditions and different people.'

The Reverend J.P. Mokgethi-Heath

An Anglican priest, Reverend Mokgethi-Heath is Policy Advisor on HIV and Theology for the International Department of the Church of Sweden. He was also a member of the GIN Interim Steering Committee. Having served as a parish priest in the Diocese of Johannesburg from 1995, he co-founded the International Network of Religious Leaders Living with or Personally Affected by HIV and AIDS (INERELA+) in 2002 and served as executive director. By January 2013, when he took up his post in Sweden, the network had grown from an initial membership of eight to a global network with more than 10,000 members from all faiths.

He also serves on the HIV strategy group for the Ecumenical Advocacy Alliance, the international reference group of World Council of Churches' Ecumenical HIV and AIDS Initiative in Africa (EHAIA), and as a member of the UNAIDS reference group on HIV and Human Rights.

Having tested HIV+ in 2000, when his immune system was already seriously compromised, he was blessed to be accepted for a medical trial that saved his life. In the following years, he was burying people who had no access to treatment while doctors and scientists in the West were saying, 'You can't give ARVs to Africans because they don't have watches.' In South Africa, as in many other countries, stigma was rife. Out of this emerged the internationally respected activist.

Reverend Mokgethi-Heath says, 'It is universally recognized that religious leaders have a unique authority that plays a central role in providing moral and ethical guidance within their communities; indeed, their public opinions can influence entire nations. INERELA+ looks to empower its members to use their positions within their faith communities. They need to do so in a way that breaks silence, challenges stigma and provides delivery of evidence-based prevention, treatment, care and support services.'

His role in the 2015 Human Dignity and Human Sexuality stream was to drive the development of the resource packs, facilitate dialogue and to maintain and nurture the momentum of the discussions that made history over several wintry days in Uppsala.

The Global Interfaith Network (GIN)

The Global Interfaith Network (GIN) was initiated by sixty-eight people from thirty-five countries at the 2012 World Conference of the International Lesbian, Gay, Bisexual, Trans and Intersex Association (ILGA). It was further consolidated at a spiritual retreat in January 2014 and subsequent ILGA World Conference in Mexico City the same year.

The network is registered in South Africa and its secretariat is based in Johannesburg, which offers easy access to the rest of Africa and the other continents.

The Global Interfaith Network (GIN) grows apace as it strives for a just world – one in which the dignity, faith, spirituality and human rights of persons of all sexes, sexual orientations, gender identities and expressions (SSOGIE) are honoured, supported and protected.

Notably, the main contributors to this book are GIN members. The focus is on developing leadership in diverse communities of faith through strategic collaboration, alliance building, creating safer spaces, education, networking and training in religious dialogue. The aim is to transform religious attitudes regarding sexual, gender and bodily diversity.

GIN also seeks to leverage international human rights bodies to protect and promote the human rights of lesbian, gay, bisexual, transgender and intersex (LGBTI) people, as well as inclusive faith voices and traditions. It works to ensure that the human rights for people of all SSOGIE are protected, and that their spirituality is acknowledged and nurtured.

A mix of individuals and organizations, GIN engages in work that accounts for the role that faith, spirituality and cultural traditions play in social and legal status. It is committed to using religious beliefs and traditions to ensure that the views, values and rights of people of all SSOGIE are recognized, respected and valued.

Haven Herrin, who chairs GIN's Steering Committee, tells of how at the 2012 ILGA World Conference, the founders of GIN boldly embraced a seat at the intersection of human rights, religion, violence and spiritual liberation. 'We were convinced that our faiths can be a source of healing, community, and frameworks despite being the cause, excuse or weapon for so much trauma, violence, structural and legal oppression.'

Herrin also speaks of an emboldened belief that GIN can shift and transform what once seemed like an intractable opposition. 'The insights and new strengths we glean when we work across geographies and across traditions are exciting. And as we peel back the nominal differences between the arguments posed by various religions, we find that the driving forces are actually the same at root. Lunges for power and domination are fuelled by false hierarchies that assign morality to our embodied experiences.'

Devdutt Pattanaik

Devdutt, a practising Hindu, has authored the introductory essay in this book, as he had for the previous book in the series, *I Am Divine, So Are You*. He writes, illustrates and lectures on the relevance of mythology in modern times. He defines mythology as 'subjective truth of a people expressed through stories, symbols and rituals'. He has written more than thirty books and 700 articles, including two based on queer themes: *Shikhandi and Other Tales They Don't Tell You* (Zubaan) and *The Pregnant King: A Novel* (Penguin).

The Reverend Loraine Tulleken

Rev'd Loraine Tulleken is an international freelance journalist and editor based in South Africa.

Professor Emerita Riffat Hassan

Professor Riffat Hassan is a Pakistani-American theologian and a leading Islamic feminist scholar of the Qur'an. Internationally acknowledged as a pioneer of Islamic feminist theology, she has done much to promote women's rights in Muslim societies and to combat 'honour' crimes against women in Pakistan. Her work after the 11 September 2001 terrorist attacks is credited with building bridges between the US and the Muslim world.

During her thirty-three years as a professor of religious studies at the University of Louisville, she was known for teaching that the Qur'an, the holy text of Islam, is a 'Magna Carta' of human rights, including absolute women's equality. She supports a non-rigid interpretation of the Qur'an, arguing that while it is the word of God, words can have different meanings. She believes the meaning of the Qur'an should be determined through hermeneutics, i.e., an examination of what its words meant at the time it was written.

Because the God of Islam is just, she also speaks of an 'ethical criterion' that rejects the use of the Qur'an to perpetrate injustice. Dr Hassan supports abortion rights and access to contraceptives for Muslim women, saying that the Qur'an does not directly address contraceptives. Instead, Islam's religious and ethical framework leads to the conclusion that family planning should be a fundamental right.

Born in Lahore, Pakistan, to an upper-class Sayyid Muslim family, she had a comfortable childhood, but was affected by the conflict between her father's traditional views and her mother's non-conformism. For most of her life, she hated her father's traditionalism because of his views of gender roles, but she later came to appreciate it because of his kindness and compassion.

As a girl she attended Cathedral High School, an Anglican missionary school, and later St Mary's College at Durham

University, England, where she studied English and philosophy. Her PhD from Durham University is for her thesis on Muhammad Iqbal, about whom she has written frequently.

Dr Hassan also taught at the University of Punjab in Lahore from 1966 to 1967, and worked in Pakistan's Ministry of Information and Broadcasting from 1969 to 1972. In 1972, she immigrated to the US with her daughter. Other schools she has taught at include Oklahoma State University and Harvard University.

In February 1999, she founded the International Network for the Rights of Female Victims of Violence in Pakistan, which works against the so-called honour killings. She has argued that these killings are a distortion of Islam and that the whole idea that women are inferior is a result of the mistaken belief among Muslims that Eve was created from Adam's rib. In the Islamic creation story, they were created at the same time.

Rabbi Jay Michaelson

Dr Michaelson is a US national voice of progressive Judaism and long-time LGBT activist. The author of five books and more than 300 articles on religion, sexuality, law and contemplative practice, he is a contributing editor to the *Daily Beast* and the *Forward* newspaper. His 2011 book, *God vs. Gay? The Religious Case for Equality*, was an Amazon bestseller and Lambda Literary Award finalist.

A professional LGBT activist for fifteen years, he founded two Jewish LGBT organizations, and has supported the work of LGBT activists worldwide at the Arcus Foundation, the

Democracy Council, and his new project at the *Daily Beast*, Quorum: Global LGBT Voices. His advocacy work has featured on NBC, MSNBC, CNN and NPR, and in the *New York Times*.

He holds a PhD in Jewish thought from Hebrew University, a JD from Yale Law School, and non-denominational rabbinic ordination. He has held visiting positions at Brown University, Yale University, Harvard Divinity School and Boston University Law School, and is currently an affiliated assistant professor at Chicago Theological Seminary. His academic articles have been published in journals including *Theology and Sexuality* and the *Yale Law Journal*. He has given named lectures at Reconstructionist Rabbinical College, Pacific School of Religion, Drew University and the Academy of Jewish Religion.

The Reverend Rowland 'Jide' Macaulay

Reverend Jide is the founder and CEO of House of Rainbow CIC (community interest company). He was the director of RJMM.CO.UK, a consultancy offering education and support with regard to human rights vis-a-vis sexual minorities of African descent. He has more than twenty years' experience in the politics of sexual orientation and gender identity in Africa, which at one time led to calls for his execution in Nigeria.

He is also the founding pastor of the House of Rainbow, Lagos, Nigeria, and London, the United Kingdom – missions introduced in 2006 and 2010 respectively. Their primary vision is to reach out to sexual minorities through education, advocacy, reconciliation and capacity building.

Raised in Nigeria, he was ordained deacon in the Anglican Church in London, and holds a degree in law, MA in practical theology and a postgraduate certificate in pastoral theology.

This dynamic and inspirational speaker, poet, pastor and preacher has authored several poetry and devotional books. He also writes for various Christian and secular journals. His focus is spiritual activism with a major link to the inclusion and reconciliation of sexuality and spirituality. He also advises on immigration and human rights, especially the right to religion for lesbians, gays, bisexuals, transgender and intersex people.

Now a globally acknowledged expert on LGBTI and human rights, Reverend Jide is currently a board member and trustee at Kaleidoscope Trust, the UK, and a deputy chair of the Interim Steering Committee of the GIN.

Imam Ludovic-Mohamed

Dr Ludovic-Mohamed is a French Muslim born in Algeria and is known as Europe's 'gay imam'. An acknowledged intellectual, he is an expert on the Qur'an and an HIV activist. A member of the Department of Anthropology at the EHESS (French school for advanced social studies), his second PhD is on Islam and gender diversity. He also did a master's degree in cognitive psychology at the École Normale Supérieure and a PhD in the social psychology of religions at the University of Nantes, France.

His thesis addresses radically alternative Islamic LGBT corporalities and religiosities, as the vanguard of new Islamic liberation theologies. He focuses on LGBT Arab-Muslim organizational emergence mainly in Europe, but also in north and south Africa as well as the US. His fields of expertise include Muslim communities in Europe and the diaspora, and social grammars concerning norm negotiation around gender, sexuality, the public sphere in relation to alternative liberation theologies and mystical branches of Islam, such as progressive, inclusive Islam and Sufism.

He founded his first NGO, the Children of AIDS, for which he embarked on a year-long trip across the globe. A second organization, HM2F, was founded in January 2010. It means 'Homosexual Muslims of France'.

In 2012, shocked to find that no imam would bury a transsexual Muslim or marry interfaith and gay couples, he opened a gay-friendly mosque in Paris. There, Muslims are treated as equals regardless of their sexual orientation, sex or ethnicity. He also married, making same-sex marriage history in France.

That same year his book, *Le Coran et la chair* (translated into English as *Queer Muslim Marriage*), was published. It tells of his personal journey of faith as a Muslim homosexual. In it he argues, 'There is nothing about homosexuality that "goes against nature" according to one interpretation of Islam. Quite the opposite,' and also, 'I believe that if the Prophet Muhammad was alive, he would marry same-sex couples.'

Introduction:
God in Capitals

By Devdutt Pattanaik

- Role of Culture
- The Karmic Burden
- Different Interpretations of the Word
- Evolving Notions of Religion

Two men love each other romantically and sexually. It's organic. Their hearts, bodies and minds just connected. There was no planning, no discussion, no debate, no negotiation, no choice. It just happened. The two are happy. They exist in an ecosystem of many other humans. Do they need other people's permission to continue? Do they need the approval of someone beyond, the one who created all that exists – God? Would these feelings exist if God had not created them? Why then does one need God's approval? Or maybe this is a test, a trap laid by Devil, so that we are drawn to a path not approved by God?

These are questions asked by many gay men, who happen also to be Christian, Jewish or Muslim. Similar questions are also asked by gay men who happen to be Hindu, Buddhist, Jain or Sikh – or Daoist, Confucianist, agnostic or even atheist.

Not only gay men, these questions are also asked by lesbians and bisexuals and transgenders, by everyone queer, by everyone who is unable to conform to the conventional ideas of gender and sexuality where men are men, women are women, and they are supposed to come together only to breed children.

1.1 Role of Culture

Before we seek permission from culture, or religion, or priests, or God, let us understand the role of culture.

Culture is humanity's reaction to nature. Nature terrifies us – it makes us feel we do not matter, as though we are only food for the predator, nothing else. Culture is created, based on stories, to give our lives meaning, to make us feel valuable, like we matter. Loving cultures find stories to accommodate the unfamiliar, the accidental, the shocking, the rare. Insecure cultures find stories to avoid all unfamiliarity, the unpredictable, the discomforting and the outlier. Religion is a rich source of stories that informs culture, with the power to make culture more nourishing, more comforting, more loving. Unfortunately, it fails to achieve that, especially in matters queer.

Many people get offended when religion is called a set of stories. This is because stories are seen as false, as myth. This understanding of stories dates back to the nineteenth century, when there was the assumption that truth is out there, and the rest is stories. This truth was initially known only to priests, the custodians of religion. Those who believed in the stories of one God mocked those who believed in the stories of many gods. Later, scientists claimed to know the truth, and so mocked even those who believed in one God.

Today, in the twenty-first century, with wider appreciation of human psychology and diversity, we know that ideas such as many gods, one God, no god are all stories told to make sense of the world and give meaning to life. We cannot live without stories. Religion provides us stories with deep roots to our soul. That makes us better humans. It enters the territory that science cannot understand – of fears and yearnings that defy measurement.

This book focuses on stories that come from religions that speak of one true God. And how they give meaning to those whose desire does not align with dominant heterosexual patterns. The title, *Behold, I Make All Things New*, comes from the Bible, from the Book of Revelation, where Christ says he will destroy the old world and create a new world, for he is the alpha and the omega! As the title states, this book seeks to refresh the relationship between the lore of one God and the lives of queer people. For this relationship is a fractured one.

The conventional and popular understanding is that God wants humans to be heterosexuals. That makes non-heterosexual behaviour a sin, or 'haram'. However, this has been challenged by the authors of this book, who have a deep understanding of the scriptures themselves and of the world around them. They show that people have misunderstood, deliberately or otherwise, the scriptures and that there is no dissonance between scriptures and the queer life.

1.2 The Karmic Burden

The subcontinent of India gave birth to stories where the idea of one God does not play a prominent role. Greater value is placed on diversity – and this is rooted in the idea of rebirth, and karma. Karma is action as well as reaction – what we do and its repercussions. We are obliged by nature to experience the repercussions of our actions. This obligation is called the karmic burden. Each one of us carries a different karmic burden based on the deeds of our past lives. This shapes our body, our mind, and the circumstances in our life. Depending on how we respond in this life, a new set of karmic burdens is created that shapes our next life. Since each one of us has a different karmic burden, we look different, we feel different, we think different, and we experience different challenges and encounter different opportunities. No one is the same and so there cannot be a common god or a common path.

Buddhism, Jainism and Hinduism offer paths to shed the karmic burden through meditation, austerity and devotion. Hinduism alone speaks of one god: this god, however, manifests in myriad ways to satisfy myriad needs. So, Hinduism is monotheistic as well as polytheistic, and the two terms are fluid so that one is many and many is one.

When the lore of one God came into India in the form of Islam first and then Christianity (except in some coastal pockets that traded with the Middle East), it was baffled by the myriad gods of India. The followers of these religions viewed the stories of the gods as falsehood and used the word 'myth' for them. For they believed in one God, one message, one path for all of humanity – a very different model for meaning.

In ancient India – in fact, around the world – religious folks were primarily monks and priests who spent every waking moment immersed in the idea of God. The common folk revered them. They revered different kinds of holy people. The idea of becoming a member of a religious order and ignoring, tolerating or rejecting all other religions emerged as part of tribal politics: no god but the tribal God.

It is first seen in the idea of the jealous God in Judaism, then in the idea of the true son of the loving God in Christianity, and in the final prophet in Islam. Here, the one God tells you how to live life. You don't need another god. In fact, there is no other god. Infidelity and disobedience are frowned upon. This God, we are told, wanted men to be men – which means, be attracted only to women – and women to be women – which means, be attracted only to men. But that is not entirely true.

1.3 Different Interpretations of the Word

Just as many gods and many paths and many karmic burdens create many different doctrines, the word of one God (and the stories around Him) is open to many different interpretations. And some interpretations, based on deep study, are considered authoritative and others are not. And the difference in interpretation has meant divisions in communities.

So, the believers in one God – who descend from Adam and Eve, and who see Abraham as the first prophet – are divided into the followers of Judaism, which believes the final prophet is yet to come; the followers of Christianity, which believes the final prophet was Jesus, who was in fact the son of God; and the followers of Islam, which believes the final prophet was Muhammad.

Further, the followers of Judaism are sub-divided into various groups, each with a different reading of how God wants us to live our life. Thus, nearly all Israeli Jews self-identify with one of four sub-groups: Haredi (ultra-orthodox), Dati (religious), Masorti (traditional) and Hiloni (secular). The same is true of

Christians: Catholics, Protestants, Orthodox, Ultra-orthodox. And the same is true of Islam: Sunni, Shia, Sufi. Each group claims that its interpretation is most informed and most correct.

Despite this diversity, the communities do not embrace diversity. Hence, capital letters are used for god: God, indicating it is absolute and true. God's word is spelt 'Word'. This use of capitals is found only in the Latin script, not in the Hebrew or Arabic scripts. But the idea of one absolute, external, non-human-dependent truth – ontological truth – permeates the major religions of the world. Scholars are, therefore, constantly seeking the approval of God in all matters, including queer.

This stands in contrast to karmic faiths, where all truth is epistemic, born in the human mind. Breaking free of the mind leads to complete loss of individual self-identity. This is liberation: nirvana (oblivion) of Buddhism, kaivalya (omniscience) of Jainism, and moksha (union of the one with the infinite) of Hinduism. Scholars here paid attention to the queer, not as something inherently wrong, but merely to ensure it did not disrupt the life of the householder or hermit.

In karmic faiths, the queer is natural, but may not be accommodated culturally, depending on the level of wisdom (pragnya, in Buddhism) and empathy (karuna) of the individuals involved. In faiths based on the idea of one God, the question is whether the queer is God's creation or the Devil's. And if part of God's creation, how must it be accommodated in culture. In many Islamic traditions, those 'men who do not function as they are designed to' are allowed to serve as passive sexual partners to men and serve in women's quarters with the freedom to step into the men's space too. But what does 'men who do not function as they are designed to' mean? The feminine and submissive male homosexual or the cross-dressing transgender? Here scholars are divided.

1.4 Evolving Notions of Religion

The problem is that these scriptures were written in times that did not have access to knowledge, which we have today, about gender and sexuality. The orthodox will reject this assertion as they believe the Talmud, the Bible, the Qur'an contain universal knowledge. Also, modern scholarship has questioned the traditional translations and readings of the holy books. Scholars have pointed out how ideas have been excluded and suppressed with the passage of time, and how ideas that seem to be timeless are actually rather contextual. We assume that Sharia laws based on the revelations to Prophet Muhammad (Qur'an) and the life of Prophet Muhammad (Hadith) have always been around, but they were actually codified only 150 years ago by the Ottoman Empire.

Today, we realize the complex relationship between society, biology and psychology. That 'masculine' (gender) is different from 'male' (sex), which is different from 'feeling desire for a woman' (sexuality). How does one reconcile these ideas discovered and/or invented in the twentieth century with customs and beliefs that evolved over the past 3,000 years in the case of Judaism, 2,000 years in the case of Christianity and 1,400 years in the case of Islam? These are questions that are being raised and answered in this book. For religion has to evolve with culture. The fixed ideas of God, Word and Prophet have to energize and empower this transformation.

We live in a global world where we cannot say my truth is the truth. We have to work with other truths – collaborate rather than compete with them. Our truths have to inform other people's truths. Other people's truths have to inform our truths. In my work, I use the word 'myth' for our expanding truths. If fact is everyone's truth and fiction is nobody's truth, myth is somebody's truth. So, read this book keeping in mind:

Within infinite myths is an eternal truth
Who sees it all?
Varuna has but a thousand eyes
Indra, a hundred
You and I, only two.

2

In the Name of God: A Letter to Muslims, Jews and Christians

By Riffat Hassan

- Merciful and Compassionate God
- Equality Before God
- The Ethical Criterion
- Sexuality and Spirituality
- Belief in Tawheed
- Conclusion

Bismil-laah ir Rahmaan ir Raheem (In the Name of God, the most merciful and gracious, the most compassionate and the dispenser of grace)

As-salaamu 'alay-kum (Peace be unto all of you)

This 'group letter' that I, a Muslim woman, have been honoured to write, is addressed, first and foremost, to Jews, Christians and Muslims, who cherish their respective religious traditions. It is written at a time when our world is bitterly divided. Extremism, bigotry and hatred are leading to horrendous acts of terror, brutality and destruction. Violence has become so rampant that it has benumbed our sensitivities in varying degrees.

Events like the shooting at the Army Public School in Peshawar, Pakistan, for instance, have caused massive shock waves throughout the world. On 16 December 2014 the Tehrik-i-Taliban massacred 132 children, ranging from the age of eight to eighteen. There was also the attack on the Charlie Hebdo weekly newspaper in Paris by the Al-Qaeda Branch in Yemen. That resulted in twelve deaths on 7 January 2015.

Such acts of aggression indicate, without doubt, that something is dreadfully wrong with the state of the world. The fact that the gunmen were shouting *Allahu Akbar* (God is the greatest) as they went about killing, further demonstrates the depravity of those who invoked the name of God who is Rahmaan and Raheem – terms that signify the highest degree of mercy, compassion and grace.

Surah 5: *Al-Maa'idah:* 32 reiterates a command given to 'the children of Israel'. It is also applicable to Christians and Muslims. Namely, that the unjust killing of one human being is tantamount to the slaying of all humanity, whereas saving the life of one human being is like saving the life of all humankind.

The current situation raises questions profoundly troubling to many people. They are – or should be – particularly troubling to Muslims, Christians and Jews, who believe that God's spirit has been breathed into them. This makes them the recipients of special capabilities as well as responsibilities. Muslims have been told by the Qur'an, which they regard as the Word of God, that human beings have been appointed khala'if al-'ard (God's vicegerents on Earth), who must take care of the Earth which sustains us. They are also commanded to strive to develop their potential to the fullest, having been created by God *in the finest configuration* (Surah 95: *At-Tin:* 3); they are to be ever-mindful of the Qur'anic world view enshrined in the resounding words of Surah 53: *An-Najm:* 43: *Towards God is your limit*, which are embodied in the beloved Islamic tradition: 'Create in yourselves the attributes of God.'

2.1 Merciful and Compassionate God

God has many attributes. Islamic mystics often talk about God's ninety-nine names, each of which has particular significance. Which of God's many attributes should Muslims, Jews and Christians strive to inculcate in themselves? There are diverse, even opposing, schools of thought or theological perspectives in our three religious traditions. However, central to our concept and experience of God is that God is merciful and compassionate. Thus, all of the ways in which God responds to us, including actions and judgements, are marked by mercy.

The Qur'an places great emphasis on God's justice, which is understood in two different ways. One is called *'adl* which means 'to be equal, neither more nor less'. Explaining this concept, A.A. Fyzee, an expert on Islamic law states: 'In a court of justice the claims of the two parties must be considered evenly, without undue stress being laid upon one side or the other.' Evenly balanced scales are the emblems of *'adl* or legalistic justice.

The second kind of justice enjoined by the Qur'an is called ehsaan. This literally means 'restoring the balance by making up a loss or deficiency'. In order to understand this concept, it is important to know that the Qur'an envisages the ideal society or community as ummah. It derives from the word *umm* (mother). The symbols of a mother and motherly love and compassion are also linked with the two attributes most characteristic of God, namely Rahmaan and Raheem from the root R-H-M (womb) common to Arabic and Hebrew.

The ideal ummah cares about all its members just as an ideal mother cares about all her children. She knows that they are not equal and have different needs. Showing undue favour to any child would be unjust. But a mother who takes into account the special needs of a child, who is challenged in some way, does not act unjustly. She exemplifies the spirit of ehsaan or compassionate justice by helping to restore the balance with regard to this child.

That God is always just, is unequivocally affirmed by the Qur'an. Every Surah, except one, begins with the words Bismil-laah ir Rahmaan ir Raheem (In the Name of God, the most merciful and gracious, the most compassionate and the dispenser of grace). This invocatory prayer is repeated by Muslims not only when they recite the Qur'an but prior to the start of any important activity in their daily lives.

In the context of God's mercy, there are two remarkable verses (12 and 54) in Surah 6: *Al- An'am* which deserve particular attention. Verse 12 reads: *Say: Unto who belongs all that is in the heavens and on earth? Say: Unto God, who has willed upon Himself the law of grace and mercy.* Verse 54 reads: *And when those who believe in our messages come unto thee, say: Peace be upon you. Your Sustainer has willed upon Himself the law of grace and mercy.*

The eminent Muslim scholar, Muhammad Asad, in his translation and explanation of the Qur'an, points out that the phrase 'God has willed upon Himself as a law' (kataba 'ala nafsihi) occurs in the Qur'an only twice — and in both instances with reference to God's grace and mercy (*rahmah*).[1] None of the other divine attributes have been similarly described. This exceptional quality of God's grace and mercy is further stressed in Surah 7: *Al-'A'raf:* 156: *My grace overspreads everything*, echoed in the authentic tradition (Sunnah) in which, according to the Prophet (Muhammad), God says, 'Verily, My grace and mercy outstrips My wrath' (Bukhari and Muslim).

The theme of God's mercy, which is universal and without boundaries, is one of the grandest themes of the Qur'an. It finds many expressions. For instance, Surah 2: *Al-Baqarah* states in verse 185: *God wills that you shall have ease, and does not will you to suffer hardship*, and in verse 286: *God does not burden any human being with more than he is well able to bear*; Surah 3: *Al-'Imran* states in verse 74: *God is limitless in His great bounty*, and in verse 150: *God is your protector and He is the best of helpers*; Surah 4: *An-Nisa'* states in verses 25–28: *God is much-forgiving, a dispenser of grace ... God wants to turn to you in His mercy ... God wants to lighten your burdens*; and in verse 64: *God is Oft-returning, Most Merciful*; Surah 5: *Al-Maa'idah:* 7 states: *God does not want to impose any hardship on you, but wants to make you pure, and to bestow upon you the full measure of His blessings*; and Surah 6: *Al-An'am:* 147 states: *Limitless is your Sustainer in His grace.*

God's mercy to humankind is also powerfully illustrated in the Qur'an in verses which are of foundational significance in Islamic mysticism. For instance, Surah 2: *Al-Baqa-rah:* 186 states: *If My servants ask thee about Me – behold, I am near: I respond to the call of him who calls, whenever He calls unto Me*; Surah 27: *An-Naml:* 62 asks a rhetorical question: *Who is it that responds to the distressed when he calls out to Him, and who removes the ill (that caused the distress), and has made you inherit the earth?*; Surah 40: *Ghafir:* 60 states: *Your Sustainer says: Call unto Me, (and) I shall respond to you*; and Surah 50: *Qaf:* 16 points to the closeness between the Creator and humanity: *Verily, it is We who have created man, and We know what his innermost self whispers within him: for We are closer to him than his neck-vein.*

God's mercy, compassion and grace are emphasized as much in the sacred texts of Jews and Christians – the Hebrew Bible and the New Testament – as they are in the Qur'an. Some of the references to God's mercy in the Hebrew Bible are more detailed than others. For instance, Psalm 103 on 'God is Love' states in verses 8–12: *God is merciful and gracious, slow to anger, and plenteous in mercy. He will not always chide: neither will He keep his anger forever. He has not dealt with us after our sins; nor rewarded us according to our iniquities. For as the heaven is high above the earth, so great is His mercy toward them that fear Him. As far as the east is from the west, so far has He removed our transgressions from us.* Reference to God's abundant and everlasting mercy are found in many Psalms.[2]

For Christians, in addition to the strong affirmations of God's mercy, compassion, grace and loving-kindness in the Old Testament, numerous New Testament statements reiterate the same core belief. Jesus makes the mercy of God a mirror for his disciples. As Luke 6:36 points out: *Be compassionate as your Father is compassionate.* The pivotal role of God's mercy and grace is emphasized in the accounts of the life of Jesus, the acts of his apostles as well as in the epistles.[3] In this context, reference may be made to a number of New Testament verses.[4]

2.2 Equality Before God

Remembrance of God's mercy, compassion and grace is a source of deep solace and succour to believers in the Islamic,

Jewish and Christian traditions. So, why have I devoted so much time to this theme in a letter written in the context of an interfaith dialogue on human sexuality?

The answer lies in what I have learnt in more than four decades, both in the classroom and in the larger world. I began my career as a feminist theologian in 1974, and my engagement in interfaith dialogue in 1979. In both areas I was for many years a solitary Muslim woman confronted with formidable challenges. There is one that I would like to mention. It concerns the issues of human dignity and human sexuality, which constitute the theme of this dialogue.

On the basis of my faith as well as my research, I had come to believe that according to the normative teachings of the Qur'an – the highest authority in Islam – women and men are equal in the sight of God. But where was this equality to be found in the world? Growing up in Pakistan's patriarchal culture, exacerbated by feudalism and tribalism, I was intensely aware of the injustice, oppression and suffering to which the vast majority of girls and women in my society were subjected. It was regarded as self-evident in this society – as well as in Muslim communities worldwide – that women were inferior and subordinate to men.

'Islamisation' took place in the Muslim world in the aftermath of the Iranian Revolution in 1979. Negative ideas and attitudes towards women were institutionalized through the promulgation and implementation of manifestly anti-women laws. The challenge for me was how to bridge the huge chasm between – on the one hand – God's compassion towards girls and women (as towards all marginalized people) and concern about safeguarding their fundamental rights, and – on the other hand – the actual life situation of a large number of Muslim women, who constituted, perhaps, the most disadvantaged minority in the world.

Since Muslims are profoundly 'People of the Book', i.e., the Qur'an, it became a major part of my task as a feminist theologian to analyse Qur'anic texts pertaining to women-related issues. Interpretations of these texts had been done almost exclusively by Muslim men, Muslim women – like Jewish and Christian women before them – having little or no opportunity to acquire knowledge of their own religious texts. The ontological, theological, sociological and eschatological status of Muslim women had been defined by men, many of whom had a markedly patriarchal mindset. In order to do an exegesis or interpretation of women-related Qur'anic texts from a non-patriarchal perspective, I had to develop my own hermeneutics or methodology of interpretation.

The Qur'an is in Arabic, which (like Hebrew) is a Semitic language. Each word has a root with multiple meanings. So, the criteria of linguistic accuracy and philosophical consistency were an important part of my hermeneutics. Linguistic accuracy required me to determine what particular words meant in seventh century Hijaz where the Qur'an was revealed. Determining philosophical consistency involved analysis of particular terms, which occurred in multiple contexts to determine if there was consistency, or otherwise, in the usage. For example, 'Adam' occurs twenty-five times in the Qur'an.

2.3 The Ethical Criterion

Thirdly, there is what I called 'the ethical criterion', which I considered to be the most important part of my hermeneutics. Muslims regard the Qur'an as 'the Word of God', which is the last and final authority in all matters. I believe that over and beyond 'the Word of God' is God, that in order to understand 'the Word of God' one must take into account the intention of the author, i.e., God. In my view, what lies at the core of the Qur'an is its ethical framework. This is a set of moral principles which enable human beings to fulfil the categorical imperative mandated by God, namely, *'al -amr bi'l ma 'roof wa'n nahy 'ani'l munkar* (to enjoin the doing of what is good or right and to forbid the doing of what is evil or wrong).

I see ethics as central not only to the Islamic, but also to the Jewish and Christian religious world views. In my study of the prophetic figures at the start and heart of Judaism, Christianity and Islam – Abraham, Jesus and Muhammad – I have been particularly struck by two distinctive characteristics they had in common. The first was their absolute faith in, and submission to, God who was most merciful, most compassionate and most gracious. The second was their deep spirituality from which flowed a morality that embodied the most important attributes of God.

The example of the prophetic figures I have mentioned is very different from what we find in much of human history or of religion in general. The law of the jungle – might is right – has been far more dominant than the moral edicts of God, who is most merciful, most compassionate. This is true even in the case of the three Abrahamic faiths. The passionate moral impulse of their originators receded as these faiths became institutionalized religions. They were more concerned with strengthening and protecting their respective territories than in establishing just and compassionate communities.

In recent decades, the rapid increase in extremism, particularly in militant groups engaged in horrendous crimes, has led to stigmatisation of Islam since many of the terrorists identify themselves as Muslims. I define a Muslim as one who lives according to the will and pleasure of God, who is Rahmaan and Raheem. Those who act in violation of God's most essential attributes and moral imperatives cannot be considered Muslim. Those who aggress upon the rights of others have placed themselves outside the boundaries of God-centred religions.

Pakistan, my country of origin, has had more terror attacks than any other country. I am sick at heart when I think of how Malala was shot (but saved through God's mercy) and 132 innocent schoolchildren murdered in cold blood. I mourn for those who have been killed and am outraged at the total inhumanity of the killers. I feel a compelling need to tell the world that the goals which motivate those who commit the most heinous of sins and crimes have nothing to do with Islam.

Muslims, like Christians and Jews, and adherents of other religions, have human flaws and shortcomings. But it is important to remember at a time like this that belief in God *as* Rahmaan and Raheem is the foundation on which the lives of tens of millions of Muslims are built. The overwhelming majority of Muslims in the world are as different from Tehrik-e-Taliban, al-Qaeda and the terror outfit that has the audacity to call itself Islamic State, as their Christian brothers and sisters are from the Nazis.

Islam, Christianity and Judaism, like many other religions, have several dimensions. These include the ritual, mythological, doctrinal, social and political. Within its own sphere of applicability, each dimension offers what is meaningful and important to those who are committed to these traditions. But history shows that there have been times when a particular dimension has acquired dominance, while another has become less important.

Today, for instance, frequent references are made to 'Political Islam' or the politicisation of Islam. It is my considered judgement that in the context of the current state of our world, it is the ethical dimension of religion, which is the most crucial. It is needed not only for establishing the parameters within which these issues should be examined, but also for keeping the focus on what is beneficial or harmful for human beings. My judgement is based upon my life experience as a feminist theologian-activist. I am taking the liberty of sharing this experience because it illustrates how ethics can be used to empower those who are marginalized and disadvantaged. It can also arouse the consciousness and conscience of those who discriminate against them.

For the past forty years I have sought to demonstrate, first to Muslim women and then to the communities in which they live, that according to the Qur'an, God has given them fundamental human rights. These cannot be abolished by any individual, group or agency. I have travelled the world to educate Muslim girls and women about normative Islamic teachings enshrined in the Qur'an and the practice of the Prophet of Islam, which relate to all aspects of their life. Difficult and dangerous as this mission has been, I have always believed that this was the only way of bringing about the internal and external empowerment of Muslim women.

Here I would like to mention that a very large number of Muslim women have three characteristics: they are poor, illiterate and live in a rural environment. The lives of many of them are fraught with every kind of hardship. However, their faith in God does not waver and Islam continues to sustain them. It also constrains them since they are conditioned to believe that Islam requires them to obey and serve men.

I have addressed all kinds and classes of Muslim women in all sorts of settings globally. I have made them aware of basic Qur'anic ethics such as their right to life, education, freedom, physical well-being and socioeconomic justice. And I have pointed out that the restrictions imposed on them in the name of Islam are cultural and not God-sanctioned.

I know that my words reached many women. I saw their eyes and souls light up as they began to see that it is God's will and desire that they should engage in *jihad fi sabil Allah* (striving in the cause of God) for their liberation from the shackles that bind them. Muslim women, empowered by the ethics of the Qur'an to strive for their own self-actualization, often become the catalysts for the moral development of the cultures in which they live.

As a university professor of religious studies with a special interest in issues related to women and gender, I had done substantial study of human sexuality in the context of the world's major religions. However, prior to being asked to participate in the Festival of Theology, I had not done a focused study of, or reflection on, the issue of homosexuality in general, nor in the particular context of Christianity, Judaism and Islam. It had always seemed to me to be a very complicated subject. My long struggle to build a solid theological case for women's equality with men in the Islamic tradition, and to demonstrate that, since women and men were equal in the sight of God, they also had to be equal in society, had been filled with difficult challenges. It has taken a heavy toll on me in many ways.

When I began my work in Islamic theology of women, I was happy to see that Muslim women, in general, had made much progress since 1974. But I could not forget that there were still very large groups, who lacked knowledge of their God-given rights. They were still unable to stand up and be counted in their patriarchal communities. At seventy-one, I wanted to be free of the fray in which I had been engaged for four decades. I wanted instead to focus on my own inner journey. But how could I abandon the cause that had been my life's most passionate quest? I felt that I still had a lot of work to do. I prayed to God to heal and strengthen me physically so I could continue the struggle.

When I received Dr Anna Karin Hammar's invitation to speak at the pre-Festival dialogue, I did not know, at first, how to respond. She was very gracious and understanding, knowing that being a feminist theologian in Muslim culture had already put me in jeopardy in a number of ways. She did not want to add to my life's difficulties, and would have been understanding if I had sent my regrets. But there was something, perhaps her loving thoughts and trust in me, perhaps something in my own deeper psyche, that made me feel an extraordinary thing had happened. As an academic I was greatly daunted by the task. I had not done an adequate study of the issue of homosexuality in terms of all the pertinent religious texts or of the increasing body of literature emanating from a large variety of disciplines. However, I felt called to accept the invitation and to embark on a new journey.

In the short time at my disposal before going to Sweden for the pre-conference workshop, I began a course of intensive study of important books and articles. I sought the guidance of my learned friends who specialized in Jewish and Christian sources and interfaith dialogue. I turned to those who gave me spiritual direction through meditation and prayer. At the conclusion of this process, I sat down to write this letter. Not with any definite outline but with the prayer *Bismil-laah ir Rahmaan ir Raheem*. I trusted that God would show me the way and help me to say what I should say.

2.4 Sexuality and Spirituality

Human sexuality has been much debated in most religious traditions, including those of Judaism, Christianity and Islam. A look at the history of how it has been viewed, from older religious traditions (e.g. Hinduism, Buddhism, Judaism, Zoroastrianism) to later ones (e.g. Christianity, Islam), shows attitudes ranging from highly positive to highly negative. Sexuality, in its broadest sense, refers to the 'quality of being sexual'. It is regarded affirmatively by the Jewish and Islamic traditions. This is because the creation of human beings as sexual as well as sexually differentiated creatures is believed to be an integral part of God's plan for humankind.

Unlike dualistic traditions, whether religious or philosophical, these traditions do not see sexuality as the opposite of spirituality. However, views about sexuality found in the Christian tradition appear to be very different from, and far more complex than, those found in the Jewish and Islamic traditions.

Prior to looking at the views of homosexual relations found in the three traditions, it is important to understand how sexuality has been seen by them in the context of heterosexual marriage of which both the Islamic and the Jewish traditions are highly affirming. The Qur'an encourages all Muslims, who are able and willing, to marry a 'virtuous' or 'chaste' man or woman, regardless of the difference is status or wealth between them. It describes marriage as a sign of God's mercy and bounty to humanity. As Surah 30: *Ar-Rum:* 21 states: *And among His* (God's) *signs is that He created for you mates from among yourselves that you might find restfulness* (and satisfaction), *and He has engendered between you love and mercy: surely, in that are signs for people who think.*

Traditional Judaism views marriage as a contractual bond commanded by God. A man and a woman come together and create a relationship in which God is directly involved. (Deuteronomy 24:1) Islamic marriage is regarded as a social contract based on the mutual agreement of the two spouses. Although marriage is not regarded either as a sacrament or as a covenant in Islam, the Qur'an refers to it as *a most solemn and serious pledge.* (Surah 4: *An-Nisaa':* 21)

Many scholars of religion point out that heterosexual marriage has not been viewed positively in the Christian tradition since the earliest days of the church. Karen Armstrong, eminent historian of religion, observing that celibacy was seen as 'the prime Christian vocation', states:

> Jesus has urged his followers to leave their wives and children (*Luke* 14:25–26). St Paul, the earliest Christian writer, believed that because Jesus was about to return and inaugurate the Kingdom of God, where there would be no marriage or giving in marriage, it was simply not worth saddling yourself with a wife or husband. This, Paul was careful to emphasize, was simply his own opinion, not a divine ruling. It was perfectly acceptable for Christians to marry if they wished, but in view of the imminent second coming, Paul personally recommended celibacy.
>
> The fathers of the church often used these New Testament remarks to revile marriage but accepted,

albeit grudgingly, that marriage was part of God's plan. St Augustine taught that originally in the Garden of Eden, married sex had been rational and good. But after the Fall, sexuality became a sign of humanity's chronic sinfulness, a raging and ungovernable force. It was viewed as a mindless, bestial enjoyment of the creature that held us back from the contemplation of God. Augustine's doctrine of original sin fused sexuality and sin indissolubly in the imagination of the Christian West. For centuries this tainted the institution of matrimony.

Augustine saw his conversion to Christianity as a vocation of celibacy. His teacher, St Ambrose of Milan, believed that 'virginity is the one thing that keeps us from the beasts'. The North African theologian Tertullian equated marriage with fornication. 'It is not disparaging wedlock to prefer virginity,' wrote St Jerome. 'No one can compare two things if one is good and the other evil.'

Martin Luther, who left his monastery to marry, inherited Augustine's bleak view of sex. 'No matter what praise is given to marriage,' he wrote, 'I will not concede that it is no sin.' Matrimony was a 'hospital for sick people'. It merely covered the shameful act with a veneer of respectability, so that 'God winks at it.' Calvin was the first Western theologian to praise marriage unreservedly, and thereafter Christians began to speak of 'holy matrimony'.

The present enthusiasm for 'family values' is, therefore, relatively recent. In the Roman Catholic Church, however, priests are still required to be celibate. Whatever the official teaching about the sanctity of marriage, the ban on artificial contraception implies that sex is only legitimate when there is a possibility of procreation. For most of its history, Christianity has had a more negative view of heterosexual love than almost any other major faith.[5]

Having looked briefly at attitudes towards heterosexual marriage in the general historical context of Judaism, Islam and Christianity, I would like to point out that all three religious traditions developed in patriarchal cultures. This coloured their views regarding women. Almost three decades ago, in trying to understand why so many Muslims, Christians and Jews believed that women were inferior and subordinate to men, I had identified three foundational theological assumptions in which this is rooted. They are, firstly, that God's primary creation is man, not woman. Created from man's rib, she is derivative and secondary ontologically. Secondly, woman, not man, was the primary agent of what is customarily described as the 'Fall', or man's expulsion from the Garden of Eden. Hence all 'daughters of Eve' are to be regarded with hatred, suspicion and contempt. Lastly, woman was created not only *from* man but also *for* man, which makes her existence merely instrumental and not of fundamental importance.

My research has demonstrated that the above assumptions are completely unwarranted in the light of the Qur'anic teachings relating to women. Moreover, a number of Christian and Jewish feminist scholars have challenged the traditional interpretations of the Genesis texts cited in support of these assumptions.

Our collective work has certainly made a difference in academic discourse relating to the issue of woman–man equality in the Jewish, Christian and Islamic traditions.

It has also been a source of enlightenment and empowerment for women and men who believe that the spirit of God has been breathed equally into all human beings. Not only are all human beings essentially equal in terms of their creation, they are also equal recipients of a great gift conferred by God, the most merciful and compassionate Creator and Sustainer of the universe. In one of its most beautiful and powerful verses, the Qur'an cites God's resounding proclamation: *Now, indeed, We have conferred dignity on the children of Adam.* (Surah 17: *Al-'Israa': 70*).

The scholarly repudiation of theological assumptions which have been used for centuries to systematically reduce women to a less-than-fully-human status is certainly to be celebrated. But what is to be done about the troubling fact that many Muslims, Christians and Jews continue to regard the inferiority and subordination of women to men as self-evident? Dualistic thinking viewed the world as consisting of two fundamentally different entities: mind and matter. Deifying the former while denigrating the latter, it identified men with mind and spirit. Women were linked to base corporeality. This thinking, which permeated many religious and philosophical traditions, caused untold damage to women through the ages. It still affects the mindset of many Christians, Jews and Muslims, though they may not always be conscious of this.

The Islamic tradition inherited not only the anti-women biases present in Christianity and Judaism, but also those predominant in pre-Islamic Bedouin culture. In it there was a concept of honour that belonged only to men. But it could be put in jeopardy by women if their behaviour, especially in a sexual context, was regarded as inappropriate. Since 1999, I have been involved in building an international coalition against 'honour killings' of girls and women, especially in Pakistan, which is, most unfortunately, the world's leading country in such brutal crimes. My study of crimes of honour made me realize how pre-Islamic ideas of 'honour', which had been totally rejected by Islam, had become a part of Muslim culture in general.

Amnesty International pointed out that in Pakistan honour crimes were supported by many people, including those responsible for the enforcement of law and justice. In my strenuous campaign against the mutilation and murder of a large number of girls and women, I used whatever facts I could gather about particular crimes. But in the end I had to remind not only the criminals but also those who promoted and supported them that they were violating God's essential attributes of mercy, compassion and justice. They would have to account for their actions on the Day of Judgment.

2.4 Patriarchal Culture and Homosexuality

My primary reason for doing a brief overview of attitudes towards human sexuality that have figured prominently in the

Jewish, Christian and Islamic traditions is to point at the deep biases that come to the fore as one delves into the subject. The discrimination, defamation and disclamation being felt today by our homosexual brothers and sisters in many communities have been experienced for centuries by women in heterosexual marriages. This happened whether they were seen in positive terms, as in the Jewish and Islamic traditions, or negatively, as in much of the Christian tradition.

All major religious traditions have developed in patriarchal cultures where men were in power and in a position to degrade women. Patriarchy may not hold sway in the same way today as it did in earlier times – at least in a number of Western societies. However, the bitter fact remains that there is inequality in power between those who hold authority in religious matters in most traditions and those who do not. This leads to oppression which cannot be deemed to be pleasing to God who is most merciful, compassionate and just.

Historically, there were a number of reasons, including biological, psychological, socio-cultural, economic and political, for the lower status of women in most Christian, Jewish and Muslim societies. The most deadly justification for this degradation was in religious terms, as my analysis of the three foundational assumptions in the foregoing narrative shows. With reference to our homosexual sisters and brothers, there are two main reasons that are generally given to justify the negativity shown towards them. The first, which in my opinion is the more important one, is 'religious'. The second focuses on what is 'natural'. Oftentimes the two reasons are used in conjunction. My brief remarks about these two reasons are given below.

Jews, Christians and Muslims who reject homosexuality on religious grounds cite texts from their respective scriptures. The Jewish texts used most often to condemn homosexuality are found in Leviticus 18:22 and 20:13. Professor Dr Johanna W.H. van Wijk-Bos, a Dutch theologian and Presbyterian minister teaching at the Louisville Presbyterian Theological Seminary, says the Christian text which contains the strongest condemnation of same-sex relations among women and men is Romans 1:18–32.[6]

The texts which Muslims use in condemnation of homosexuality are taken from the story of Prophet Lut (Lot) in the Qur'an, and are found in Surah 7: *Al-'A'raf:* 80–81; Surah 11: *Hud:* 77–79; Surah 15: *Al-Hijr:* 67–72; Surah 21: *Al-Anbiyaa':* 71, 74; Surah 26: *Ash-Shu'araa':* 165–168; Surah 27: *An-Naml:* 54–55; Surah 29: *Al-'Ankabut:* 28–29. Another verse sometimes cited in this context is Surah 4: *An-Nisaa':* 14–15.

Much has been written about the texts, especially in recent years. Traditional interpretations have been challenged by modern scholars who believe they need to be reformed. Knowing that scriptural texts have been hugely influential in moulding societal attitudes towards homosexuality, reformist thinkers of varying quality have analysed them in a variety of ways. Some have pointed out the intricacies of the language, and sought to show that other and better interpretations should be considered. Others have referred to a number of factors such as the historical, sociological, political and philosophical. They argue that these should be revisited to arrive at interpretations which are more in line with modern religious consciousness.

In an article entitled, 'Who says homosexuality is a sin?' Josh Gould cites an ancient quote by Rabbi Meir Baal Hanes: 'Any interpretation of scripture which leads to hatred or disdain of other people is illegitimate.' In the same vein, Karen Armstrong, the moving spirit behind the worldwide launching of a Charter of Compassion in November 2009, has stated: 'If your understanding of the divine made you kinder, more empathetic, and impelled you to express sympathy in concrete acts of loving-kindness, this was good theology. But if your notion of God made you unkind, belligerent, cruel, self-righteous, or if it led you to kill in God's name, it was bad theology.'[7]

Being a Muslim and coming from a tradition which regards the Qur'an as its highest source, I know the vital importance of scriptural texts in the lives of believers. When I began my Odyssean venture to develop the discipline of feminist theology in Islam, I knew that to win the battle for the recognition of Muslim women's God-given rights, each cited Qur'anic verse would have to be challenged and reinterpreted.

As I write this letter, I am all too aware of the fact that a similar battle will have to be fought with regard to the scriptural texts in the Christian and Jewish traditions. But there is neither time nor space here for this. Furthermore, I have learnt from my thirty-five years of engagement in Jewish-Christian-Muslim interfaith dialogue that it leads more often to theological wrangling than to a deepening of compassion for persons of other faiths.

The struggle to liberate scriptural texts from traditional, negative interpretations is not an easy matter for Jews, Christians and Muslims. Having trodden this path, I know how hard it is. Nonetheless, I encourage reformist scholars in the Jewish, Christian and Islamic traditions to follow the example of the Muslim modernist reformers of the past two centuries. Their rallying cry was: 'Back to the Qur'an, forward with Ijtihaad.' What they meant by this was that they had to purge their traditions of all those elements, which had overlaid and obscured the divine imperatives enshrined in the Qur'an. It was the search for the ethical principles which reflected God's essential attributes. Forward with 'Ijtihaad', which means 'independent reasoning', indicated that they would use their reason (which according to the Qur'an is God's special gift to humanity) to implement these principles to create God-centred societies.

I would like to share the wisdom of poet-philosopher Muhammad Iqbal, the most outstanding Muslim thinker since the death of Jalaluddin Rumi in 1273, who has had a formative influence on my life and work. He noted that '... things have changed and the world of Islam is today confronted and affected by new forces set free by the extraordinary development of human thought in all its directions'. Then he made a statement of extraordinary significance:

The claim of the present generation of Muslim liberals to re-interpret the foundational legal principles, in the light of their own experience and altered conditions of modern life, is in my opinion, perfectly justified. The teaching of the Qur'an that life is a process of progressive creation necessitates that each generation, guided but unhampered by the work of its predecessors, should be permitted to solve its own problems.

The second reason cited by those who oppose homosexuality, both on religious and secular grounds, is that it is not in accordance with 'nature'. This is being challenged by an increasing number of people from different disciplines and vocations. They do so largely on the basis of new developments in science and understandings of human personality. Reference is sometimes made to the 'old brain' and the 'new brain' which coexist uneasily in today's human beings. In her book *Twelve Steps to a Compassionate Life*, Karen Armstrong describes the evolution of the latter from the former and what this means in the modern way of life. She states:

There is no doubt that in the deepest recess of their minds, men and women are indeed ruthlessly selfish. This egotism is rooted in the 'old brain' bequeathed to us by the reptiles that struggled out of the primal slime some 500 million years ago. Wholly intent on personal survival, these creatures were motivated by mechanisms that neuroscientists have called the 'Four Fs': feeding, fighting, fleeing, and – for want of a more basic word – reproduction. These drives fanned out into fast-acting systems. They alerted reptiles to compete pitilessly for food, to ward off any threat, to dominate their territory, seek a place of safety, and perpetuate their genes.

To paraphrase: Armstrong reasons that our reptile ancestors were interested only in status, power, control, territory, sex, personal gain and survival. Homo sapiens inherited these neurological systems, located in the hypothalamus at the base of the brain. Thanks to them our species survived. The emotions they engender are strong, automatic and 'all about me'. Over the millennia, however, human beings also evolved a 'new brain', the neocortex. It is home to the reasoning powers. It enables us to reflect on the world and on ourselves, and to stand back from instinctive, primitive passions.

But the Four Fs continue to inform all our activities. These instincts are overwhelming and automatic. They are meant to override our more rational considerations. Armstrong points out that 'much of the twentieth century was certainly red in tooth and claw, and already the Four Fs have been much in evidence in the twenty-first ... And yet human beings continue to endorse ideologies that promote a principled, selfless empathy.'

A thought-provoking response to those who view homosexuality as 'unnatural' or against human nature has been made in the first comprehensive book on gay, lesbian and transgender Muslims by Dr Scott Siraj al-Haqq Kugle, a gay Muslim scholar, who teaches Islamic studies at Emory University.

Again, I paraphrase: modern psychiatry increasingly holds that sexual orientation is an inherent part of an individual's personality. Elements affecting it may be genetic, influenced by hormonal balances in the womb and shaped by early childhood experiences. The cumulative effects unfold during adolescence and early adulthood. Most psychiatrists in the West (and increasingly among professionals in Muslim communities) assert that one's attitude towards one's sexual orientation is largely cultural. But they add that orientation itself is not cultural. So the behaviour deriving from one's sexual orientation is subject to rational control and clinical modification. The underlying sexual orientation is not. In premodern times, philosophers also observed that sexual orientation was largely determined outside the choice of the individual. As professionals in Muslim communities slowly adopt clinical approaches based on research and modern medicine, they advocate a non-judgemental approach. At the same time, neo-traditionalist Muslims caricature homosexuality as a crime, a disease, or an addiction, and they have a wide audience.[8]

Despite the new data that has emerged, and is increasing, regarding the nature and causes of sexual orientation, in my opinion, a number of Jews, Christians and Muslims, open to re-examination of the traditional view, would agree that 'the specific origins of sexual identity and its etiology are still imperfectly understood'.[9]

While the debate continues between those who condemn homosexuality on the basis of the reasons stated above, and those who oppose them, same gender relationships have received social and legal recognition in many countries. They include Australia, Belgium, Canada, Denmark, France, Germany, Hungary, Iceland, Israel, the Netherlands, Norway, Portugal, South Africa, Spain, Sweden and the United Kingdom.

As pointed out by William Stacy Johnson:

> The new politics of gay recognition has come dramatically into conflict with the older politics of social control. In response to gay and lesbian demands for inclusion in the institution of marriage, others have insisted that changing the definition of who has access to marriage will have bad consequences for society as a whole. Although Europe and Canada have managed the political transition from control to recognition with relatively less social upheaval, in the United States the move toward recognising same-gender relationships has led to a formidable backlash.[10]

We live in strange times reminiscent of Dickens' memorable words at the start of *A Tale of Two Cities*:

> It was the best of times, it was the worst of times, it was the age of wisdom, it was the age of foolishness, it was the epoch of belief, it was the epoch of incredulity, it was the season of Light, it was the season of Darkness, it was the spring of hope, it was the winter of despair, we had everything before us, we had nothing before us, we were all going direct to Heaven, we were all going direct the other way.

While the 'formidable backlash' against gay marriages mentioned above was going on, the US Supreme Court was making landmark decisions. They would lead to what *Time* magazine has referred to as 'one of the most rapid and dramatic political shifts in US history'.[11] The article predicted that 'by summer, same-sex marriage rights will be law of the land'.

The die was cast in 1996, when the Supreme Court struck down Colorado's law, ruling for the first time that gay people cannot be discriminated against through law, no matter what the majority of voters might think. In 2003, the court went further, ruling that moral teachings are not sufficient reason to deny homosexuals the freedom to form intimate relationships. These two concepts led directly to the 2013 opinion in which the justices struck down the Defence of Marriage Act (DOMA). The court ruled that the Constitution bars the federal government from treating opposite-sex marriages differently from same-sex marriages in states which legalize both. Now the court will apply the same reasoning to state laws. Does the Constitution allow states to discriminate when Congress cannot? Can the fourteen states that still ban same-sex unions refuse to recognize those performed in other states?

Justice Anthony Kennedy, the dominant voice in the court's gay rights cases for two decades, left no doubt about his thinking in his 2013 majority opinion: 'No legitimate purpose' exists to justify a law 'to disparage and to injure' same-sex couples. DOMA 'instructs all federal officials, and indeed all persons with whom same-sex couples interact, including their own children, that their marriage is less worthy than the marriage of others'. The implications of such strong language are clear. Polls show that the majority of Americans are willing, even eager, to see the court take the final step.

The making of laws which protect vulnerable and marginalized persons from discrimination and harm is a highly significant event. Having seen the promulgation of laws which eroded the foundations of the human rights of Muslim women in Pakistan and other Islamic countries, and the devastating impact of these laws on so many precious lives, I am so thankful knowing that my gay sisters and brothers in the US will soon have the same legal rights as other Americans. But is the securing of legal rights – important as they are – all that these brothers and sisters want, or deserve, to have?

I am particularly concerned about my Muslim gay brothers and sisters. More especially if they are living in Islamic countries where homosexuality is condemned for reasons already mentioned. Also, because it is seen as part of the evil of 'Westernization' that has been imposed on them by erstwhile political colonizers or through the influx of mass Western culture in the modern era of cultural colonialism. There is no prospect of any gay rights movement arising in the Islamic world, where the human rights of the majority of women are still unrecognized, though their empowerment is one of the highest priorities of donor agencies in all Muslim countries. What can be done to bring about a change in Muslim societies and communities towards those who are homosexual or transgender?

I reiterate my belief that in order to open the hearts, minds and spirits of those who cherish the religious traditions of Judaism, Christianity and Islam, it is necessary to focus on God, Rahmaan and Raheem. I have cited many references to the infinite, unbounded mercy and compassion in texts that are very dear to believing Muslims, Jews and Christians. I have also referred to two Qur'anic verses, which declare that God has willed on Himself the law of grace and mercy. Such a law has, however, not been willed on human beings to whom the gracious Creator has granted the gift of freedom of will. God's mercy to human beings is shown through the moral guidance given to them. I quote below some Qur'anic texts that have profound ethical implications in the context of our dialogue.

In Surah 49: *Al-Hujurat:* 13, the Qur'an tells us that diversity has been created by God for a reason. *Behold! We have created you all out of a male and a female, and have made you into nations and tribes, so that you might come to know one another. Verily, the noblest of you in the sight of God is the one who is most deeply conscious of Him. Behold God is all-knowing, all-aware.*

Referring to the creation of all human beings from a male and a female, Muhammad Asad points out that several major Qur'anic exegetes have understood this to imply that the equality of biological origin reflects the equality of human dignity common to all. Explaining the phrase 'know each other', Asad says all belong to one human family, without any inherent superiority of one over another.

He connects this idea with the exhortation, in the two preceding verses, to respect and safeguard each other's dignity.

In other words, men's evolution into 'nations and tribes' is meant to foster rather than to diminish their mutual desire to understand and appreciate the essential human oneness underlying their outward differentiations. Correspondingly, all racial, national or tribal prejudice is condemned – implicitly in the Qur'an, and most explicitly by the Prophet who said, 'All people are the children of Adam, and Adam was created out of dust.'

It is worth quoting the two preceding verses. They show that God prohibits believers from engaging in immoral activities. Examples include derision, defamation, mockery and insulting others through offensive name-calling. Nor may we invade the privacy of others or speak ill of them in their absence.

O you who have attained to faith! No men shall deride (other) men: it may well be that those (whom they deride) are better than themselves; and no women (shall deride other) women: it may be that those (whom they deride) are better than themselves. And neither shall you defame one another, nor insult one another by (opprobrious) epithets: evil is all imputation of iniquity after (one has attained to) faith; and they who (become guilty thereof and) do not repent – it is they, they who are evildoers.

O you who have attained to faith! Avoid most guesswork (about one another) – for, behold, some of (such) guesswork is (in itself) a sin; and do not spy upon one another, and neither allow yourselves to speak ill of one another behind your backs.

In these verses as also in Surah 4: *An-Nisaa':* 148–149, and Surah 24: *An-Nur:* 16–19, the Qur'an decrees that all human beings must be protected from slander, ridicule and backbiting. This fundamental human right belongs as much to our gay brothers and sisters as to anyone else. Muslims, who do not honour it, are in violation of what God, Rahmaan and Raheem has mandated.

The Qur'anic statement that creation of diversity is a part of God's design requires deep reflection. Stating that 'there is a moral purpose behind the single God's creation of different and seemingly contradictory human types', Scott Siraj al-Haqq Kugle observes: 'Our human diversity is often cause for exclusion and violence, but it is actually God's way of challenging us to rise up to the demands of justice beyond the limitations of our individual egoism and communal chauvinism.'

It is important to refer to the Qur'an's attitude towards religious diversity, particularly among adherents of monotheistic traditions, in this interfaith dialogue. In his book *An Historian's Approach to Religion*, the noted historian Arnold Toynbee said all three religions, with their common historical root, have a tendency towards exclusivism and intolerance. They also ascribe to themselves an ultimate validity. This means that historically, Jews, Christians and Muslims have each tended to assume that they had a highly privileged, if not exclusive, relationship with God.

This is an assumption that has often led to triumphalism and the trivialization of the 'other'. It is categorically rejected by the Qur'an in a verse that is repeated twice, in Surah 2: *Al-*

Baqarah: 62 and Surah 5: *Al-Maa'idah:* 69. It has, in my opinion, no precedent in any religion: *Verily, those who have attained to faith (in this divine writ), as well as those who follow the Jewish faith, and the Christians, and the Sabians – all who believe in God and the Last Day and do righteous deeds – shall have their reward with their Sustainer; and no fear need they have, and neither shall they grieve.*

The core message is that what matters to God is not the 'label'. Whether one calls oneself an adherent of the Islamic, Jewish, Christian or any other God-centred religion, *anyone* who believes in God, in accountability for one's actions in this world on the Day of Judgment, and performs good deeds, will be rewarded by God and protected from fear and grief.

Surah 33: *Al-Ahzab:* 35 refers explicitly to both men and women in the context of their relationship to God: *Verily, for all men and women who have submitted themselves unto God, and all believing men and believing women, and all devout men and devout women, and all truthful men and truthful women, and all men and women who are patient in adversity, and all men and women who humble themselves (before God), and all men and women who give charity, and all men and women who fast (and have self-restraint), and all men and women who are mindful of their chastity, for all men and women who remember and remember God unceasingly; for them (all) has God readied forgiveness and a mighty reward.*

God does not judge different religious groups on the basis of the names which they attach to themselves. Nor does God judge individuals on the basis of their sexual identity, social, political or any other affiliations. Regardless of how Muslims have interpreted the specific texts in which they ground their

condemnation of homosexuality, it is the essence of what God is
— most merciful, most compassionate, most gracious, most just
— that must lie at the core of their faith and ethical framework.

The Message of the Qur'an is regarded by many contemporary
Muslim scholars as the best English translation and explanation
of the Qur'an. In his foreword, Muhammad Asad refers to the
two fundamental rules of Qur'anic interpretation. He states:

Firstly, the Qur'an must not be viewed as a compilation
of individual injunctions and exhortations but as one
integrated whole. It is, as an exposition of an ethical
doctrine in which every verse and sentence has an
intimate bearing on other verses and sentences. All of
them clarify and amplify each other. Consequently, its real
meaning can be grasped only if we correlate every one of
the statements with what has been stated elsewhere in its
pages. We try to explain its ideas by means of frequent
cross-references, always subordinating the particular to
the general and the incidental to the intrinsic...

Secondly, no part of the Qur'an should be viewed
from a purely historical point of view. All its references to
historical circumstances and events — both at the time of
the Prophet and in earlier times — must be regarded as the
illustrations of the human condition. They are not ends
in themselves. Hence, the considerations of the historical
occasion on which a particular verse was revealed must
never be allowed to obscure the underlying purport of
that verse.

It is my earnest hope that the truth and wisdom of Asad's words will reach not only Muslims who love the Qur'an, but also Jews and Christians who love their own scriptures. All of us are guilty, in some measure, of focusing on particular passages in our sacred texts rather than on seeking to understand their relationship to the larger context or the meaning of the text in its entirety.

Karen Armstrong observes:

> In fact, everybody reads the Bible selectively. If people followed every single ruling to the letter, the world would be full of Christians, who love their enemies and refuse to judge other people, which is plainly not the case. Christians would also be obliged to eat Kosher meat (*Acts* 15:20) and stone their disobedient sons to death (*Deuteronomy* 21:18–21) … The Bible must be read with care. It is not a holy encyclopaedia giving clear and unequivocal information. Nor is it a legal code that can be applied indiscriminately to our very different society. Lifting isolated texts out of their literary and cultural contexts can only distort its message. Instead, we should look at the underlying principles of biblical religion, and apply these creatively to our own situation.

I would like to remind Muslims that a large part of the Qur'an's concern is to free human beings from the chains that bind them: traditionalism, authoritarianism (religious, political, economic), tribalism, racism, classism or caste system, sexism and slavery. Recognising the human tendency towards dictatorship and despotism, the Qur'an states in categorical terms in Surah 3: *Al-'Imraan:* 79: *It is not conceivable that a human being unto whom God had granted revelation, and sound judgment, and prophethood, should thereafter have said unto people. 'Worship me besides God' but rather (did he exhort them), Become men of God by spreading the knowledge of the divine writ, and by your own deep study* (thereof).

The Qur'an says, with undiluted emphasis, that God, Rahmaan and Raheem, did not give the Prophet of Islam the right to command that his followers follow him rather than God. This has profound implications for Muslims. Islam has no Church that can institutionalize the edicts of its leaders. It cannot excommunicate those who do not obey its traditions and regulations. This means that no one other than God has the right to limit human freedom, as stated in Surah 42: *Ash-Shura':* 21.

2.5 Belief in Tawheed

The cardinal principle that underlies Islam is belief in Tawheed. It is enshrined in the words so beloved of Muslim mystics: *laa ilaaha il-Allah* (There is no god but God). Of great importance in this statement is the contrast between 'laa' which represents the negation of everything that is not God, and 'illa' which affirms the oneness and allness of God. As A.M. Schimmel says, this contrast has been from early times a subject of interest to many 'speculative minds who discovered not only a strictly dogmatic meaning, but also a deeper mystical truth in the confrontation of the *'laa"* and the *'illa"'*.

Many Muslim mystics held that it was not possible to find God until one had renounced everything that was not-God. A similar idea was expressed by Nathan Soderblom who was the Church of Sweden Archbishop of Uppsala between 1914 and 1931, and the recipient of the 1930 Nobel Peace Prize. As he said:

> No is also needed. Without No there will be no proper Yes. For then all that denies and destroys, degrades and delays what is right and good would be allowed to remain unattacked and unabolished. That is why a No is necessary in the moral warfare of the individual, in the evolution of religion and in the history of the race.[12]

In the context of Tawheed, the Qur'an makes many references to Prophet Abraham's passionate, dedicated quest for God. Referring to his special virtue in this regard, the Qur'an states in Surah 16: *An-Nahl:* 120–122: *He was devout to God, turning away from all that is false, and was never of those who ascribe divinity to aught beside God.* Prophet Abraham's demolition of the idols worshipped by his people sets a model for all who revere this great Prophet who is equally important for Jews, Christians and Muslims.

Iqbal, in his historic lectures on *The Reconstruction of Religious Thought in Islam*, referred to Tawheed as 'the foundation of world unity', and stated: 'From the unity of the all-embracing

Ego (God) who creates and sustains all egos follows the essential unity of all mankind.' In his view, 'The essence of Tawheed as a working idea is equality, solidarity and freedom.' Pointing out that Islam does not recognize the 'tyrant overlordship' of either 'the sceptered monarch or 'the surpliced priest', Iqbal cites the example of the Prophet of Islam who translated the principles deriving from God's Unity and Sovereignty into terms of actual living:

He shattered every ancient privilege,
And built new walls to fortify mankind,
He breathed fresh life in Adam's weary bones, Redeemed the slave from bondage, set him free.[13]

Iqbal is the foremost reformist thinker of the modern period and is regarded as 'the spiritual founder' of Pakistan, the only country in the world that was created in the name of Islam. He was deeply aware of, and profoundly saddened by, the fact that 'the pure brow of the principle of Tawheed has received more or less an impress of heathenism, and the universal and impersonal character of the ethical ideals of Islam has been lost through a process of localization'. The fact that in his own career as a political thinker Iqbal rejected this 'process of localization' shows that for him the ideas implicit in Tawheed were a living force – a practical not just a theoretical necessity.

Explaining Iqbal's unshakable loyalty to Tawheed, Halide Edib, Turkish writer, scholar and public figure dedicated to women's emancipation, observes insightfully in her book:

> To whatever political creed the Muslim may belong, his ultimate loyalty must be to the One God who cannot be symbolised by material objects or by ideas. This point was best expressed by the Muslim members of the 'Front Populaire', in the French colonies. They lifted their fists like the rest of their comrades, giving the sign of their political creed, but added to it the lifting of their index finger to the sky. The last is the sign common to all Muslims: 'There is no God but one God...' is always said with that gesture meaning God to be above and beyond all terrestrial ideas and symbols.[14]

Through his powerful message articulated in poetry and prose in Farsi, Urdu and English, Iqbal had motivated millions of Indian Muslims to struggle to actualize the ideal of Tawheed in practical terms. But his words and vision have been deliberately excluded from public discourse in Pakistan which owes its existence to him. This was done by the country's self-serving power wielders who wanted to keep the people subservient, so that they would not challenge them or claim their own rights.

The moral, intellectual, social, cultural, economic and political degeneration that characterizes today's Pakistan is also evident, in varying degrees, in the Muslim world in general. The challenge posed to contemporary Muslims by Iqbal, whose philosophy is rooted in the ethical vision of the Qur'an, is to return to laa ilaaha il-Allah. What this means is that they must reject all that is in opposition to God even if it is a belief, an idea, an attitude, a custom, a practice, or anything else that has been hallowed by religious or cultural traditions. They must not deify symbols of authority or false gods that claim total allegiance. Those who worship what is not God are sternly rebuked in Surah 12: *Yusuf:* 40: *All that you worship instead of God is nothing but (empty) names which you have invented – you and your forefathers – (and) for which God has bestowed no warrant from on high.* This verse contains a critically important statement: *Judgement (as to what is right or what is wrong) rests with God alone.*[15]

We are living in a world in which hatred and fear of Islam is assuming near-cosmic proportions amongst many non-Muslims. The majority of Muslims are acutely troubled by the increasing violence in their own societies. I feel very strongly that bearing witness to laa ilaaha il-Allah in word and deed, and inculcating in ourselves the essential attributes of God, who *is* Rahmaan and Raheem, is the most important religious challenge that we face today. I believe that it is possible to reform Muslim societies and communities. We need to internalize and fulfil the constantly reiterated Qur'anic commandment to be compassionate to those who are vulnerable to physical, emotional, psychological hardship. The same applies to those subjected to social, economic and political injustice. Persecution is commonly inflicted upon those who are marginalized and unable to exercise the fundamental rights that God has granted to all human beings.

The Qur'an gives us a serious warning in Surah 29: *Al-'Ankabut: 1–3: Do men think that on their (mere) saying, 'We have attained to faith', they will be left to themselves, and will not be put to a test? Yea, indeed, We did test those who lived before them; and so, (too, shall be tested the people now living; and) most certainly will God mark out those who prove themselves true, and most certainly will He mark out those who are lying.*

As a Muslim I believe that we are called upon today to prove our faithfulness to God by committing ourselves to the cause and service of those individuals and groups in our communities, who face the greatest jeopardy and difficulties. They certainly include our gay sisters and brothers. Impelled and compelled by the Qur'an's ethical injunctions, many of which I have cited in this letter, we must stand up for their dignity and safety. We must make the effort to connect with their humanity, to listen to their story, to share their suffering and joy. As a Muslim I believe that love is not a word, it is a deed. We must demonstrate through our actions that our hearts are open to our gay brothers and sisters, and that we stand side by side with them in the loving presence of God, Rahmaan and Raheem.

Jews and Christians, who also believe that God is most merciful and most compassionate, have an ethical mandate similar to that of Muslims. With reference to the Jewish tradition, Karen Armstrong observes: 'Throughout the Pentateuch, the priestly writers insist on God's compassionate care for the creatures: all are pronounced good, exactly as he made them. Even those animals declared "unclean" in the cult must be left in peace and their integrity respected.'

Love is the central focus of the primary commandments given by Jesus in Mark 12:30–31. This is the first: *Listen, O Israel, the Lord our God is the one Lord, and you must love the Lord your God with all your heart, with all your soul, with all your mind and with all your strength. The second is this: You must love your neighbour as yourself. There is no commandment greater than these.*

In Matthew 5:44, Jesus commanded his followers to love even their enemies because God is merciful to good and bad people alike. As Armstrong says:

In the New Testament, Jesus goes out of his way to consort with those whose sexual lives were condemned by the self-righteous establishment. According to Jesus, nobody has the right to cast the first stone in these matters. For centuries Christians failed to live up to this inclusive mandate and found it hard to accept their sexuality. Eventually, however, they learned to overcome their prejudice in favour of celibacy, and realized that heterosexual marriage could bring them to God. The current attempt to recognize homosexual partnerships is ... the latest development in the long struggle to bring sexuality in the ambit of the sacred.

The strong emphasis on God's mercy and compassion in the Qur'an, the New Testament and the Hebrew Bible makes it self-evident that all humans, irrespective of sexual identity, are recipients of God's unbounded grace. Jews, Christians and Muslims must recognize what this means in terms of their interaction with their brothers and sisters, who are gay, lesbian or transgender. For me as a Muslim, the meaning is very clear. I must be merciful and compassionate towards all, especially towards those who are suffering. But I am also called upon to live up to the principle embodied in laa ilaaha il-Allah. I must say no to what is not in conformity with God's mercy, compassion and justice.

At an existential level I believe that what is truly important in our world and in our lives are intimate human relationships and not sexuality, whether heterosexual, homosexual or transgender. If a relationship is based on mutual love, compassion, respect, trust, protection and fidelity, it is to be celebrated, for it is certainly one of God's greatest blessings to be cherished forever. On the other hand, if a relationship is characterized by selfishness, abuse, exploitation, cruelty, oppression and disloyalty, it is not something to celebrate. In fact, if one of the partners in the relationship is in danger of being harmed by the other, as is unfortunately a very common occurrence, intervention becomes a moral duty.

2.6 Conclusion

I would like to end my letter to you – my sisters and brothers who are Muslim, Christian and Jewish – with the same words with which I began it: Bismil-laah ir Rahmaan ir Raheem (In the Name of God, the most merciful and gracious, the most compassionate and the dispenser of grace) and the earnest request that we should all, individually and collectively, include it in our daily prayer and meditation.

To my gay sisters and brothers, I send my blessings and the immortal words of Rumi who invites us all to a higher place beyond the reach of common humanity:

Out beyond ideas of wrongdoing and rightdoing,
There is a field. I'll meet you there.
When the soul lies down in that grass,
The world is too full to talk about.
Ideas, language, even the phrase 'each other'
Doesn't make any sense.[16]

Was-salaam (Peace be unto you)

I Am a Woman

Riffat Hssan

I am a woman
with the eternal heart
of a woman
who, like Othello,
loved not wisely
but too well.

I am a woman
with the eternal heart
of a woman
living in a world
in which the rules
are made by men —
and where men can
break all the rules
and yet be gods

saviours and saints
martyrs and heroes
but where if women
break the rules
made by men
broken by men
they cannot live
without being shamed
slandered and abused
beaten and hurt
scourged and stoned
burned and buried
alive and damned.

I am a woman
with the eternal heart

of a woman
born to love
living in a world
in which when men
love – they are called
princes and knights
poets and mystics

or at the worst – perhaps –
lunatics;
but when women love
then love becomes
a mortal sin
for which they must
give up their life –
for when a woman
is guilty of
a mortal sin
– the sin of loving –
then she must die
so that the jealous
god of love
may be at peace.

I am a woman
with the eternal heart
of a woman

living in a world
in which there are
a number of men
and also some women
who cannot love;
and since love is
what makes us human
and gives us life
these men and women
are callous and cold,
cruel and cowardly
though they wear
the masks of sages
and madonnas
and cherubs;
and they are always
ready to strike
my eternal heart
because I dare
to live and love.

I am a woman
with the eternal heart
of a woman
who has endured
so many births
and so many deaths

so that the seed
of life and love
may not be
destroyed by those
who in the name
of god of love
who does not love

want to create
a loveless world
a lifeless world
full of tombs
where one cannot hear
the sound of life –
the laughter
of a little child
warm from the womb
who wants to live
and wants to love
and to whom
an eternal-hearted woman
is what god should be.

I am a woman
with the eternal heart
of a woman
the bearer of life
the nurturer of life

the protector of life
I can give life
because I am not
afraid of pain
for I know that love
is always pain

even joyful love
is ringed with pain
and no one can love
who cannot embrace
with heart and soul
the pain of living
the pain of loving.

I am a woman
with the eternal heart
of a woman
and I can suffer
again and again
the pain of loving
men and women
who do not love
who will tear
my heart and soul
to little shreds
and who will put

my life-carrying body
upon death's bed
in order to placate a god
who says he is
the god of love
but who abhors
both life and love
and who demands
a sacrifice – my sacrifice –
and says that I
must slaughtered be
just like an animal
helpless and trapped
whose blood is spilled
so that the sins
of those who kill
may be forgiven.

I am a woman
with the eternal heart
of a woman
and though I may be
tormented and abandoned
dishonoured and disowned
scourged and flogged
stoned and burned
and buried alive

I will never
be a martyr
I will never
be a victim
I will never
be a loser
I will always
be a survivor
I will always
be a winner
I will always
be triumphant

for though I go
I will return
and though I die
I will live again
forever and forever
for I am a woman
with the eternal heart
of a woman
and since my heart
is made of love
and love is eternal
embodied in creation
leading to resurrection
though all else will burn

with the funeral pyre
in the flames of the fire
my eternal heart
will never to ashes turn

and like a phoenix I will
   rise again
and like a phoenix
I will be reborn.

3

A Jewish Perspective

By Rabbi Jay Michaelson

- Introduction

- Biblical Values Affirming Sexual Diversity

- Leviticus

- Sodom and Gomorrah

- Love Between Men in the Bible

- The Gifts of Sexual Diversity

- An Invitation to Conscience

3.1 Introduction

'GOD versus Gay' is a myth. Taken as a whole, the vast majority of biblical texts set down fundamental values such as the importance of love, justice and compassion. Those values, in turn, urge a narrow reading of the two Hebrew Bible verses which seem to talk about same-sex intimacy – a reading restricting the text to only one form of sexual expression, only by men, and only in extremely limited contexts with nothing to do with lesbian and gay lives as they are lived today. Such readings, of various types, have been adopted by all but Orthodox movements of Judaism – representing about 80 per cent of the American Jewish population. Unsurprisingly, Jews are the religious group most likely to support marriage equality, LGBT non-discrimination protection, and other LGBT rights issues, with support generally in the 75–90 per cent range.

And yet the myth persists.

As a rabbi and long-time LGBT activist, I have counselled many religious young people who are terrified of having to choose between happiness and their religious way of life. Within Orthodox and Ultra-Orthodox communities, children are still being disowned, lives are being squandered and hateful legislation is still promoted.

Before I came out, I was certain that being openly gay would spell the end of my religious life. I was an Orthodox-practising Jew, and the practice gave meaning and shape to my life. I repressed my sexuality, acting out occasionally but regretting it afterwards. I tried, for years, to change. Eventually, after ten years in the closet I had had enough. The pain, isolation, loneliness and shame had grown so great that I was ready to forsake my religion for the sake of my happiness.

What I found was a shock.

Coming out was the doorway to greater religious faith and joy than I had ever imagined. My relationship with God and my religious community grew stronger. My spiritual path began to unfold, my prayer life began to awaken. My love for other human beings slowly unfurled and expanded. Coming out was not the end of my religious life, but the beginning of it.

'God versus Gay' – and I will be writing here of sexual orientation, rather than gender identity, though many of the same issues are implicated – isn't just a false dichotomy. It's a rebellion against the image of God itself. Just imagine lying to everyone you know all the time. Imagine feeling that your soul, your way to love and relationship and delight, is distorted, evil and broken. Imagine believing that because of something you cannot change God hates you. What would you do? If you are like me, you would do everything you could to change this awful part of yourself. You would construct ever more elaborate masks that hopefully conceal the dark truth. When all else fails, you will consider ending your life.

Where do these feelings come from? Whose fault is it that, in the United States of America, 40 per cent of gay teenagers consider suicide – four times as many as straight kids? Ours, of course. The paradox is searing: you're making the wrong choice, because homosexuality is a sin, but you're so sick, you can't make the right one.

Behold, I Make All Things New

Some believe that self-hatred and contradiction is required by a loving God. They think that God wants 5 per cent of human beings to hate themselves, repress themselves and consider killing themselves – all because of a trait, an aspect of their souls.

But this cannot be if we take seriously the fundamental values of our religious tradition. The sanctity of relationship, love of God and of our neighbours, the holiness of life, the importance of justice and compassion demand that those of us who are LGBT live full lives. These values also demand that others become supportive, loving allies. If the Divine Word is a tree of life, whose paths are pleasant, how could it lead to the tyranny of the closet and the threats still experienced by gay people around the world?

Culture/Visibility

Before turning to religious material, though, we must first take a deceptively simple step: admit the existence and dignity of gay and lesbian people. Even in the twenty-first century, denial of this existential reality is still a frequent tactic. There are still those who insist that homosexuality is a 'lifestyle', a choice or a pathology, and that all of us who feel it in our souls are deluded, perverted or worse.

Fortunately, if religion provides much of the impetus for this wilful ignorance, it also provides a remedy. Personal experience, personal testimony and meaningful communication within one's faith community are part of every Western religious tradition. Evangelicals offer their life's stories as witness to the operation of grace in their lives. Rabbis base their legal decisions on both the weight of precedent and the tenability of law in people's lives. Listening to our neighbours counts, religiously.

All this is based on experience, on meeting the 'other' and acknowledging him or her. The common denominators are openness, honesty, conversation and sacred religious values applied to the sacred task of understanding Scripture, tradition, reason and experience. To deny the testimonies of millions of people is an aberration, an unjustified departure from the norm of religious conversation.

And, if religious communities negate lesbian/gay voices, many are prepared to reciprocate. They abandon religion as part of their journey to self-acceptance. Who can blame them? If doors are shut in one's face for decades, eventually one stops knocking.

But sexual diversity is real. The question is how religious people should respond to this reality. Authentic religion never hides its head in the sand. Religious communities have capably revised their doctrines regarding non-European people, women and other formerly marginalized groups in light of clearer understandings. So are we invited to engage with the reality of sexual diversity.

To be sure, that reality is also more complicated than words like 'gay' and 'lesbian' indicate. Every study of human sexuality, from Kinsey onwards, reveals it to be more like a continuum than a duality. Indeed, many people, especially women, experience their sexuality as bisexual or in some other fluid way.[1] Even for those who experience their sexuality as a continuum, 'choice' is surely not the right word to convey the essence of sexual identity. I choose what clothes to wear and what to eat for lunch. Bisexuals and those of more fluid sexuality do not 'choose' to fall in love. They do not 'choose' to possess their sexual identities. Thus, even where there are aspects of volition and ranges of possible partners – more common among women than among men – there are also elements of depth, essence and soul.

Moreover, several scholars and theorists have suggested that our tendency to focus on genitalia and sexual intercourse may, itself, be part of the problem. Women's sexuality may be more fluid and not necessarily expressed in genital, erotic contact. For example, Adrienne Rich, in her influential essay, 'Compulsory Heterosexuality and Lesbian Existence',[2] argued that we should focus less on genital acts among women and more on how romantic or affectionate pairs of women formed a kind of 'lesbian continuum' and created alternatives to 'compulsory heterosexuality'.

Lillian Faderman has persuasively shown how 'romantic friendships', which may or may not have had a sexual component, were often women's primary emotional – and 'erotic' in the general sense – ties.[3] It is more fruitful historically and does less violence to women's experience to recognize and appreciate instances where they are able to construct alternatives to compulsory heterosexuality, rather than try to fit women's intimacy into artificial binaries that privilege male experience.

It is also true, as I have remarked already, that our current categories of homosexuality, gay, lesbian, bisexual and so on are of relatively recent coinage. In the academic world, a debate rages about whether sexuality is socially constructed, or whether it is an essential, trans-historical fact of life. It yields more heat than light. On the one hand, we know from visual evidence such as pottery, paintings and textual evidence that same-sex behaviour has existed since the dawn of human expression. On the other hand, we also know that it has been construed differently by different societies. For example, as recently as 200 years ago, many men in many cultures would not consider themselves 'gay' simply because they engaged in sexual relations with other men as long as they took the insertive, 'active' role. This was because sexual identity was defined not by the gender of one's partner but the role one took in intercourse.

As certain as we are that same-sex behaviour has taken place everywhere across time, we are equally sure it has been understood in terms very different from our own. Thus, as we turn to our religious traditions for information regarding homosexuality, we must do so with the understanding that 'homosexuality' and 'heterosexuality' did not even exist as categories until relatively recently. Even the term 'sodomy' wasn't invented until the eleventh century. To say 'the Bible forbids homosexuality' is as ridiculous as saying 'the Bible forbids the Internet'.

This does not mean that we have no recourse to sacred text. Its categories are different from our own, and that is an important point. Even if 'gay' people did not exist since time immemorial, people similar to gays have. Sexual diversity is, as we'll see later, one of the great gifts of human experience –

a great gift that God has given us. As pioneering gay activist Frank Kameny first said, gay is good or, at least, it has the same potential for good as other forms of sexuality.

But before we can agree or disagree with that assessment, we must first accept the fact that sexual diversity exists. It is an ineluctable part of the souls of millions of people around the world.

What is religiously significant isn't how anatomies bump up against one another but how the souls of lovers intertwine. This knowledge may only be gained first-hand or from direct testimony. What differentiates homosexuality from bestiality, incest and the rest? Love, of course. The presence of mutuality, kindness and caring in relationship; the holiness of sacred companionship. There are plenty of published sources to consult but the real 'sources' must be your own soul, and the testimonies of others who are lesbian or gay. And to explore how the mainstream religious traditions validate and celebrate same-sex love, we must first acknowledge it.

Naturalness

The second threshold in the progress of our investigation is to understand this: homosexuality is natural. The sentence is simple, true and supported by scientific evidence. Yet, we in Western religious communities are so used to hearing it is unnatural, disordered or against the will of God that it may seem surprising, even blasphemous, at first. It remains a primary campaign slogan of the religious right. The 'natural family' is the code word at the United Nations and elsewhere for promoting heterosexual, monogamously married couples with children, above all other family configurations. 'Gender complementarity' is still used in religious statements about the moral wrongness of homosexuality.

All of these claims (such as 'lifestyle' and 'choice') attempt to render LGB people invisible. And it is pointless to proceed with our exploration of the religious value of sexual diversity if these threshold issues are not met. Thus, we queer people must first establish that we do, in fact, exist.

In fact, sexual diversity is part of the fabric of nature. A fabric for theists, woven by God. Same-sex behaviour is found in guppies, macaques and penguins – not to mention over 100 species of mammals, from apes to elephants. Put in stark religious terms, sexual diversity is part of God's plan.

Often, when one asserts the naturalness of homosexuality, a second question immediately arises: what purpose does it serve? But why there is homosexuality in nature is a different question from whether there is. Clearly, our attempts to answer the 'why' will be speculation: *Where were you when I laid the foundations of the Earth?* (Job 38:4) The point is not 'it is in nature, therefore it is good' but just 'it is in nature'.

Moreover, many traits remain mysterious even within a given frame. Some aspects of physiology readily lend themselves to explanation, like tigers having sharper teeth than cows. But many others are not easily explained. We cannot pretend to know the 'mind' of evolution, let alone the mind of God. Rather, the central point is the naturalness and existence of homosexuality in nature.

In the past two decades, considerable evidence has amassed for the biological basis of sexual orientation. The research is well summarized and synthesized in the recent book by Simon LaVey, *Gay, Straight, and the Reason Why*. Specifically, the region of the brain most responsible for sexual behaviour is different in gay men and straight men, with the former's more closely resembling that of women. The evidence suggests that a combination of genetics, birth order and the levels of sex hormones circulating during foetal life causes this different brain structure to develop. Brain structure among transgender people has not been studied as widely, but preliminary results are similar. Sexuality is thus a physical characteristic with psychological effects. Nor are its effects limited to sexual choice. Secondary physical characteristics that generally distinguish gay people from straight may even include fingernail length. The differences between gay and straight children manifest before puberty.

Many species display homosexual behaviour and several have individuals with durable preferences for same-sex partners. In Paul Vasey's study of macaques, for example, female pairs were shown to exist and endure without any particular necessity. Farmers know that some rams prefer other rams. We now know that the rate of homosexuality among sheep is about 10 per cent, and the rams have the same difference in brain structure found among gay men. The behaviour of the bonobos, among our closest genetic relatives, has been known for decades. In short, we cannot deny the reality of sexual diversity by pretending it does not exist. It does. The religious question is how we are to understand it.

As for 'the reason why', we don't know. Some scientists have suggested that, perhaps, homosexuality exists in nature because it is advantageous for communities to have some members more concerned with care of other people's children or with the community as a whole. This is called the 'kin selection' model. Interestingly, this scientific theory accords with some human communities, which have given special roles to gender-variant people. The 157 Native American tribes regard them as sacred 'third-gendered' people with special abilities as healers, shamans or warriors. The fa'afafine of Samoa, essentially homosexual men, help with child-rearing.

Other models suggest that male homosexuality is actually an enhanced sexual attraction to males that may be of biological advantage to females, or that some percentage of homosexuality among animal populations helps promote group cooperation and cohesion.

Still other scientists have observed that in animal species close to our own, sexuality performs many functions other than reproduction. Bonobo apes, for example, engage in sexual behaviour to build all kinds of relationships, to establish power, and, apparently, for fun. They also have one of the most peaceful of primate cultures. In this context, sexual variance could serve as an ordering mechanism for societal structures.

Obviously, it would be unwise to extrapolate human norms from animal behaviour. 'Natural' does not mean morally good, but it does mean that the view that homosexuality is unnatural is at odds with the facts.

I also appreciate the scientific evidence of the physical nature of homosexuality in humans and its common appearance among animals. As someone who cares deeply for the natural world, I like knowing that my sexuality is not an aberration and is connected to the rhythms of life around me. It is useful to me that scientists can now measure the structure of my brain to verify the inclinations of my heart. Useful perhaps, not essential.

Indeed, what seems most 'unnatural' is the norm of heterosexual monogamy, which is not present in the Bible, unlike polygamy, prostitution, arranged marriage and marriage to young children. The 'family values' of the Bible are one man with many wives, several concubines and many, many children. These norms lasted through the time of Christ.

Recall, too, that the Hebrew Bible is not burdened with the Pauline doctrine, in which what is 'natural' (physin) does not mean 'according to biology' but rather 'according to the proper hierarchy of male and female'. Namely, women must always be passive and men must always be active. For Paul, as for two millennia of Christian history, part of the 'natural law' is that men should always dominate women. This was not different from how Roman society encouraged certain forms of male homosexual behaviour, but demanded that the more privileged partner take the 'active' role. Adult free males could penetrate slaves (of any gender), and men could penetrate women. But, as Bernadette Brooten says, 'free, adult males ought never to be passive, and women should never be active … [and] should they transgress these boundaries, society deemed their behaviour contrary to nature'.

In fact, Paul's language is strikingly similar to that of the Jewish/Hellenistic philosopher Philo, who said that in Sodom (i.e., Rome), 'they accustomed those who were by nature men to submit to play the part of women'. Contrary to popular clichés about ancient Rome, this was stigmatized even then. For example, Julius Caesar was relentlessly mocked for assuming the receptive role in his relationship with Nicomedes, the King of Bithynia. Doing this relative to a slave or man of inferior rank was actually criminalized.

In an age of female presidential candidates, do we still believe that for women to ever 'rule' over men is 'unnatural'? Of course not. Notwithstanding their claims to scientific objectivity, categories like physin are culturally specific, and most of us have already set aside this particular iteration of it.

There is one final consequence of the naturalness of homosexuality: the appreciation of the complexity and beauty of nature, with sexual diversity being part of it. *The heavens declare the glory of God, and the firmament tells of the work of God's hands.* (Psalm 19:1) *Lift your eyes and look to the heavens: Who created all these? God, who brings out the starry host one by one, and calls them each by name.* (Isaiah 40:26)

Appreciating the beauty and diversity of nature humbles and inspires us. Sexual diversity is another one of these works. What God has created, we are invited to appreciate, marvel at, preserve and explore. God is described in the Jewish tradition as the *meshaneh habriyot*, the one who varies creation. Sexual diversity is as much a part of the variety of nature as are mountain vistas and snowstorms and sun showers. Some flowers are red, others yellow; some feathers are brown, others blue. Nature loves variety, diversity and plenitude.

Just as the heavens declare the glory of God, so too do the infinite permutations of human intimacy, and their correspondingly infinite capacities for love. We inhabit a sensual universe filled with delight, and capable of great sanctity. That sexual diversity is natural means that it does exist; that it is not something apart from the order of nature. On the contrary, it is part of something wondrous, something beyond the capacity of the mind to frame, beyond the capacity of speech to articulate. It is a mystery why we humans love the way we do, and how powerfully love tugs us towards reconciling heaven and Earth.

Reading Religiously

Finally, to explore what religious traditions have to say about sexual diversity requires a specific kind of reading. All of us, of course, bring preconditions to ancient biblical text. Perhaps, you don't believe in 'God', or understand the word differently from how I do, or do not understand it at all. On the other hand, maybe you believe it is impossible for the Bible to be wrong, not only on its surface but even as interpreted by tradition. Maybe, you've had the heavy books of the Bible thrown at you so many times that you have no interest in picking them up and opening them.

All of these views are understandable, legitimate and not to be denied. But the invitation here is to look afresh at a few biblical texts together, because they tell us something crucial about human relationships, and/or at least tell us something about how Christian and Jewish traditions conceive them. This matters even if you are not religious. At the very least, whatever one's views about God, the Bible or religion in general, these traditions have shaped how we live, and continue to inform moral judgements. The verses retain an immense power to inform and inspire. But at its best, religion takes the inescapable realities of our human lives and connects them to our deepest values. Birth and death, eating and drinking, and the ethics of commercial life. All of these are grist to the mill, because religion and spirituality are meant not as Sunday hobbies but as ways of life itself. A spirituality that is not at home in hospital wards, ancient forests and shopping malls, and which says nothing about how we are to relate to each other, is not a real spirituality.

Nor can we only focus on the 'good' texts. In a moment, we will look at Genesis 2:18–25, which talks about love and companionship. If those verses were all that our religious traditions had to say about human relationships, the answer would be fairly simple. For most people, *a man ... shall hold fast to his wife*. In some cases, a woman shall hold fast to hers. And in some others, a man shall hold fast to another.

But, of course, it's not so simple, because many people sincerely believe that certain other verses – Leviticus 18:22, Romans 1:27 – rule out the possibility that Adam and Steve can be a couple allowing for grace, love and holiness. Later, we will see that these few verses are obscure, ambiguous and certainly do not contemplate loving, committed relationships. But, first, we need to build a larger context in which to understand them.

We do this all the time. Consider the most basic of ethical norms: not to kill. This one of the Ten Commandments is quite clear, and its two words – *lo tirtzach* in Hebrew – do not admit of any exceptions. Yet we all know that, for better or for worse, there are exceptions. For example, most people (and, clearly, biblical texts) believe it is justified to kill in self-defence, or as part of a just war. No verse exists in a vacuum, even when it is as unequivocal and clear as *Thou shalt not kill.* How much more so, then, for a handful of biblical verses which are ambiguous in their wording and intent.

The 'bad' verses have plenty of ink devoted to etymology, cultural context, Hebrew and Greek. In those traditional communities still not reconciled with sexual diversity, they still get plenty of airplay. But no interpretation has any grounding without our fundamental religious values. A talented biblical commentator can twist words to mean whatever she wishes them to mean; 'The devil can cite Scripture for his purpose.'[4] What differentiates a linguistic game from a sincere engagement with sacred text is how much is at stake. How sincere are our intentions? How careful are we? How connected are we to our fundamental values?

The question is not whether gay people can find a way to weasel around Leviticus's verses, or whether anti-gay people can use them as a brickbat. It is what our deepest shared values tell us about the nature of same-sex relationships. In some ways, that is a harder, longer conversation. It is also deeply rewarding. Engaging with these fundamental values, in text and in conscience, reminds us how important they are. Being gay, or having a gay relative or parishioner, may be the reason for our inquiry, but it is important for everyone. It is a sacred act.

3.2 Biblical Values Affirming Sexual Diversity

Companionship

'It's Adam and Eve, not Adam and Steve.' We've all heard the cliché, and know its meaning: that whatever nature has to say, God has said that male and female complement one another, that only a man and a woman may marry.

Yet the pairing of Adam and Eve was the solution to a problem. In the more detailed version of the Creation story, they don't just appear on the stage; human coupling is the result of Divine fidgeting. God creates the human being, but then has to tinker with the original plan, because of the first flaw. What is that problem?

Loneliness. *It is not good for humans to be alone*, God says in Genesis 2:18. In context, this is a shocking pronouncement. Six times, God had remarked how good everything was: light, heaven and earth, stars, plants, animals. The entirety of Creation is *very good*. Yet suddenly something is not good, something which all of us experience in our own lives and which we all strive to transcend: the existential condition of being alone.

Loneliness is the first problem of Creation, and love comes to solve it. The biblical writer (or writers) looks around the world and finds a natural environment filled with radical beauty. It is a world that is 'good' for one chapter and seventeen verses.

Notice too that Eve is not the first solution for Adam's aloneness. God first presents him with every animal in the world. But none suffices. Only then does the story of Genesis 2 tell us that God took the rib from man to make woman. Only human companionship solves the existential problem of aloneness – the first problem our religious traditions set out to address.

Finally, notice that Eve is not created, in this narrative, to make children with Adam. Indeed, Eve's femininity is not even essential to be an *ezer kenegdo* – a 'help-meet', someone able to be with Adam on equal terms and be a companion to him. Of course, procreation is also a central value, and it is articulated later in the text, but this story, on its terms, is about companionship.

I know how 'Adam and Eve' has been used as a weapon against gay people (and women), but I read it as validating the importance of human love and companionship. If one has had the experience of love (of a partner, of a community, of God), then one can know what this verse is really about. What is read in Genesis becomes inscribed in the heart: that human relationship is the bridge across existential loneliness.

For most people, this love is experienced in a relationship between a man and a woman. For about 5 per cent of people this love is found in a relationship between two men, or between two women. For others, love may be found in either kind of relationship, and sexuality may be experienced as fluid.

During my teens and twenties, as I struggled with my sexuality, I had relationships with women, and, as much as I was able, fell in love. But something was always 'off', even though at the time I couldn't quite identify it. After ten years of wrestling, cajoling, self-hating, self-judging and finally a serious car accident I finally admitted the truth: if I wanted true love, the kind that the *Song of Songs* sings about, my Eve would have to be a Steve.

It was not easy to admit. As I have said, I was raised a Conservative Jew, but I had taken on Orthodox Jewish practice in my twenties, like many young people searching for a more holistic and committed form of Jewish life. And I thought that 'coming out' would spell the end of my religious life.

But what some folks don't understand about 'the closet' is that it is not just a set of walls around sexual behaviour. It is a net of lies that affects absolutely everything in one's life: how you dress, who you befriend, how you walk, how you talk. And, more importantly, how you love. How can you build authentic relationships with anyone – friends, family – under such conditions? If you are religious, how can you be honest with yourself and your God if you maintain so many lies, so many walls running right through the centre of your soul?

Sexuality is about much more than sex. It's about love. How we love, whom we love, how open we are with the channels of love in our lives. These affect much more than the gender of the person we are kissing. And when those channels are blocked it affects everything. In my case, it stopped me from being a writer and chasing other professional dreams. Even the novels I wrote alone in my apartment at night had to be carefully hidden, since they might be interpreted as 'gay' and tarnish my reputation. This is existential loneliness, and I believe I understand what the biblical writer may have intended. I remember it.

Love

Love is more than the solution to the conundrum of aloneness. Throughout the Bible it is celebrated as the consummate human activity, a gateway to holiness. *Anyone who fails to love can never have known God, because God is love.* (1 John. 4:8) As Cardinal Basil Hume wrote, 'Every experience of love gives us yet another glimpse of the meaning of love in God himself. Human love is the instrument we can use to explore the mystery of love which God is.'[5]

When we speak of human dignity, or 'the transcendent nature of the human person and the supernatural vocation of every individual',[6] when we speak of being created b'tzelem Elohim – in the image of God – we point to our capacities for thought, creativity and intimacy. We are speaking of our capacities for love.

Sexual diversity is really affective diversity, emotional diversity, spiritual diversity. How we love one another shapes how we love God. Sexuality – hetero, homo and of every other form – is not simply lust. It is an expression of what makes us most human. The *Song of Songs*, whether read literally or allegorically, is a beautiful, erotic love song. It may at once describe earthly and divine affection.[7] Of course, it is a heterosexual love song. It is also a transgressive one – in scholar David Carr's words, 'a forbidden love that risks discovery'.[8]

The Shunamite woman is dark-skinned, but insists on her beauty. This is despite the conventions of the times; the love affair is basically an interracial one. And there is a remarkable equality and autonomy between the man and the woman in the poem. It's also contrary to the various theories that men and women 'complete one another' and thus only heterosexual unions are complete. The couple in the *Song of Songs* are equals to, not complements of, one another.[9]

When we apply this intense valuing of love and relationship to the question of same-sex attraction, then clearly, as with Genesis 2:18, our religious traditions argue strongly in favour of sanctifying loving relationships. Ambiguous verses elsewhere may proscribe certain forms of sexual expression. But we must read them as narrowly as possible so they may be reconciled with the overwhelming weight of religious teaching on the holiness of love.

What we are really talking about is the most fundamental message of Western religion: *Choose life*. (Deuteronomy 30:19) We are not like the death-obsessed culture of ancient Egypt, with its mummies and pyramids. We are blessed with the capacity to live, to drink from the well of life for a short period.

Behold, I Make All Things New

As the *Song of Songs* tells us, love is stronger than death. To choose life is to say yes to the world, which religious people believe God has created.

Love is fundamental. When we see two people in love, or if we are lucky enough to experience love for ourselves, we know this to be true. Somehow, even the poetic heights of a Shakespeare or a Sappho cannot convey the immanence of love itself, the lightness it brings to the heart. Perhaps, we are best leaving definition to the neuroscientists.

It is not good to be alone. It is worse to exile oneself, or one's dear ones, to loneliness. If *Genesis* and our conscience are guides, then we must see that people in love with one another, building homes and perhaps families together, is religious. It is preferable to people anonymously cruising for sex in public restrooms. The alternatives are affirmation and sanctification on the one hand, rejection and distortion on the other.

Ethically, we human beings are all invited to curb our sexual appetites some of the time. But none ought to be forced to tamp down our libidos *all* of the time. This smashing down of the saplings that God has planted runs counter to every religious teaching about the importance of love, intimacy and human connection. It may seem as though a few biblical verses prohibit same-sex relations. But experience has shown that not to be the case. So, our readings of those verses are in need of correction.

There is no conflict between same-sex intimacy and the Bible, which exhorts us towards love and human intimacy. An open, honest sexuality does as well. The Bible warns us against aloneness; and the experience of aloneness. It has a handful of verses condemning a narrow band of sexual behaviour. So long as that band is kept as narrow as the text allows, there is no conflict between a religious life and a gay one. On the contrary, the real conflict is between religion and repression.

If there is one thing that distinguishes the faith of the Abrahamic religions, it is their emphasis on love. After all, what do we really mean when we use the word 'God'? We have different interpretations of the word, different textual traditions, different theologies and different conceptions of what God is or isn't. Do we believe or not? Is it all a grand delusion or the most important truth there is?

But beneath these many differences, to have God in one's life is to say yes to the world as an expression of love.

All of us experience the world as a series of 'its': books, chairs, mountains. Some of us experience the world as one big 'it'. But the religious have the experience of You. Whatever our theology, whether this You is separate from the world or within it, immanent or transcendent, ineffable or knowable, this personalization and the love that naturally flows from it is the essence of the religious life.

Love, like God, is unprovable. Human beings experience love and it has little to do with external realities. Our beloved isn't really more wonderful, beautiful and kind than every other person on the planet. It just seems that way. So, too, the inanimate objects we casually say we 'love' are not really special or precious. We make them so.

Likewise, with the love of God, theologies, proofs, stories, myths, arguments seem beside the point. I don't think any of us really cares about the age of the Earth or the meaning of evolution. We care about love and associate it with this or that belief about the world.

There is, for religious people, a further aspect of love, beyond, or perhaps within, the love among people. It is boundless, unconditional, undeserved and seeming to drip from every leaf in the forest and every particle of air. The spaciousness of this most transparent love is the texture of religious life itself. In the mere ringing of a bell, in the briefest movement of wind, mystics of all faiths find the deepest of mysteries.

In Scripture, this love is expressed over and over again, in myth, metaphor and poetry. God loves us, the Bible says, repeatedly. *For God loves the just and will not forsake his faithful ones.* (Psalm 37:28) It is a reciprocal relationship – a two-way street. God loves us, we love God. If the heart is opened, the heart is filled. It's our choice to love in return. *You shall love the Lord your God with all your heart and with all your might.* (Deuteronomy 6:5)

And I have learned this: If God loves us then God could never want the 'closet'. There is no reconciling a loving God to its tyranny. Whatever our seven verses in Old and New Testaments mean, they cannot possibly mean this. It is unthinkable, obscene.

Obviously, I do not mean to suggest that human relationships must be the same for everyone. Again, there are those who feel called to celibacy, whether out of a greater religious calling, or following the dictates of their hearts. None of this is to demean them or their choices. But to be compelled to such abstention or, worse and more likely, a life of furtive encounters is fundamentally incompatible with the concept of a loving God. The 'closet' is not really about celibacy; it is about deception, hatred and denial.

Honesty

When I lived in fear of being gay, I was afraid that I would die of AIDS, that I would never be able to have a family, that my parents would disown me. Above all, I feared losing my connection to God. I was certain that religion and homosexuality were incompatible. It is what I was taught. Moreover, I had no gay role models and the images I had of gay people were negative ones.

All this took place in the 1980s and 1990s, not the 1950s or '60s. All around me in Florida, where I grew up, and in New York, Jerusalem and Connecticut where I lived and went to school, there were gay rabbis and lesbian ministers. LGBT people of all spiritual and religious bents were sincerely integrating their spiritual and sexual selves. But I didn't know it. Even in the age of the Internet, it's possible to believe, as I did, that being gay is the worst possible thing in the world; especially if you're religious.

So I lied.

Chiefly, I lied to myself, willing myself to believe that I was bisexual or that I could master this evil inclination, as my religious tradition taught me. But I also lied to girlfriends, family members, friends and teachers. I lied to employers, to students and to casual acquaintances. I lied all the time, to everyone. Even on the rare occasions when I would sneak out of my life and into the seedy gay underworld of secrecy and sex, I would lie, making up fake names and backgrounds so that no one could identify me later.

Somehow, I believed that all this lying was in the service of God. From where I sit now, the very proposition is preposterous. *He that works deceit shall not dwell within My house: he that tells lies shall not tarry in my sight.* (Psalms 101:7–8) *Thou shalt not bear false witness.* Surely, the *seal of God is truth*, as the Jewish rabbinic saying has it. (Shir Hashirim Rabbah 1:9) Yet, from where I hid for a decade of my adult life, I thought telling the truth would end my religious life. In fact, it enabled it to grow.

The weight of lies is so invisible and omnipresent that it eventually becomes unnoticeable, until at last it is shrugged off, out of despair, desperation or even hope. I had no idea how much lighter life could be, or how the anxieties that I took for granted were unnecessary and uncommon. I realized that closeted people were often unaware of how miserable they were. So were straight people who had no idea what it is like to carry around such a secret – one that an incautious move can divulge. Catastrophe is always around the corner.

Of course, as we know from formerly closeted politicians, musicians and clergy, the deception is never as perfect as one hopes it to be. My family and some of my friends were surprised when I came out to them. Others said they'd known all along.

But in my world of lies, I had believed the deception was complete. I've already remarked at how tragic and offensive it is to hear homosexuality called a 'lifestyle', as if it is like living in the country, or enjoying golf or tennis. But the closet, in my experience, is a death-style – a slow, painful draining out and drying up of all that makes life worthwhile. Even for those of us fortunate enough to live in places where gay-bashing and state-sanctioned violence are comparatively rare.

This is true even for those closeted people who seem to be happy and successful. In my work, I have met hundreds of them. They are mostly men, successful, often married, and with varying degrees of self-awareness. Many have children, careers and lives that are filled with joy. Yet, I almost always recognize in them the same tentative anxiety I once knew in myself.

Religious people should support equality for LGBT people because more openness leads to more honesty, more holiness and more openness to spirituality. Once shame lifts, gay people are not different from straight people. Some are wild and some strait-laced; some pious and some irreverent; some devoted to building families and others less so. It is only the presence of shame that distorts sexuality into something harmful. Even the excess for which many people judge gays is the product not of homosexuality, but of homophobia.

The choice is ours, all of ours. *Let them make me a sanctuary, and I will dwell within them,* God says of the Israelites in Exodus 25:8. That is our charge, and we fulfil it, deliberately or not. Build a sanctuary that welcomes people of all sexual orientations and gender identities, and they will make freer choices, undistorted and unimpeded.

In the Jewish tradition, the danger of *chillul hashem*, the profanation of God's name, occurs anytime a religious person does something odious. Rabbis committing adultery, Orthodox Jews convicted of bribery or theft, and so on. Having spent a decade of my adult life in the closet, and a decade out of it, and witnessing the effects of religiously justified hatred of gay people, I feel certain in my heart that the anti-gay distortion of religion is a great *chillul hashem*.

Out of ignorance, and often unwittingly, we as religious communities are doing grievous harm to the very traditions we seek to uphold. And we are harming the people we love.

My religious traditions, and those of my Christian sisters and brothers, are too powerful and too ubiquitous to be so simply abandoned. Besides, such surrender comes at an unacceptable personal cost. Am I to turn my back on my own devotional practice, my own people, simply because some believe them to be beyond reconciliation with my sexual identity? No. Just as I refuse to choose God over gay, so too do I refuse to choose gay over God. The dichotomy does not hold up under scrutiny. It has revealed itself to be false, and I refuse to reinforce it.

Honesty, of course, brings about a closer relationship to God. It is also a prerequisite for authentic relationships with other people. Andrew Sullivan has written that while some may read a passage in Leviticus as prohibiting homosexual behaviour, the ninth commandment is unambiguous about not bearing false witness.[10] Surely all of us who consider ourselves followers of a religious or spiritual path know this to be true.

Whether under oath or not, it is the height of hypocrisy to pretend religiosity while practising dishonesty.

Yet, this is precisely what some would demand of religious gays and lesbians.

What choice is offered by family members who threaten to disown a gay or lesbian child? Only repression, deceit or exile. I was fortunate to have family who were willing to talk, to listen and to learn more about the reality of sexual orientation. Most importantly, my family loves me. They have never seen me as happy as I am. Now I am able to have truly fulfilling intimate relationships. But I work with people every day who are not so lucky, who feel they have to lie in order to maintain their family relationships.

For me, the quintessential 'coming out' story in the Bible is that of Joseph and his brothers. Joseph, you recall, has miraculously survived being sold into slavery (twice) and falsely imprisoned. He has ascended to the highest position of administrative power in Egypt, second only to Pharaoh. Years have gone by and now his brothers come to Egypt in desperation, as a famine has devastated their land. Joseph recognizes them immediately, but they do not recognize him. He then subjects them to a test. Would they treat the youngest, Benjamin, as cruelly as he had been treated years before?

Finally, the brothers do pass this test, and Joseph is unable to restrain himself. Genesis 45:1 uses a new word to describe what happens next: *v'hitvadah yoseph et echav* – and Joseph 'made himself known' to his brothers. This is a unique word, not found anywhere else in biblical text, and not often used in modern

Behold, I Make All Things New

Hebrew either: *v'hitvadah*. It's in the reflexive form, since it is something Joseph does to himself. He discloses himself, he reveals himself. He finally tells the truth about who he is.

It is Joseph's coming out story. He tells the truth, to himself, his brothers — and, not least, the Egyptians whom he governs. Life is going to be different for his family, and for his native and adopted nations, from now on.

Life has also changed for Joseph. Coming out is a courageous act, because inherent in the process of self-transformation is the change into the unknown. One cannot know how one's relationships or one will change, and there is no going back. The process is terrifying. Yet, as the Joseph story relates, it often becomes irresistible. When at last the truth can be spoken, there is a lifting of an invisible burden. As I have often seen, its heaviness outweighs any of the challenges one fears in advance. Not that freedom is paradise, but it does mean a deep relaxing of fear, constriction and worry. Perhaps, for the first time, there is the possibility of integrity.

These are unavoidable religious values. Anyone who styles themselves religious must favour them. As between a reading of Scripture that promotes deceit, and one that promotes honesty, which is the one that best accords with our fundamental values? As between an outdated and pseudo-scientific distortion of Holy Writ and one that accommodates both our best understanding of the nature of human sexuality and our deep commitment to the values of truthfulness, intimacy and love, which biblical interpretation is far-fetched and which the plain meaning of Scripture?

We read Scripture honestly when our reading promotes this as well as justice, compassion, love and holiness. We read Scripture plainly when we stop twisting ourselves and our sacred texts to conform to a mould they were never meant to inhabit. Of course, I have doubts. But each time I come back to first principles. What really matters?

However we understand the word 'God', what is it that God could be said to want? Time and time again, I come back to these core teachings and values, truthfulness high among them. I cannot understand a loving God who wants human beings to lie, cheat and be degraded. Whereas I can easily understand fallible human beings being confused about sexuality and scripture. As much as the affirming readings of Leviticus, Romans and Corinthians may seem at odds with the traditional ones, the repressive readings of those texts are far more at odds with traditional values.

So it is not that doubts do not arise. They do, and they ought to. But there is a clarity that emerges in the process of discernment. There is a security in those truths that we humans can scarcely apprehend. These are the truths of science, of experience and of religious teaching, all of which point in the same direction. And they are the truths I have known in my own spiritual practice and my own relationships with others. Known, not as dogmas taken in from outside, but as lived truths, which I know by their resonance in the soul. This is so because life is precious, and fleeting; that moments of being and transcendence are possible; that cruelty is evil and compassion good; that there is a love accessible simply by resting in a truth that cannot be expressed.

Justice

Justice – justice, shall you pursue, demands *Deuteronomy* 16:20. This is the Hebrew Bible's call: not to oppress the stranger, to set up just courts that judge people fairly, to proclaim *liberty throughout the land.* (Leviticus 25:10) It is echoed by the prophet Isaiah; *The Spirit of the Lord is on me, for God has anointed me to preach good news to the humble, to bind up the broken-hearted, to proclaim freedom to the captive, and liberation to the prisoner.* (Isaiah 51:1) And by Micah, who tells us *to act justly and to love mercy, and to walk humbly with your God.*[11] (Micah 6:8)

One sometimes hears of a sinister 'homosexual agenda' being advanced by some secretive, powerful cabal of gay activists. Really? What is that agenda? Well, politician Barney Frank, at a 2010 news conference playfully described it this way: 'to be protected against violent crimes driven by bigotry, it's to be able to get married, it's to be able to get a job, and it's to be able to fight for our country. For those who are worried about the radical homosexual agenda, let me put them on notice. Two down, two to go.'[12] (A reference to the repeal of the US 'Don't Ask, Don't Tell' policy.)

In other words, the 'radical homosexual agenda' is a myth. What most gay people want is just to be treated equally and fairly. Indeed, the very language of 'radical homosexual agenda' is itself part of the defamation that gay people rightly complain of. It is part of the demonization of sexual minorities.

The Bible is exquisitely clear on how we are to relate to minorities in our midst. *The stranger that dwells with you shall be to you as one born among you, and you shall love him as yourself; for you were strangers once in the land of Egypt* (*Leviticus* 19:34) and *You shall not mistreat a stranger, nor oppress him: for you were strangers in the land of Egypt.* (*Exodus* 22:21) We are asked to recall that those we would demonize, those we would 'other', are people just like us. The mandate to justice comes from a reminder of our own shared experience of oppression. Israelites, too, were strangers once – minorities, persecuted and enslaved. We may be comfortable now, but we are commanded to remember that this was not always the case, and to act appropriately.

Thus, the biblical command to justice merges with the mandate to empathize. We are called upon to remember what it is like to be oppressed, to try to get to know the group that is being disfavoured. Maybe, we are not widows or orphans ourselves but we are asked, by our religious traditions, to empathize with them. To imagine what it is like to stand in their shoes.

All of us have a tendency to favour the in-group over the out-group. Lately there have even been scientific studies which have measured this on a hormonal level.[13] And so the Bible calls us to remember that all of us are the 'other' in one way or another. Either in our own past, as in the case of the Israelites, who once were slaves, or in the remembered past of our ancestors. This is especially true in the case of minorities.

It is precisely when a majority of people have a certain view that protection of minorities is most necessary.

These commandments are not only applicable to sexual minorities. They apply to all the 'strangers', who dwell among us. Indeed, many gays and lesbians have found common cause with other minorities in their struggles against interlocking and intersectional oppressions. But there is something unique about gays and lesbians. The 'stranger' may be within one's own family. Remember, few gay people grow up with gay parents. Most grow up in heterosexual families and majority-heterosexual communities. Gay people often know what it is like to be a stranger even within their own homes.

Ethnic and religious minorities generally have families and communities that are 'like them'. Sexual minorities do not.

As such, the mandate to love the stranger imposes a higher responsibility because the stranger may be within. In the church pew, as a preacher inveighs against homosexuality. Around the dinner table, when someone makes an anti-gay joke. In the junior high school where bullies pick on 'sissies'. The act of empathy is made actual in the everyday experience of the person next to you who you don't yet know is gay.

3.3 Leviticus

So, what about Leviticus?

The important fact about the 'bad' verses in Leviticus is not that they mean one thing or another, but that they are ambiguous. This, I will prove beyond a doubt in this section. I will show

Leviticus can be read in any number of ways. For example, 18:22 can be read as forbidding all same-sex behaviour on the part of men or women. It can be read broadly or narrowly or anywhere in between.

But if Leviticus itself is ambiguous, my claim is that only the narrow reading is in accord with our shared fundamental values. That is why the preceding section comes before this one. On its own, many readings of Leviticus 18 are possible. But in the context of Genesis 2:18, or the way integrity opens the heart to the sacred, the only ones that make sense are those which read it narrowly. Those interpretations which accord with our fundamental values, promote life and sanctify righteous living are superior to those which do not. Our guiding question must not be 'which reading do I prefer?' or 'which reading seems the most likely?' but rather 'which reading is plausible and accords with our fundamental values?'

Leviticus 18:22, the Hebrew Bible's most notorious prohibition on homosexual behaviour, is often read in a vacuum, as if it is floating in the air. But have you ever read it together with its preceding verse? See if this changes the flavour: *And you shall not give any of your seed to set them apart to Molech, neither shall you profane the name of your God: I am the LORD. And as a man you shall not lie the lyings of woman. It is a toevah.*

Let's analyse each word in turn.

First, there is the Hebrew word 'et'. 'Et' is untranslatable, it is a grammatical signal that the next word is a direct object. Often, you see this part of the verse translated as 'Do not lie with a man as you would with a woman,' but 'with' is not the meaning of 'et'. If the Bible wanted to say 'with' it would use the word 'im'. 'Et' suggests something about the nature of the prohibited act. It is something done to a person, or at a person.

This has led some commentators to interpret Leviticus 18:22 as being about sexual violence, or sexual degradation. The interpretation is basically about 'making a man into a woman', which in biblical times was a humiliating and degrading act.[14] That would mean that this verse is no more about a loving same-sex relationship than a prohibition on rape is about a loving opposite-sex one. This is not my precise reading but it is certainly justified by the word 'et'. Just reading the verse literally tells us that this prohibition is not about love, but about sexual objectification.

Second, and so hidden in plain sight that many people don't notice it at all, there is the word 'man'. Leviticus 18:22 is only about men. It was never, in Jewish law at least, expanded to include women. The later prohibitions on lesbianism derived themselves from an entirely different source, an obscure verse. It is about not following 'the practices of Egypt' which was interpreted first by rabbinic legend, then by medieval casuistry, to prohibit lesbian sexual activity.[15]

Until the twelfth century, lesbianism was only as problematic in Jewish law as, say, wearing a bikini. It was seen as immodest, perhaps lewd, but never a violation of biblical law. In the Christian tradition, one statement in the New Testament (Romans 1:26–27) does mention women. As we shall see, it probably has more to do with women being dominant sexually than lesbianism. And let us remember that the story of Sodom is about male rape, and Paul's words in Corinthians about men having sex with men. To group gay men and lesbians together, in terms of religious values, is a huge misplacement. At least half of the people we now call 'homosexual' are not covered by this prohibition. Leviticus 18:22 has nothing to do with women.

The third important term in the verse is *mishkevei ishah*, which literally means 'the lyings of women'. This may seem obvious – don't lie with a man as you lie with a woman – but its scope is not clear. The Hebrew words *tishkav* ('lie') and *mishkevei* ('ishah') are basically the vulgar words for sex. When the Bible refers to making love, it uses the word *yada*, as when Adam 'knew' Eve his wife.

Moreover, biblical and Jewish law regard this 'lying' as requiring penetration by a penis. For these sources that is what 'sex' is. Without penetration, there isn't any sex. *Mishkav zachar* (the lying of a man) means penetration; *mishkevei ishah* means being penetrated.[16] Thus Rashi, perhaps the most well-known of the Jewish commentators, states that there are two ways to 'lie' with a woman (i.e. vaginally and anally). That is what is prohibited here. Since only one of those 'lyings' is possible with a man, what is prohibited here is anal sex.

This is an important detail. It forms the basis for the current understanding of the verse in some religious Jewish communities because it allows for gay people to be fully included, even while maintaining the literal biblical law. Anal sex is prohibited by the Torah, this view holds, but other forms of sex are not.

Now, many sexual activities are prohibited for straight (married) people too. For example, according to Jewish law, men and women may not have sex during the woman's menstrual period. But do rabbis go around inspecting the private lives of married couples, asking when women are menstruating? Of course not, that would be offensive. So, this opinion holds, just as we don't intrude on the private lives of straight people, so we don't intrude on the private lives of gay people.

We assume that married gay couples are observing the law, i.e., not having anal sex and we don't inquire any further. That's between the couple and God. Since other forms of male sexual activity are permitted, this allows us to bless same-sex unions while maintaining a strict interpretation of Leviticus 18:22. (Contrary to stereotype, about a third of gay men do not regularly engage in anal sex.[17]) In this way, we can maintain Leviticus 18:22. We can even maintain that it sets forth a prohibition on all male intimacy, and still fully welcome same-sex couples and perform same-sex unions. We only need to read the verse according to its plain meaning: that *tishkav* means anal sex and only that.

The last key word of the verse is, in my opinion, the most important: *toevah*. While lecturing and teaching across the country, I have been amazed at how everyone thinks they know the meaning of this obscure Hebrew word. Abomination, right? Isn't that what it says in the Bible?

No. Whatever *toevah* means, it definitely does not mean 'abomination'. As best as I can tell, 'abominations' are things which should not exist on the face of the Earth: three-legged babies, oceans choked with oil, and maybe Cheez-Whiz. Indeed, this is how many religious people regard gays and lesbians.[18] The word 'abomination' is found in the King James translation of Leviticus 18:22. The translation reads: *Thou shalt not lie with mankind, as with womankind: it [is] abomination.* Yet this is a misleading rendition of the word *toevah*, which means something permitted to one group, and forbidden to another. Although there is (probably) no etymological relationship, *toevah* means taboo.[19]

The term *toevah* (and its plural, *toevot*) occurs 103 times in the Hebrew Bible. It almost always has the connotation of a non-Israelite cultic practice. The primary *toevah* is *avodah zara*, foreign forms of worship (often called 'idolatry'), and most other *toevot* flow from it. The Israelites are instructed not to commit *toevah* because other nations do so. Deuteronomy 18:9–12 makes this quite clear: *When you come into the land that YHVH [Yahveh] your God gives you, do not learn to do the* toevot *of those nations. Do not find among you one who passes his son or daughter through the fire; or a magician; or a fortune teller, charmer, or witch … because all who do these things are* toevah *to YHVH and because of these toevot YHVH your God is driving them out before you.*

Elsewhere, Deuteronomy 7:25–26 commands: *you shall burn the statues of their gods in fire. Do not desire the silver and gold on them and take it onto yourself, else you be snared by it, for it is a toevah to YHVH your God. And you shall not bring toevah to your home.* Six verses in Deuteronomy further identify idolatry, child sacrifice, witchcraft and other 'foreign' practices as *toevah*.[20] Deuteronomy 32:16 is typical. Prophesying Israel's unfaithfulness, Moses said: *They provoked God with foreign things, angered him with* toevot. *Toevah* is serious, but in a particular way: it is an idolatrous transgression of national boundary. It is certainly not 'abomination'.

Toevah is used four times in Leviticus 18 – once to refer to male homosexual acts, and then thrice as an umbrella term. As in *Deuteronomy*, the signal feature of *toevot* is that the other nations of the Land of Israel do them: *You shall therefore keep my statutes and my judgements, and shall not commit these* toevot ... *because the people who were in the land before you did these* toevot *and made the land impure (*tameh*).'* (Leviticus 18:26–27; see also *Leviticus* 18:29) The term is repeated with reference to homosexual activity in Leviticus 20:13.

Toevah is also culturally relative. For example, there are things which are *toevah* for Egyptians but perfectly acceptable for Israelites. Genesis 43:32 states that eating with Israelites is *toevah* for Egyptians. Genesis 43:34 states that shepherds are *toevah* to Egyptians yet the sons of Israel are themselves shepherds. In *Exodus* 8:22, Moses describes Israelite sacrifices as being *toevat mitzrayim-toevah* of Egypt though obviously Israelite ritual is not an 'abomination.'

So, if:

(1) *toevah* is a culturally relative taboo related to the boundary between Israelite and foreign, and (2) male anal sex is specifically called a *toevah*, unlike other prohibitions (e.g. incest), then (3) male anal sex is a culturally relative taboo related to the boundary between Israelite and foreign.

This isn't about 'abomination' or nature or even morality. It is about a ritual purity law that distinguishes Israelites from foreigners.

Elsewhere the Bible bears this out. The Books of Kings and Chronicles use *toevah* nine times to refer to acts that other nations did in the Land of Israel.[21] Ezra 9:1, 9:11 and 9:14 use the word in exactly the same way. In all these cases, *toevah* refers to a foreign cultic behaviour wrongly practised by Israelites and Israelite kings. Get it?

The prophet Ezekiel uses the term toevah a record-setting thirty-nine times to refer to idolatry,[22] usury,[23] haughtiness and pride,[24] heterosexual adultery[25] and violence.[26] He also uses it as a general term for foreign acts or transgression in a cultic context.[27]

In one extended passage (Ezekiel 8:1–18), Ezekiel is taken on a visionary tour of *toevot*, all of which have to do with idolatry, including women weeping for the goddess Tammuz and men worshipping the sun. This extended passage, with six mentions of *toevah*, links the term in every instance with *avodah zara*, or idolatry.

In five instances, Ezekiel mentions *toevah* together with both idolatry and *zimah* or *znut*, lewdness.[28] This strongly suggests that the nature of sexual *toevah* is not mere sexual activity, and certainly not loving intimate expression. It is sexuality in a cultic context. Likewise, in Deutronomy 19:19, which labels as *toevah* sacrifices bought through prostitution or 'the price of a dog', a biblical euphemism for a male cultic prostitute.

Other prophetic writings follow suit. Jeremiah associates *toevah* with idolatry[29] and unspecified transgression.[30] Malachi (2:11) uses the term to refer to the Israelites having 'married the daughter of a foreign god'.

In rare cases, *toevah* can mean other things. Deuteronomy 17:1 uses it to refer to the sacrifice of a blemished animal. Deuteronomy 22:5 calls cross-dressing (which in contemporary Orthodox Jewish law includes women wearing pants) a *toevah*, though, like Leviticus 18:22, this may also be connected to cultic sexual practices. Remarriage (i.e. of the same two people) is *toevah* according to Deuteronomy 24:4.

The sole ethical use of the term in the Torah is in Deuteronomy 25:16, in which the use of unequal weights and measures is called *toevah*. Psalm 88:9 poetically invokes the term, by way of analogy, for being alienated from one's friend: *You have taken me far from my acquaintance; made me a toevah to him, put away, and I cannot come out.* Isaiah uses it to refer to the sacrifices of hypocrites,[31] as a taunt against earthly power,[32] and, once again, idolatry.[33]

The only major exception to this biblical trend, and it is a unique case, is the Book of Proverbs. *Toevah* is used twenty-one times to refer to various ethical failings. These include the ways, thoughts, prayers and sacrifices of the wicked.[34] Mentioned are pride,[35] evil speech,[36] false weights,[37] deviousness,[38] lying,[39] scoffing,[40] justifying the wicked and defaming the righteous.[41] Scholars have proposed varying theories as to why Proverbs is unlike the overwhelming majority of other cases, though we may never know for sure.

Aside from Proverbs, *toevah* has nothing to do with ethics, and everything to do with cultic behaviour, idolatry and foreign ritual. However, we may understand this type of transgression, it is certainly not 'abomination' in the modern sense.

Incidentally, the King James Version uses the term 'abomination' for not just *toevah* but also the related terms *sheketz, pigul* and *nivash*, as many as six times in New Testament texts.[42] One of these variant uses has led to the website godhatesshrimp.com, which makes posters that say: 'God Hates Shrimp' (Leviticus 11:10–13) in the form of 'God Hates Fags'. Biblically, they are correct; strange that we never see angry protests in front of a seafood restaurant.

Finally, it is noteworthy how *toevah* is used in Leviticus 18:22. The chapter describes several sexual sins, then mentions Molech worship (a form of Canaanite idolatrous practice), then says that male anal sex is specifically *toevah*, then describes the whole list of sins the Canaanites performed as *toevot*.[43] Now, imagine if a similar structure were used today. Imagine if someone said to you, 'Don't kill, don't steal and don't eat the cheese – it is spoiled.' The first two instructions have no conditions; they are universal prohibitions. The third one, though, provides a reason for the ban, implying that when the cheese isn't spoiled, the ban would not apply. Likewise, here. Leviticus says very clearly: no incest, no idolatry and no male anal sex because it is *toevah*. It's almost as if Leviticus is going out of its way to specify that male anal sex is prohibited because it is a Canaanite cultic practice.[44]

Which it was.

We learn from Deuteronomy 23:27 and I Kings 14:24 that the Canaanites had *qedeshim*, sacred prostitutes, both male and female, who would enact the role of a god or goddess in an ecstatic, sexual ritual. Campaigns against cultic prostitution were undertaken by King Solomon[45] and King Josiah.[46] Similar forms of cultic prostitution were found in Babylonians, as recorded by Herodotus,[47] and elsewhere in the Ancient Near East.[48] Especially since Leviticus 18:22 follows Leviticus 18:21, it seems clear that what is being forbidden here is what the Bible is always interested in forbidding: idolatry.

Indeed, as we shall see in the cases of Romans, Corinthians and Timothy, what appear to be regulations of homosexuality are always about idolatry. They are also about demarcating a sharp boundary between lascivious, pan-sexual, idol-worshiping pagans on the one hand, and Jews and Christians on the other.

It is no coincidence that the primary Pauline condemnations come in letters to the Romans and Corinthians. Their cities were known as the most licentious places in the empire. Israelites and, later, Christians are told not to do what the other nations do, which includes these idolatrous forms of sexual practice. Idolatry is the source of sin, especially sexual sin, in apocryphal books such as Wisdom of Solomon (see 12:23 and 16:4). And every one of the biblical texts supposedly about homosexuality are actually about idolatry and boundary making between communities.[49]

The view that Leviticus 18:22 is really about cultic prostitution also accords with the general context of the verse in the Book of Leviticus. Leviticus 18 is part of a large section of the Torah which describes the boundaries of pure and impure, Israelite and Canaanite, proper and improper worship, and which follows upon the death of Aaron's sons following their offering of 'strange fire'. In other words, while the language of *toevah* strongly suggests a connection to idolatry, the overall context of the verse does as well.[50]

Taboos may still be important. As a religious Jew, I don't eat shrimp. But for most Christians, Levitical taboos (like not eating shrimp) were nullified by the coming of Christ. If this is just some ancient cultic taboo, then it no longer has applicability. More generally, understanding the nature of the prohibition as being against cultic prostitution certainly helps me understand how Leviticus 18:22 relates to my own life: it doesn't. I think this literal reading of Leviticus 18:22 makes more sense than any other one. It 'wins'. Even if it only 'ties' with the anti-gay readings, that is enough. The point here is that it is plausible, and that such a reading is *necessarily* based on our fundamental values.

I repeat. All this textual investigation doesn't take place in a vacuum. It happens in a context in which children are killing themselves because of 'God versus Gay'. If I had to take a tortured, roundabout reading of Leviticus, I would do that. Because a tortured reading of one verse makes more theological sense than the torture of young gay people.

But I don't even have to do that. All I have to do to remove the false stigma of 'God versus Gay' is read the verse closely, literally and attentively. Leviticus 18:22 admits of many meanings. One of them is that it is a prohibition of male anal sex in the context of idolatry. That meaning accords with our fundamental religious values. Therefore, it is holy.

3.4 Sodom and Gomorrah

The most infamous story of homosexuality in the Bible – the story of Sodom – is not about homosexuality at all.[51] Indeed, the 'sin of Sodom' was understood in biblical texts to be ethical rather than sexual. The term 'sodomy' was invented in the eleventh century as a legal classification for specific sins of Catholic priests. The association between Sodom and homosexuality did not begin in the Church until the fourth century. Like the word 'abomination', the term 'sodomy' is a misleading part of the myth of 'God versus Gay'.

Most of us know the Genesis 19 story well. God is preparing to destroy the cities of Sodom and Gomorrah, but will spare them if ten righteous people are found. Two angels (in the form of men) come to Sodom and Lot meets them at the gates, inviting them to stay with him overnight. They reluctantly do so and Lot makes them a feast. *But before they lay down,* Genesis 19 continues, the men of the city surround the house and demand *bring them out to us and we will know them,* a phrase clearly understood sexually.[52]

Lot goes out, begs *please, my brothers, do not do evil,* and offers his own virgin daughters instead. The citizens refuse, saying, *we will execute judgment on the one who has come to stay [with you], and now we'll do worse to you than them.* They press Lot back against the door, and are on the verge of breaking through the door when the angels grab Lot and pull him inside. They smite the men of Sodom with blindness. Quickly, the angels help Lot's family escape. Sodom and Gomorrah are destroyed by fire and brimstone.

The Hebrew Bible almost univocally understands the sin the Sodomites committed in terms of ethics and hospitality, not sexual morality. But even before turning to those texts, if we were to read the story of Sodom with fresh eyes, it is obvious that homosexual rape is the means, not the end, of Sodom's wickedness. Genesis 19 clearly contrasts Lot, who goes above and beyond the requirements of hospitality, with the Sodomites, who do the reverse.

Lot insists that strangers dine and rest with him; the Sodomites seek to humiliate them. This emphasis on hospitality is entirely of a piece with what we know of the Ancient Near East where hospitality was a core value. There were no Holiday Inns. Hospitality was essential for survival. Its presence or absence tells us much about the ethical character of people. Treating guests properly is no minor virtue. It is of paramount concern to the Hebrew and Christian Bibles.[53]

Moreover, the story of Sodom is in a section of the Bible where hospitality and ethics are central themes. Only one chapter earlier, Abraham had welcomed three men to his tent, and the text spends five verses on the details of the menu he prepares.

Indeed, after departing, these men look towards Sodom, suggesting they may be the same messengers. (The Hebrew word *malachim* is less supernatural than 'angels', as they appear in the next chapter.) Right after Abraham's bargaining with

God on behalf of Sodom comes the story and its aftermath. And right after that comes yet another story of hospitality. This time of Abraham and Sarah's visit to Gerar. There, Abraham, fearing that King Abimelech will kill him in order to obtain Sarah, tells him that Sarah is his sister.

These Genesis chapters are about variations of hospitality: Abraham's and Lot's generosity, the wickedness of Sodom, and Abraham's fear that Gerar would act similarly. The male Sodomites' interest in men is incidental. If they were raging homosexuals, Lot would not offer his daughters in return. Homosexual rape is the way in which they violate hospitality – not the essence of their transgression.

Reading the Sodom story as being about homosexuality is like reading the story of an axe murderer and saying it is about an axe.

This is even clearer in the 'literary echo' in Judges 19.[54] There, a Levite is travelling with his concubine, and staying at a house in Gibeah. As in the story of Sodom, the Levite is threatened by a Benjamite mob that wants to 'know him'. His host offers his own daughter; the mob refuses. Finally, the Levite hands over his concubine to the mob, who raped and 'abused her' all night long. (Judges 19:25)

This horrible story, which concludes with the Levite killing and dismembering the concubine, is meant to tell of the degradation of Israel prior to the institution of the monarchy. But in mirroring the story of Sodom, it also tells us that it is not the gender of the angels or the Levite that matters to the mob.

It is the use of sexual violence to degrade and humiliate. The Benjamites are neither 'gay' nor 'straight', and neither are the Sodomites. Both are predators, humiliators and dehumanizers.

Consider a recent example. In 1997, several New York City policemen viciously beat Abner Louima and 'sodomized' him with the handle of a bathroom plunger. Do we think for one minute that the policemen were 'gay'? Obviously not. They were using anal rape as a means of degrading Louima. Likewise, appallingly clearly, in the case of Sodom.[55]

Other texts of the Hebrew Bible bear this out.[56] Sodom's wickedness is connected to cruelty, injustice and deceit – never homosexuality.

Jeremiah 23:14: *I have seen also in the prophets of Jerusalem, a horrible thing: they commit adultery, and walk in lies: they strengthen also the hands of evildoers, that none returns from his wickedness: they are all of them unto me as Sodom, and the inhabitants thereof as Gomorrah.*

Amos 4:1–11: *Hear this word, children of Bashan, that are in the mountain of Samaria, which oppress the poor, which crush the needy, which say to their masters, Bring, and let us drink. I have overthrown some of you, as God overthrew Sodom and Gomorrah.*

Repeatedly, Sodom is linked with oppression of the poor, crushing the needy, and ethical wickedness – never sexual immorality. Elsewhere, Sodom and Gomorrah are mentioned as placeholders for idolatry,[57] wickedness in general,[58] or as evidence of God's divine wrath.[59]

Ezekiel 16:49–50 specifically defines the sin of Sodom. *Behold*, the prophet writes in God's voice, *this was the iniquity of your sister Sodom: pride, fullness of bread, and abundance of idleness was in her and in her daughters, neither did she strengthen the hand of the poor and needy. And they were haughty, and did* toevah *before me, and I took them away as I saw fit.*

Even if we assume that *toevah* here refers to the specific *toevah* of Leviticus 18 and 20, and not to the other 101 times the term is used in the Bible, then male anal sex is one of the six sins of Sodom. It is, at most, no more central to 'sodomy' than are pride, gluttony, sloth and economic injustice. Yet even this is a wild stretch of interpretation.

As we saw in the previous chapter, the word *toevah* is used thirty-nine times in the book of Ezekiel, but he never once refers to homosexuality. Moreover, he lists five specific injustices as the 'sin of Sodom'. So, there is basis not to read homosexuality into the description of Sodom's sin. It may come from somewhere, but it doesn't come from the Bible.

Indeed, the sole biblical reference to sexual immorality connected with Sodom occurs in the short New Testament epistle of Jude. Even then the reference is to licentiousness, not homosexuality. His homiletical purpose is to preach against contemporary heretics.

Classical Jewish sources follow the same pattern. The Babylonian Talmud, for example, associates Sodom with abuse of strangers, pride, envy, cruelty to orphans, theft, murder and injustice.[60]

And, as collected by Rabbi Steven Greenberg in his landmark book on Judaism and homosexuality, *Wrestling with God and Men*, there are many Jewish legends of Sodom that depict it as an extraordinarily rich, stingy and cruel city.[61] (See, e.g., Genesis

Rabbah 42, 49; Leviticus Rabbah 5, Numbers Rabbah 9.) Indeed, as Greenberg notes, only a single classical Jewish text, the *Avot de Rabbi Nathan*, links Sodom with homosexuality. And then only in one of two surviving editions. The rest discuss Sodom at length, but never make the association.

Really, how could the tale of Sodom, a story about rape, be interpreted as condemnation of any relationship, no matter how loving, between men? Does the story of how King David spies on Bathsheba and arranges for her husband to be killed in battle (2 Samuel 11:2–5) mean that all heterosexual relationships are similarly depraved? And what about the 'echo' in Judges 19? Since the men of Gibeah rape the (female) concubine, does that mean that all 'heterosexuality' is forbidden by the Bible? Obviously not. The evil of the Sodomites is rape, inhospitality, cruelty and violence. To suggest that it is homosexuality is offensive.

The Bible condemns many things in the story of Sodom. But homosexuality is not one of them.

3.5 Love between men in the Bible

David and Jonathan

Our investigation would not be complete if we did not discuss the Hebrew Bible's clearest expression of same-gender love, the story of David and Jonathan. No, David was not 'gay'. He had numerous love affairs with women (often troubled and ethically dubious), as well as one with a man. But labels are not the point; this is a tale of two men who were in love with one another, who expressed that love physically, and who form an essential part of the Bible's overall depiction of earthly and divine love.

Parenthetically, I wish also to acknowledge the story of Ruth and Naomi as one of the Bible's rare explorations of love between women. Ruth is clearly devoted to her mother-in-law, and her poetic words *Wherever you go, I will go* have been an inspiration to lovers of all configurations over the centuries.[62] In the case of Ruth and Naomi we have two women who vowed to live together for life. They loved each other deeply and adopted each other's extended families as their own. They relied on each other for substance – as do many lesbian women today.

Instead of condemning these relationships, the Bible celebrates them, giving them their own book in Scripture.[63] In focusing more extensively on David and Jonathan, I certainly do not want to repeat the mistakes of many other male scholars who overlook, distort or minimize these sacred, loving relationships among women.

Nor do I propose the story of David and Jonathan as a commentary on the meaning of Leviticus. The Hebrew Bible contains both legal and narrative material, and often the two contradict one another. For example, Deuteronomy 7:3 explicitly forbids an Israelite from marrying foreign women. Yet King Solomon did and the text does not judge him for doing so. The dietary laws of Leviticus seem in direct contradiction with the menu offered by Abraham to the angels in Genesis 18:8. Abraham and Sarah were half-siblings (Genesis 20:12); their marriage transgresses the incest laws of Leviticus 18:9– 11. Likewise with Moses's parents, who were nephew and aunt. (Exodus 6:20 vs. Leviticus 18:12)

The Hebrew Bible does not speak with one voice, and we should not assume the priestly writer (or Writer) of Leviticus has the same agenda as the author(s) of the Book of Samuel. Leviticus does not prohibit Samuel, who does not undermine Leviticus. These are two voices in the biblical conversation. What the David and Jonathan story does tell us is that the Bible knew of, and presented affirmatively, a wide range of emotional and erotic possibilities for its male heroes, and that all of us have something to learn from them.

The story of David and Jonathan begins in the first Book of Samuel, chapter 16. God tells the prophet Samuel that God has rejected Saul as king of Israel, and instructs Samuel to anoint a son of Jesse in his place. Samuel passes over all seven of Jesse's elder sons, finally coming to the youngest, David, a teenaged shepherd described in I Samuel 16:12 as *beautiful to the eyes and good to behold*.

David is anointed with oil, and *the spirit of God came upon David from that day forward*. Yet just as the Holy Spirit comes to David, it departs from Saul, who is soon *troubled by an evil spirit from God*. Saul's servants suggest that he find someone to soothe him by playing the harp. Eventually they bring him *David and God is with him*. David is now described not merely as a shepherd but as a skilful musician, valiant warrior, man of war, wise in speech, and an attractive man, *and so, David came to Saul and stood before him, and he loved him very much, and he became his armour-bearer.*

Now, the term 'armour-bearer' – *nosei keilim* – is an important one, and would be immediately recognized by a contemporary reader of the book of Samuel. In Mediterranean cultures of the time, the armour-bearer is essentially the hero's sidekick. Ancient examples include Achilles and Patroclus in the *Iliad*, and Gilgamesh and Enkidu in *The Epic of Gilgamesh*.[64] (For a contemporary analogue think of Batman and Robin.)

Moreover, it was widely understood that the hero would be older, stronger and generally in love with the younger sidekick. This love had a sexual component, though, as in other love affairs, the sexual aspect was only a part of the overall relationship. In Greece, the relationship was one of erastes (the older, dominant partner who would take the 'active' sexual role) and eronemos (the younger partner who would take the 'receptive' role). It is immortalized on vases, in poetry and throughout the culture, which also gave us democracy, philosophy, athletics and the dramatic arts.

The armour-bearer relationship appears several times in the book of Samuel. In Chapter 16, Saul's son Jonathan has an armour-bearer, who speaks to him in surprisingly amorous language: *Do all that is in your heart; turn, and I am with you as your own heart.* (I Samuel 16:7) Later, when Saul dies in Chapter 31, his armour-bearer falls on his sword. (I Samuel 31:5) Clearly, the relationship is a close, personal bond. Now, whether it included a sexual bond, as it did elsewhere in the Mediterranean context, is not specified. But as scholars Susan Ackerman and

Theodore Jennings point out, this was a familiar, conventional relationship at the time.

Moreover, the erotic element in it is hinted at here by the fact that David's sole qualification for the job is that he's good-looking. After God's spirit descends on David, he is regarded in other ways. Before that, he seems to be chosen purely because he is attractive. But all this is prologue – let's get back to the story.

In the next chapter, the Philistines, the Israelites' great enemy, unveil their great and terrible hero, Goliath. All the Israelites are terrified of him, including King Saul, but David, who originally went to the front lines to deliver cheese to the Israelite warriors, is unafraid. He tells Saul that *the Lord who delivered me out of the paw of the lion, and out of the paw of the bear, will deliver me out of the hand of this Philistine.* David even rejects Saul's armour, and faces Goliath with just a staff, a sling and five stones. Goliath is insulted that the Israelites have sent a mere boy to fight him – but, as we all know, David slays him and leads the Israelites to a routing of the Philistine army.

David returns a hero, and is installed in the royal court. Now the story takes a turn: *when [David] finished speaking with Saul, the soul of Jonathan was knit with the soul of David, and Jonathan loved him as his own soul ... Jonathan and David made a covenant, because he loved him as his own soul. And Jonathan stripped himself of the robe that was on him, and gave it to David – and his sword, and his bow, and his girdle.* (I Samuel 18:1–3)

Like his father, Jonathan has fallen in love with David but, unlike Saul's, this love is described in passionate terms.

Jonathan's soul is knit together with David's, and Jonathan loves him dearly. And then, curiously, he strips naked. Why? Some readers of the story suppose this is a sexual reference.

But if we place Jonathan's act in the context of the armour-bearer relationship, it begins to make more sense. Saul has already adopted David as his armour-bearer. Now Jonathan has done the same thing. The text is setting up a love triangle between the three men, but emphasizes that Jonathan's love of David is different from Saul's. David doesn't do anything for Jonathan; he is not being hired to play the harp. Jonathan loves him freely, and in a much deeper way than Saul does.

Meanwhile, Saul becomes jealous of David, who is being lauded as a hero by the Israelites, and plots against him. David is made an army captain, and Saul promises his daughter Michal in marriage if David emerges victorious, all the while hoping the Philistines will kill him. Yet David triumphs, and marries Michal who, like Jonathan, has fallen in love with him. (Michal's love is not described in similarly powerful terms; the text in 18:20 merely states *And Michal, Saul's daughter, loved David.*)

David's two lovers, Jonathan and Michal, each save his life from their vengeful father. First, Saul tells Jonathan that David should be killed, but Jonathan, the son of Saul, *delighted in David very much* (I Sam 19:1) and pleads successfully on his behalf. Then, after Saul becomes enraged again, Michal helps David escape from the royal court – through a window, no less – into the wilderness. In Chapter 20, Jonathan visits him, promising *Whatever your soul asks, I will do it for you*. David is terrified, and, at his request, the two make an alliance, Jonathan promising to notify him of any threats to his life.

Verse 17 then reads: *And Jonathan added, to swear his love to David, because he loved him as he loved his own soul.* Jonathan and David have already sworn their military pact; this, the text specifies, is in addition to that. It is a pact of love. And notice throughout that it is Jonathan who is in love with David, not necessarily the reverse.

At this point David is obtaining various tangible benefits from Jonathan who gains nothing in return. Once again the text goes out of its way to describe Jonathan's love for David as something more than mere friendship and certainly more than an alliance.

Saul knows it too. When David fails to appear at court for a feast, Jonathan makes an excuse for him. Saul replies, enraged: *You perverse and rebellious son! Behold, I know that you have chosen the son of Jesse to your shame, and the shame of your mother's nakedness! For as long as the son of Jesse lives on the Earth, you and your kingdom shall not be established.* (I Samuel 20:30–31) Now, the second line of Saul's admonition frames Jonathan's action in dynastic terms but the first is clearly sexualized. Jonathan has chosen David to his shame – the Hebrew root is *bushah*. As if that weren't clear enough, Saul emphatically calls Jonathan 'perverse' and adds that his love affair with David is to the 'shame of your mother's nakedness' – *ervat imecha*, a term that unambiguously refers to sexual sins. Back in Leviticus 18, the prohibitions on incest use identical language: *ervat imecha* appears in verse 7. There is no question, reading verse 30, that Saul is scolding Jonathan for a shameful sexual relationship.

Of course, Saul may simply have been insulting Jonathan. But it isn't just this one insult. For three chapters, the text has been repeating how much Jonathan loves David, and how he went beyond the bounds of an armour-bearer relationship, beyond the bounds of a personal alliance. Given that the conventional armour- bearer relationship already included an erotic element, and that Jonathan went above and beyond convention, is it really likely that Saul was just making it all up?

Jonathan and David's last meeting, as David is about to go into hiding, is recorded at the end of Chapter 20: *David came up from the south and fell on his face to the ground, and bowed three times. And each man kissed one another, and each man cried with one another, until David gained composure. And Jonathan said to David: Go in peace, as the two of us have sworn in the name of God, saying God will be between me and between you, and between my seed and your seed, forever.* (I Samuel 20:41–42)

This is the last time the two would see one another alive. For the next ten chapters, the book of Samuel recounts David's flight from Saul, their occasional encounters, and finally Saul's and Jonathan's death in a battle with the Philistines. As such, the scene is heartbreaking. Jonathan has by now risked his own life for the man he loves. Even David is moved to tears. Indeed, when Jonathan dies, it seems that David finally realizes how much Jonathan meant to him. His lamentation, contained in 2 Samuel 1:18–27, is famous even today. It reads, in part: *How the*

mighty are fallen, in the midst of the battle! Jonathan, gone upon Your high
places. I am grieved for you, my brother Jonathan, you were so dear to me.
Your love for me was more wonderful than the love of women. How the
mighty are fallen, gone are the instruments of war.

Thus, ends the story of David and Jonathan. But the tale has
a postscript. David eventually honours the covenant he made,
giving to Jonathan's son Mephibosheth the ancestral lands of
Saul, which came into David's possession during the civil war
that marked the first several years of his kingship. (II Samuel
9:1–13) What, then, are we to make of it? Certainly, religious
traditions have appreciated the depth of David and Jonathan's
'friendship'. The rabbis of the Talmud said it was the epitome
of selfless love, for example. (Mishna Avot 5:1) But is there
more than that?

As we have already seen, to simply export concepts of 'gay'
and 'homosexuality' from our period to the Ancient Near East
would be ludicrous. Obviously, Jonathan is not 'gay'. Not only
did he have a son (and thus an unnamed wife as well), but
the way in which an Ancient Near Eastern prince would have
understood his love of a young warrior is different from how
gay and lesbian people understand their loves today.

We may be fixated, today, on whether David and Jonathan
'did it' or not, and we may search in vain for evidence. But this
is our problem, not theirs. What is clear is that Jonathan loved
David in an intense emotional way that is far more than mere
'platonic' love or friendship, as those terms are understood
today. Both he and Saul had relationships with David that
would conventionally have been understood as including an

erotic element. The covenant Jonathan makes with David is explicitly described as being above and beyond the political alliance they make *v'yosif*. The text says that Jonathan added something extra.

The story has been used for centuries as a code for homosexual love affairs, such as those between Philip II and Richard the Lionheart as well as Edward II and Piers Gaveston. Both of which were described in contemporary histories with allusions to David and Jonathan. Their love was an inspiration for artists including Michelangelo and Donatello, both of whom had sexual and emotional relationships with men.[65] Oscar Wilde cited it at his trial.[66] Contemporary scholars including Theodore W. Jennings Jr., Tom Horner, John Boswell, David Halperin, Martti Nissinen, Rabbi Steven Greenberg, Susan Ackerman and Jean-Fabrice Nardelli have understood the tale of David and Jonathan to include clear references to sexuality. Nissinen even speculated that more overt references may have been edited out.[67] Some have even suggested that the 'pact of love' between David and Jonathan should be considered a marriage. As Tom Horner put it:

Cannot two men be good friends, without the issue of homosexuality being raised? Yes, they can. But *when* the two men come from a society that for two hundred years had lived in the shadow of the Philistine culture, which accepted homosexuality; *when* they find themselves in a social context that was thoroughly military in the Eastern sense; *when* one of them – who is the social superior of the two – publicly makes display of his love; *when* the two of them make a lifetime pact openly; *when* they meet secretly and kiss each other and shed copious tears and parting; *when* one of them proclaims that his love for the other surpassed his love for women ... we have every reason to believe that a homosexual relationship existed.[68]

Is there nothing in between? Must there be either sexual intercourse or 'friendship'? Taking a cue from the 'lesbian continuum' discussed above, surely, we would all agree that what Jonathan felt for David can be described as a *romantic* love with erotic overtones, whether or not it blossomed into sexual activity. And surely that is more important.

As we explored earlier, the very notion that 'homosexuality' can mean both an orientation towards romantic connection, and a physical sex act, is part of the problem. It reduces love to sex, and reduces gay people to what we do with our genitals. This is demeaning, irreligious and offensive. What matters here is that Jonathan loved David. This love was an essential part of the story of David's ascent to kingship – and that, traditionally, this is God's plan, and that David is the ancestor of the messiah. Jonathan's love for another man is not some bit part in the drama of the Bible. If he had not loved David as he loved his very soul, there would be no messiah.

If we try to fit Jonathan and David into our categories of gay male relationships, whether to applaud or condemn them, we will be frustrated for lack of evidence, and end up shouting at one another. Just as recently happened in the Israeli parliament, when a liberal MP quoted David's eulogy in support of a gay rights bill, and fundamentalist MPs threw things at her.

But if we allow the Bible to tell its own story, what emerges is a touching and perhaps tragic tale of one man's love for another, a deep, passionate, embodied love that ultimately shaped the most important drama in human history: the line of David, leading to the messianic redemption.

What also emerges is a biblical universe with multiple configurations of, and approaches to, sexuality, homosociality, eroticism and same-sex romantic love. LGBT people find ourselves in history. Everyone who has experienced love finds another prism through which this universal human emotion can be refracted. Yes, we can use our ideological preconceptions as blinders, and interpret this romantic story as being something other than what it is. But 'the seal of God is truth', and when the blinders are removed, the tale becomes affirming, poignant and heartbreaking.

David and Jonathan's romance prepares David for his relationship with God, seals the transmission of the Israelite monarchy to the Davidic line, and models a relationship to God that all of us might reflect upon.[69] And, since David's line is also messianic, it alters the very course of human history. It also serves to expand our horizons regarding the emotional capacity of human beings, and that is of importance to all of us.

God has chosen, if we may use that word, to appear in a world with infinite variations of love. We are far more than a rainbow of sexualities. We are countless refractions of light, each with our own hue, yet each a mote on the same beam of sunlight. And the more of those tints we can become aware of, the more of That Which Is – the 'I am that I am' that spoke to Moses from out of the fire – becomes cognisable. Not through limitation, but through endlessly astounding proliferation.

3.6 The Gifts of Sexual Diversity

Today, as LGBT human rights advance in the West but are steadily being eroded in the global South and East, the public conversation is often quite limited. On one side, many in the mainstream gay movement say that LGBT equality will not change anything. 'Just let us in,' they say. 'We will conform to traditional values and family structures and all will be well.' On the other hand, many opposed to LGBT equality predict that all hell will break lose: society will be destroyed, the family shattered.

I will explore a third option: that LGBT equality and, more importantly, LGBT difference, do have the potential to change things for the better. I will focus here on productive changes in familial/sexual ethics, the growth of religious consciousness, and how we think about religion and theology.

Ethics

Will affirming the lived testimonies of our gay and lesbian siblings, friends and community members weaken marriage and harm traditional values? Will it contribute to the decay of our society?

Unlike many of my friends and allies in the LGBT movement, I take these concerns seriously, even if they are often exaggerations. I don't think they're just expressions of homophobia or bigotry. Many people are sincerely concerned about the increasing vulgarization of our society. Many link it to changes in our moral fabric. And I am sympathetic. Our public society has indeed grown more vulgar and more crude, and I have devoted much of my professional life to offering alternatives to the lowest common denominator that often passes for 'culture' today.

I agree, then, that there are lines that distinguish wholesome values from unwholesome ones. But neither sexual orientation nor 'traditional' values are among them. Whatever your philosophy, you will find gay people, straight people and any other kind of people who agree with you. Whether someone is gay or not is not the determining factor of a good person (however you define that). Sexual orientation is just not a predictor for moral living.

Let's start with familiar family arrangements. Our best studies of same-sex families find them not only as successful as opposite-sex ones, but, in terms of raising children, often *more* successful.[70] There is unanimity among two decades of scientific studies that the sexual orientation of parents does not influence the psychological health of the child.[71] It may be common folk wisdom that a child needs both male and female role models in the house, but that is not what the data shows.

It has been borne out by evidence in countries with same-sex marriage for many years, and by the 2–6 million gay parents of 6–14 million children in America.[72] Children do better with two parents, but whether those two parents are of the same gender or not is not a determinative factor, except in cases of child abuse. (Children of lesbian parents report an astonishing 0 per cent of sexual abuse.[73]) Oh, and children of gay parents are no more likely to be gay than children of straight parents.[74] With respect to marriage, laws permitting same-sex marriage have been found to have no effect on marriage, divorce, abortion or illegitimacy rates.[75]

So much for conventional family structures. What about unconventional ones?

Conservatives are right to worry that any time we relax our standards, particularly traditional ones that have been with us a long time, we risk opening the floodgates to all kinds of dangerous and immoral behaviour. At the same time, let us remember that biblical 'family values' include arranged marriages, sex with twelve-year-old girls, concubines, polygamy and prostitution. Is this what we want for today? King Solomon, the Bible tells, had 700 wives; what could 'marriage' even *mean* in such a context?

At the time of the New Testament, girls were married off as young as eight or nine years old. Paul specifically states that women do not have authority over their own bodies. (1 Corinthians 7:4) For most of Jewish and Christian history, wives were regarded as the property of their husbands. This was the essence of marriage and remains the essence of the

Behold, I Make All Things New

traditional Jewish wedding ceremony today. Consequently, for most of history the very notion of 'rape' was inapplicable in the context of marriage.

It is also important to remember that traditional, nuclear families based on loving, voluntary marriage between two adults have only been with us for a few hundred years. Marriage has changed radically from its earlier forms. We have moved from polygamy to monogamy and from a labour-based model of marriage to a happiness-based one.[76] Arranged marriages were common throughout most of human history, with marriages often taking place when children reached adolescence.

Interreligious and interracial marriages were completely banned, and not even regarded as 'marriages'. Family constellations in Europe often included aunts and uncles and cousins, all sleeping in the same household, often in the same room. Children were raised by the entire extended family. Prior to the modern period, families were seen primarily as economic units, not romantic ones.[77] As unusual as two dads may seem, a working mom is even more so. This would have been unthinkable even a hundred years ago, let alone to the Church fathers who said that men should rule over their wives.

Intimate human relationship has always been about more than procreation. It is also about fidelity, mutuality and accountability, giving life, identity and community, intimacy and pleasure.[78] At a traditional Jewish wedding, the couple blesses God for creating love, joy and sexual pleasure. And as we saw, the 'first couple', Adam and Eve, were created for companionship, not breeding. Pleasure, bonding, support, love: these are found in opposite-sex marriages, same-sex marriages and non-married configurations of intimacy.

Every sexual act is an opportunity for ethical choice, and even for spiritual transcendence. Is a sexual encounter loving, passionate, ethical, respectful, consensual and safe? Does it celebrate the energies of the body, and invite in holiness, as you understand it? These are ethical, moral and religious questions that present themselves in all sexual experiences, whether in traditional contexts or not.

Yet ironically, there is only a small constituency interested in asking them. On the conservative side, there is a great deal of moral discourse, but only a limited range of acceptability. On the liberal side, there is a wide range of acceptability but only a limited amount of moral, ethical and spiritual discourse. Perhaps, coming to a more mature understanding of sexual diversity can help Christians and Jews heal the wounds that our traditions bear regarding sexuality in general. Christianity arose as an ascetic movement, with celibacy as its original ideal. Judaism's origins include deeply offensive notions about women's bodies. And both traditions bear their scars today.

The vulgar, puerile sexuality that marks American public life is a direct consequence of religion's inability to talk seriously about sex. We urgently need a sexual conversation which recognizes that sex may be sacred, even outside conventional boxes, and that sex may be degrading, even within them. Coming to terms with the reality of sexual diversity can help awaken our religious communities to the possibilities and perils of sexuality more generally.

This is not a new theological topic, but it is one in which new theological reflection is desperately needed.[79] For example, theologian and ethicist James B. Nelson has devoted several books to creating an LGBT-inclusive, body-affirming, responsible Christian sexual ethic. He says:

> The appropriate ethical question is this: What sexual behaviour will serve and enhance, rather than inhibit and damage, the fuller realization of divinely intended humanity? The answer ... is sexual behaviour in accordance with love ... commitment, trust, tenderness, respect for the other, and the desire for responsible communion. It means resisting cruelty, utterly impersonal sex, obsession with sexual gratification, and actions that display unwillingness to take responsibility for their personal and social consequences. This kind of ethic is equally appropriate to both heterosexual and homosexual.[80]

Lesbian theologian Carter Heyward values the erotic – being in 'right relation' – as essential to the human condition and our relationship with God. This does not mean that 'anything goes'. Quite the contrary, as Heyward writes, 'We need an ethical, or moral, apprehension of ourselves in relation that can inform our sexual behaviour by helping us understand what is right or wrong for us.' Indeed, it is the failure of mainstream religion to create an ethic that appreciates the value and power of sexuality that has led to our present state in which 'our collective body is badly abused and abusive, broken and violent'. She adds that a sex-affirming ethic 'is morally imperative'.[81]

Once again, we should not expect a single 'gay sexual ethic' to emerge from the multitude of LGBT voices active today. Some are relatively traditional, valuing monogamous relationships and opposing promiscuity.[82] Others are more radical, questioning society's assumptions about eroticism and sexuality.[83]

I have found, and felt personally, that sexuality can be ennobling or degrading. Sex has connected me to my deepest loves, desires and values. It has also caused me to feel deeply alienated. Contrary to what some might expect, most of my experience of that kind occurred when I was still in the 'closet'. This makes sense. The closet is a place of lies and self-hatred, where even short-term intimacy is impossible. Even the few sexual encounters I had during those years were furtive and covered over with shame. I couldn't let my sexual partners even know my last name, let alone anything real about me.

I was so filled with self-loathing that even the moments of release were tinged with guilt. I felt that God hated what I was doing. So I had to block God out. No wonder so many people resort to drugs and alcohol in order to have sex. If the sex you are having is shameful, you have to work hard not to feel any shame.

It is also much easier to be irresponsible, unsafe and immoral when the only kind of sexual encounters you can imagine for yourself are transitory and anonymous. Worrying about ethics is like rearranging the deck chairs on the *Titanic,* if you think that the entire sexual act is corrupted by sin. And, since you are already an inveterate sinner who deserves to be punished, why worry about HIV or AIDS? If you get it, you probably deserve it.

I have experienced all of this first-hand.

Yet, I've also experienced that same-sex intimacy can be intimately connected with ethics, ecstasy and the sacred. There are many inexplicable delights in this endlessly surprising and holy world. Sex is only one of them but it certainly is a big one. When the sex is good, God in all Her, His and Its manifestations is breathing and singing along with my partner and me.

When two become one, you can feel the joys of being human and being embodied and having a few short decades to live and love on Earth. Isn't this part of what living is *for?* That, in this short span of life, it is possible to connect in this way, to feel and to move and to embrace and to hold? And even, sometimes, to join all of this with the possibility of love. And ending the aloneness and the consummation of its opposite? Isn't this a big part of the point of being alive?

To me it is.

It is no coincidence that sexuality and mysticism share a common vocabulary, that St Theresa writhes in her ecstasy the way a lover contorts. When by chance or design the energies of the moment are right, sexual union and mystical union are parallel motions of the soul. The boundaries of the ego recede. The illusions of self are smashed. In their place is a joining with something larger, something greater.

The point is to join spirit and matter together. Indeed, it is to see that they are not separate in essence. Sexuality is perhaps the essential arena for this holy unification.

3.7 An Invitation to Conscience

Iris Murdoch wrote:

> The facts which will cure this prejudice belong to the ordinary talk of ordinary people, and should gradually become more accessible if those who know about homosexuality will refer to it sensibly, and as homosexuals gradually emerge from the demoralizing secrecy which is at present forced upon them. Doubtless, homosexuals will always be a minority and, doubtless, they will always be with us. What is needed is not more science but just more humane and charitable recognition of our right to differ from one another.[84]

This seems absolutely correct. I acknowledge that there is something to the *newness* of gays and lesbians that must give pause to a traditional believer. One reason so many religious people are conservative politically is that it involves moving slowly when considering changing the existing institutions or principles. It is why conservatives opposed civil rights for African Americans in the twentieth century.

Then again, most conservatives today favour equality for people of all races, right? We may disagree about the details but only a tiny fringe believes what virtually all conservatives believed sixty years ago: that God desires segregation of the races, and that Africans are cursed to serve Europeans because of the sin of Ham.

Conservatives and traditionalists *do* eventually change their minds, individually and collectively. Consider the role of women in our society. Even conservatives, who believe that women ought not to pursue careers and should focus only on the raising of children, say they should be educated and have the right to vote. But 150 years ago, such a view was considered radical.

Surely this is a good thing. We now understand that centuries of racism and prejudice clouded many of our moral judgements in the first half of the twentieth century. We should be deeply thankful that our religious communities have been able to evolve on this point. Most of us today would say that racism is not only bad policy but is actually immoral. It's *wrong* to have racist thoughts and support racist policies.

This means that the social activism of the twentieth century, bitterly opposed as it was, was actually *good* for religious communities. At the time, many conservative preachers condemned Dr King as a heretic, a fearmonger and much, much worse. But from our point of view today he rescued the church from itself.

Of course, no one is arguing that sexual minorities are in the same social position as ethnic or racial minorities. But we can draw lessons from one struggle to another. As in these other areas, accepting sexual diversity is good for religious communities because it is precisely the flexibility of religious values that enable them to survive and adapt.

My teachers in religious school didn't teach us to be racist, but there was plenty of prejudice to go around. In my public high school, I remember that a black kid was beaten up because he was dating a white girl. This was pretty much accepted at the time. It wasn't official school policy. We had a black principal, for heaven's sake. But it was pretty well understood that some lines weren't meant to be crossed.

Likewise, to call someone a fag in my public school was about the worst insult you could hurl. To not respond, either verbally or with violence, meant you really were a fag, which was even worse. There were one or two guys who, in retrospect, were probably gay. But even they never dared to actually admit it or bring a boyfriend to the senior prom, or anything that public – at least nothing that I saw. To be gay in my high school was something to hide, to be ashamed of. It was definitely something to lie about. Now, who was the afflicted here, and who were the comfortable?

Religious communities shouldn't fear this kind of change. We should welcome it, because it is an invitation to conscience, to self-examination. That is what the religious life is about.

Yet, I know full well that, in some communities, the opposite movement is taking place: a move towards more fear and more incitement. There are still preachers who support gay kids lying about who they are and being ashamed of their sexual identity. There are many who send them to bogus, abusive and totally ineffective 'reparative therapy' to learn how to crush and mutilate what God has created. There are even a few, who say that gay kids who are subjected to violence – and according to FBI statistics, gay people are statistically the most likely to be targets of hate crimes[85] – get what's coming to them.[86]

We need to own up to the contribution of our religious communities to that kind of violence. We can't just blame the immediate perpetrators, when they have been egged on by leaders and elders. *Of course,* it matters what preachers say in the pulpit. Isn't that why they talk in the first place? So how could we imagine that their words would *not* have an effect when they are applied to gays and lesbians?

We grow as religious people through an unlikely combination of courage and humility. It takes courage to question one's opinions, and humility to recognize that we may not be as right as we thought.

When I was a child, I talked like a child; I thought like a child, I reasoned like a child. When I became a man, I put childish ways behind me. So says Paul in I Corinthians 13:11 of his own religious maturation process. It may seem like strength to hold fast to unchanging religious beliefs, and there are times when such steadfastness is also an act of heroism. But it takes even more strength to heed the demands of our faith traditions to introspect, discern and reflect on what we thought we knew.

All of us who make religion or spirituality part of our lives are accustomed to the process of introspection. Religious Jews review our lives as part of the annual cycle of Rosh

Hashanah and Yom Kippur. But all of us involved in religious communities and spiritual practice are invited, time and again, to look inward.

Notwithstanding all the naïve pop advice to 'trust your gut', this must be tempered by love. All animals have gut reactions, but only humans (and perhaps a few others, in more limited ways) are able to reason. We are blessed with the ability to rise above our gut reactions. As some religious traditions put it, we have the sparks of God within us. The process of educating the moral conscience, of growing up religiously and ethically is, in large part, the process of applying love and reason to what we think we already knew. Love teaches us how to think justly.

I have seen this process unfold hundreds of times regarding LGBT issues. The organization Parents and Friends of Lesbians and Gays (PFLAG), for example, is largely made up of folks who have travelled this journey, from rejection to acceptance to embracing. These are ordinary people, not gay activists and not gay themselves. They once held strongly anti-gay views, for whatever reason, but were forced to re-examine those views when people they loved came out as gay or lesbian.

This journey is a painful one, but it is also blessed. It is the unfolding of the moral conscience and, in my opinion, religious consciousness at its very best. But sometimes, it comes too late. I urge you to read the book *Prayers for Bobby* by Leroy Aarons. This book (and TV movie) is the story of Mary Griffith, a devout, conservative Christian (Presbyterian), who urged her son to 'change' his sexual orientation. Bobby prayed and prayed, but could not change his sexuality. He eventually moved out of the house, but was still tormented by his inability to be accepted by his mother or by God. Eventually, Bobby killed himself by jumping in front of a truck.

The story does not end there. Mary Griffith eventually begins to question her church's teachings about homosexuality, going over some of the same verses we read so closely in part two. Her views about the nature of sexuality change. She realizes that she had been asking her son to do the impossible: to change a trait God gave him. Eventually, Griffith became an unlikely gay advocate, PFLAG member and activist in her community.

Griffith's story is tragic. Her redemption comes too late to save her son. But it is redemption, nonetheless. It is exactly what religious life is meant to be about: questioning our certainty, questioning what we thought we knew, and earnestly living in the light of God and conscience. People of faith are not called upon to be automatons. If our faith means anything, we have taken up the challenge to live unlazily, according to our hopes and ideals. Occasions that demand we do so, such as the question of equality, dignity and respect for sexual minorities, are not crises. They are invitations.

New Voices

Sexual diversity is good for religious communities because diversity in general is good for them. All of us are enriched by having multiple perspectives on God, values and how to live a meaningful life. Even when we share fundamental values, we learn from people who experience those values in different ways. This is how I have learnt from my friends who are Catholic, Muslim, Hindu, Mormon and Protestant. Not by pretending that our differences do not exist, nor by supposing that they are so great that conversation between us is not possible, but by learning precisely from our differences. There are always multiple approaches to questions of value, and seemingly infinite permutations on the life well lived.

How dull it would be if all of us shared the same gender, the same ethnicity or the same national background. On a superficial level, I know my life would be impoverished without African-American jazz, Japanese food or foreign films. More seriously, my spiritual life has been deeply nourished by encounters with other traditions and other perspectives within my own.

Valuing diversity in this way – the 'gorgeous mosaic' of ethnicities, nationalities and religions – used to be taboo. Only a generation or two ago, it was considered unseemly for black and white folks to mix, or for people of different religious communities to associate with one another. Now even conservative religious communities welcome people of different nationalities and ethnic backgrounds. Likewise, with sexual orientation.

By way of analogy, I often think about the contributions that women's and feminist theology have made to religious communities over the past several decades. The way I think about God, Torah and Israel (the foundational values in Jewish philosophy) have been hugely impacted by feminist theology. I use different liturgical language than I did growing up. It is because I internalized how relating to God only as 'King' is both insulting to many women and is a limiting way of thinking. It is one of the images Jewish people use for God, but only one. My spiritual life has been enriched by being invited to think of God as Compassionate (which in Hebrew is related to the word for womb), multi-gendered and within the world as much as beyond it.

The way I understand Scripture has been shaped by the effusion of women's Bible commentaries, legends, and myth making, all of which have appeared within the last half-century. If women were still being told that their ideas weren't worth expressing, or weren't distinctive in any way, my own spiritual life would be much poorer.

So too, I am convinced, with the voices of sexual and gender minorities. What is being called 'queer theology' has only just begun, but already it is shining new light on scripture and tradition. To take but one example: if masculinity is defined, as it often is, in terms of violence and aggression, isn't the injunction to love your enemy and turn the other cheek 'queer' as well?

Maybe, these conventional boxes of masculine and feminine flatten *all* of our experiences, not just those of sexual minorities. Maybe, the Bible is inviting all of us, particularly men in this case, to be 'queer' again – not construed narrowly in terms of sexual orientation, but understood broadly, in terms of defying conventional expectations of gender roles, and taming precisely those instincts which might be understood as gendered in one way or another.

If the Bible is asking males to curb their sexual appetites, curb their instincts to fight, and curb their desires to be as big and powerful as possible, maybe the insights of 'queer' men can be of value to all of us who take these mandates seriously. Maybe, the simple binaries of masculine/feminine don't capture the richness of who we are as human beings. Maybe, their inadequacy points to the limitations of simple yes/no, black/white, permitted/forbidden, insider/outsider reasoning generally. Maybe, the experiences of LGBT people remind all of us that our lives are more complex than simple dichotomies suggest. My point is that the 'different voices' of sexual and gender minorities have only just begun to be heard, and have the capacity to enrich all of our lives.

Of course, only the most naive believer, or perhaps the most arrogant, would pretend to *know* the purpose of every quirk of creation. Would any of us really want to tell the parents of a child with a rare degenerative disease that it is part of God's plan? Some people do, but I have always preferred a more humble approach. God works in mysterious ways, and it is human arrogance to pretend to understand Divine motives.

I approach sexual diversity in the same way. Perhaps, there is deep religious purpose to the myriad ways in which human beings and animals express their sexuality. Perhaps, over the centuries, we may even come to know more about what that is. I am more interested in exploring the *gifts* of sexual diversity than guessing the *reasons* for it. Do I know *why* God made me gay, or six foot one, or good with words? No. But I know that all of those traits carry with them certain gifts, responsibilities, risks and opportunities. This, to me, seems the more fertile line of inquiry.

And it has already begun to bear fruit. Do LGBT people, as Jung said, have a special 'spiritual receptivity'?[87] Do gay people experience (or transcend) the balance between masculine and feminine, at the heart of so many mystical and religious traditions? Are there special perspectives on the key questions of religion that are afforded to sexual and gender minorities?

Already, a generation of scholars in the discipline known as 'queer theology' have begun to open exciting lines of investigation in religious thought:[88] Carter Heyward, James B. Nelson, Robert Goss, Virginia Ramey Mollenkott, Donald Boisvert, Marcella Althaus-Reid, Irene Monroe, Daniel Spencer and Rebecca Alpert.[89] These and many, many other theologians are attempting nothing less than a recovery of the physical, embodied and erotic within religious traditions which have traditionally suppressed them.

The growing 'gay spirituality' movement has sought to articulate distinctive roles for gay men as healers, bridge builders and, in general, people able to integrate masculine and feminine in ways that are of value to everyone, with writers such as Christian de la Huerta, Toby Johnson and the great radical Harry Hay arguing that 'third gender people were and are those who were assigned responsibilities for discovering, developing, and managing the frontiers between the seen and the unseen, between the known and the unknown'.[90]

We have only begun to learn from transgender biblical scholars and theologians like Virginia Ramey Mollenkott,

Justin Tanis and Noach Dzmura.[91] Perhaps, we in Jewish and Christian communities will learn from other cultures which venerate sexual and gender minorities. For example, in many cultures, sexual and gender minorities are seen as 'in-between'. Sometimes they are referred to as 'third-gendered', or as possessing both masculine and feminine genders within them. (Cultural and psychological genders – not biological sexes, of course.)

Indeed, in many cultures, this is for the better, as we have already explored with reference to indigenous peoples around the world. From the gender-variant berdaches or winktes in Native American traditions (including Omaha, Sioux, Iban and Hidatsa people), to shamans of Siberia (including the Chukchi, Yakut and Koryak tribes), the basir of Borneo, and the male isangoma of the Zulu, people we might call gays and lesbians exist as sacred priests of the liminal, the 'in-between'.[92]

Sexual minorities are neither this nor that, and in transcending dichotomy, they enter the zone of the sacred. In a sense, the regard of these cultures for people we would identify as LGBT is not dissimilar to the view that 'queer' people fill important communal roles precisely because they are less likely to have children. It may seem strange to say so, but perhaps the overwhelming predominance of gays and lesbians in the arts is part of the same basic phenomenon as 'gay' animals helping to take care of their communities.

Ours is a hidden history, though it is made visible in everything from second century Indian stone carvings (temple of Chhapri, Chhattisgarh, central India) to countless Greek

Behold, I Make All Things New

myths (e.g. Zeus and Ganymede, Achilles and Patroclus, Narcissus and Echo, Apollo and Hyacinth) and artefacts. We are spoken of in the *1001 Nights* (sometimes called the *Arabian Nights*), the poetry of Rumi and Hafiz, and the Jewish poetry of Judah Halevy. We were part of Australian aboriginal culture, Mamluk Egypt, early modern Japan. One seventeenth century collection of short stories on the varieties of love between men, *The Great Mirror of Male Love*, is among the most noted works of literature from the period. And the love of younger men was an essential part of the Samurai way of life at the time.

In traditional Chinese society, the term longyang comes from the fourth century BCE tale of Longyang Jun and his lover. For example, the term duanxiu (the 'torn sleeve') comes from the first century BCE story of an emperor whose lover was napping on his shoulder and who tore his sleeve rather than awaken his beloved.

In India and Pakistan, the hijra, biological men whom we might call 'gay' or trans-gender (*hijra* is often derogatory; kinnar and khwaja saraa are alternatives) live to the present day in sacred intentional communities. They dress as women and venerate specific divine figures. The hijra, and the *kothi* – who act similarly to the *hijra* but do not have particular religious roles – are part of a long-standing tradition, which formed the basis of Nepal's recent recognition of 'third gender' people. Today, some hijra and kothi live on the margins of society, but others are still venerated as having special spiritual insight and power.

Gender-variant men and 'third gender' people are mentioned in the *Kama Sutra* and Mahabharata. The spectrum of perspectives on sexual minorities around the world is dazzling.

To repeat, it is not that all of these cultures venerated 'gay' people. As theorists such as David Halperin and others have stressed, words like 'gay' and 'homosexuality' are recent. They are socially constructed terms that do not apply to every form of same-sex intimacy. But in different combinations and iterations, under different labels, we sexual and gender minorities have always existed and always will.

Ultimately, love is more complex than our estimations can guess. Our religious poets have not been content with such biological determinism. They have imagined a world in which individual souls are incomplete, only becoming whole once they find their soulmates. None have pretended to reduce love to reproduction. As soon as we try to provide neat explanations for complex and beautiful phenomena, we cheapen rather than enrich the mystery of human life.

Do LGBT people have special roles to play in the unfolding of the Divine will? Undoubtedly, we do. As do people of different ethnic groups, religions, genders and nationalities. Do I know exactly what those roles are? No. Nor do I want to. I find myself most affirmed not in formulas which spell out what my role is supposed to be, but in appreciating the vast multiplicity of those potentials. If love is indeed as holy as Scripture says it is, surely this is how it ought to be.

Behold, I Make All Things New

A Christian Perspective

By Rev'd Rowland 'Jide' Macaulay

- Introduction
- It's Not in Our Culture
- It's Not Natural, It's Not Scriptural
- What the Bible Says
- Spotlight on Africa
- Justice, Bible and LGBTI Matters
- Summing Up

4.1 Introduction

This work is based on personal experiences, collective studies and training. I have also drawn from the Reformation Project studies developed by Matthew Vines and many other scholarly debates by other theologians on the issue of homosexuality. I hold a very firm pro-gay position on matters of sexuality, Christianity, faith and spirituality.

Definitions

Spirituality is the human ability to connect with a spiritual force, a connection with the Divine. This is part of life. In Africa and elsewhere it is considered spiritual food. For Christians, there is a need to reconcile with God through worship, meditation and prayer. The spiritual needs of sexual minorities are no different from that of the sexual majority. Hence, it is essential to support LGBTI people on their journey towards reconciliation of their sexuality with spirituality. Besides adding to their well-being and faith, it negates guilt and lifelessness.

Inclusive and welcoming religious communities help people deal with the aftermath of discovering they belong to a sexual minority. There is a need for education and formal acknowledgement of the existence and validation of sexual orientation and identity in order to liberate and validate individuals.

Too often, the fundamentalist argument is that the religious text forbids same-sex union, and, therefore, it is a sin. The idea is that the Divine Being approves of this prejudice under the principle of 'love the sinner but hate the sin'. This is archaic.

Sexuality is the sexual knowledge, beliefs, attitude, values and behaviour of individuals. It includes anatomy, physiology and the biochemistry of the sexual response and reproductive systems. Other factors include gender identity, sexual orientation, roles and personality, as well as thoughts, attachments, physical and emotional expression, and relationships.

Sexuality outside the dictated norm, i.e., heterosexual, is strongly denied, mystified and vilified. Too often, religious leaders and mainstream organizations reject sexual minorities. Those identified as part of a sexual minority face gigantic oppression by society, religion, the law and customs. This is particularly so in Africa where religious leaders and mainstream organizations reject sexual minorities. With the exception of South Africa, no African countries have legislative processes or powers that offer protection against discrimination or existing societal phobias.

Sexuality and sex is part of our humanity and to express such desire is human. Homosexual behaviour or lifestyle does not detract from our societal engagement and responsibility. Nor does it limit or improve our intellectual interaction.

Religion is a cultural system that creates powerful and long-lasting meaning. Many religions have narratives, symbols, traditions and sacred histories that intend to give meaning to life or explain the origin of life or the universe. They derive morality, ethics, religious laws or a preferred lifestyle from their ideas about the cosmos and human nature. In my opinion, this does not change or restrict our sexual enjoyment and exploration.

The Christian gospel is 'good news' for all people. But this has often been held back from LGBTI people. My intention is to readdress and assist in bringing back the Word and sharing of that good news to all. The good news of our Lord Jesus is also intended for those on the margins of society – those ostracized and discriminated against for whatever reason.

The most persuasive expression of the love of God is in John 3:16–17: *For God so loved the world that he gave his one and only Son, that whoever believes in him shall not perish but have eternal life. For God did not send his Son into the world to condemn the world, but to save the world through him.*[7]

A friend of mine, a deacon in the Church of England, expanded on the word 'so' which precedes 'love'. This exceptional love includes *all* God's children. It is reasonable to ask: why have we allowed the Church and its people to harbour hatred that makes the Church an awful place to be? This is not only true for LGBTI people but also, in many cases, for their friends and families.

Presently LGBTI clergy, people of faith and organizations have to seek affirmation outside the boundaries of their faith communities. Christians show such disdain for the gospel in their dealings with LGBTI people that at times I am ashamed to be called a Christian.

It is difficult sometimes to debate the right and wrong of sexuality. The assumption that all humans are born or created heterosexuals is wrong. It is unwarranted to assume that those who identify as same-gender loving are simply heterosexuals behaving badly. Sadly, this is used to justify persecution, cruel punishment and further exclusion from the good news.

Keith Sharpe, in his book, *The Gay Gospels: Good News for Lesbian, Gay, Bisexual and Transgender People* (2010), speaks of 'biblical texts of terror', those used to demonize LGBT people. He also divides the good news of hope into two 'testaments': the 'Defensive Testament and the 'Affirmative Testament'. The former signals that there is no condemnation of same-sex love to be found anywhere in the Bible. The latter helps to uncover open and hidden affirmation of LGBTI lives in the Bible. I agree with Sharpe.

Deeply worrying is the difference in the understanding of same-sex relationship between the West and the global South. The collections of scholarly materials, which I hope to draw and rely upon, are part of what I would call a great stride towards recognizing the humanity of LGBTI people in law, politics and theology. It is, however, regrettable that the Christian Church in its far right and patriarchal attitudes, continues to maintain opposition to the equality and validation of same-sex relationships. In doing so, it supports discrimination against LGBTI people by society.

My intention is also to gather many positive theological outcomes that seek to affirm LGBTI Christians. I will draw on material that is progressive and inclusive. I will seek to highlight contemporary biblical research and other progressive analyses in this debate. I will re-examine the context of biblical narratives, the understanding and virtues of LGBTI Christians, and their relationship with the Bible. I will also look at the complex relationships within Christian communities and how best to navigate the journey of reconciliation.

I believe it is not enough to use the Bible to simply determine theological faith. As we evolve and deal with many issues of life, culture and tradition, we engage in many changes. We need to understand people in the context of modern times. I am not suggesting the erosion of previous matters and how they are understood, but rather a new look, a fresh understanding. This is with particular regard to human sexuality as it brought me to engage with the Uppsala Festival of Theology.

My hope is to offer the best explanation based on my personal experience, and also of those I have helped on a journey of reconciliation. Notably, I continue to learn from progressive theological debate on the matter of homosexuality and the Bible.

Over the years, decades and centuries, the interpretation of the Bible with regard to LGBTI Christians has been ferocious. More so in the traditional global South. For example, in 2009, with the leadership of Christian ministers like Martin Ssemp, founder of the Makerere Community Church in Uganda, we saw a wave of violence unleashed by Christians on unsuspecting LGBTI people.

We have witnessed mobs in many countries such as Pakistan, Iraq, Jamaica, Uganda and Nigeria, to mention a few, claiming that it is their Christian or Islamic duty to attack those perceived to be gay. The problem remains unsolved. For LGBTI, who identify as Christian, the issues of reconciliation, inclusion, understanding and dialogue for change are extremely urgent. We can no longer bury our heads in the sand of archaic theology and expect change. *'For our struggle is not against enemies of blood and flesh, but against the rulers, against the authorities, against the cosmic powers of this present darkness, against the spiritual forces of evil in the heavenly places.'* (Ephesians 6: 12)

This theological reflection is born out of the many issues that continue to divide faith communities. Recent religio-political interpretation and condemnation of LGBTI people have aggravated the situation. My hope is also to wrestle with the misunderstanding of homosexuality in many cultures and faiths, using Christianity as my remit.

Many people come to realize they are gay or lesbian after years of anguish and anxiety. Then, their culture and faith cause them to deny their identity and preclude an authentic understanding of same-sex love. For too many, it is a journey of derailment, stress, stretch and depression.

At a tender age, I was unable to engage with Christian Scripture within the hierarchies of my religious institution and my family. I feared retribution. It has been the same for so many people that I have worked with over the years – young men and women who were afraid of their Christian communities.

For too many, their place of engagement is far removed from their faith communities. Faith leaders don't study the subject. This makes it even more difficult for LGBTI people to 'come out' and recognize who they are and where they belong.

Shortly after I came out, I happened across a book called *Pastor, I Am Gay* by Howard H. Bess, an American Baptist minister. It tells of his meeting in the 1980s with a despairing gay man and how subsequent secret research revealed the damage the Church had caused LGBTI people. Bess subsequently reached out positively with love and acceptance to the gay community in ways unprecedented and unimaginable at the time. When the church discovered this, he was fired.

Even today, there are very few places where gay people can safely engage. Only a handful of ministers are willing to publicly reach out and risk including them in their lives and ministry.

In 2013, Malcolm Johnson, an Anglican priest for fifty years, published his autobiography, *Diary of a Gay Priest: The Tightrope Walker*. Working in the East End and the City of London, he was openly gay for most of that time and never far from controversy. As rector of St Botolph Aldgate he, along with his team, was particularly involved with homelessness, HIV/AIDS and education. He considers the Church to be still a dangerous place for a gay priest.

Another fighter for the inclusion of gay and lesbian people is the Reverend Colin Coward MBE. In 1997, he started the organization called Changing Attitude, which seeks to address LGBTI issues, especially in the Church of England. The same can be said of Canon Giles Goddard, who founded the Inclusive Church organization which seeks to end all divides between people. I strongly recommend his book *Space for Grace*, published in 2008. Dr Alan Wilson, Anglican Bishop of Buckingham and author of *More Perfect Union: Understanding Same-Sex Christian Marriage*, is another clergyman who has earned many enemies within the church and beyond.

In a nutshell, the LGBTI community and its defenders have for too long attracted spiritual wickedness beyond measure. We have enemies in high places. Over the decades, the struggle for affirmation has been dogged with many assaults from, among others, American conservatives, European evangelicals and African fundamentalists. The debate on the inclusion and acceptance of homosexuals in the body of Christ is, possibly, the most divisive discourse in the history of the Church. Hence the urgency to rebuild a broken Church, remould a crushed people, and prepare the faith community for reconciliation.

In creating space for this resource, the Church of Sweden must surely have made St Paul proud. I remind you of his first letter to the Corinthians 12:1–21: *Now concerning spiritual gifts, brothers and sisters, I do not want you to be uninformed. You know that when you were pagans, you were enticed and led astray to idols that could not speak. Therefore, I want you to understand that no one speaking by the Spirit of God ever says, 'Let Jesus be cursed!' and no one can say 'Jesus is Lord' except by the Holy Spirit. Now there are varieties of gifts, but the same Spirit; and there are varieties of services, but the same Lord; and there are varieties of activities, but it is the same God who activates all of them in everyone. To each is given the manifestation of the Spirit for the common good. To one is given through the Spirit the utterance of wisdom, and to another the utterance of knowledge according to the same Spirit, to another faith by the same Spirit, to another gift of healing by the one Spirit, to another the working of miracles, to another prophecy, to another the discernment of spirits, to another various kinds of tongues, to another the interpretation of tongues. All these are activated by one and the same Spirit, who allots to each one individually just as the Spirit chooses. For just as the body is one and has many members, and all the members of the body, though many, are one body, so it is with Christ. For in the one Spirit we were all baptised into one body – Jews or Greeks, slaves or free –and we were all made to drink of one Spirit. Indeed, the body does not consist of one member but of many. If the foot were to say, 'Because I am not a hand, I do not belong to the body', that would not make it any less a part of the body. And if the ear were to say, 'Because I am not an eye, I do not belong to the body', that would not make it any less a part of the body. If the whole body were an eye, where would the hearing be? If the whole body were hearing, where would the sense of smell be? But as it is, God arranged the members in the body, each one of them, as he chose. If all were a single member, where would the body be? As it is, there are many members, yet one body. The eye cannot say to the hand, 'I have no need of you', nor again the head to the feet, 'I have no need of you'.*

4.2 It's Not in Our Culture

Homosexuality in Africa and other parts of the global South has been blamed on western European influence and colonialism. The radical intervention of technology is another scapegoat. However, homosexuality has been present in African culture throughout history and is acknowledged in many societies. Unfortunately, modern sceptics ignore factual history. African leaders believe that behaviour which deviates from normal gender roles is a phase which children go through. So, they resort to legislation.

Historically, Africa has always been the friendliest and most tolerant continent. Homosexuality and same-gender behaviour date back to before colonialism and the intervention of religion. The arrival of colonialism contributed to the mass hatred; there was also the influence of religious fundamentalism. Yet, Christianity teaches and encourages one to: *Love thy neighbour as thyself.*

Sadly, this concept has been abandoned for the sake of 'hate missions' propelled by religious leaders. Examples can be found in Botswana, Uganda, Nigeria and Malawi. Churches, mosques and other religious institutions are aiding and abetting their governments to pass laws that criminalize homosexuality. Some go as far as to propose the death penalty.

I believe my own developmental experiences as an African are no different from those of many Europeans. However, current waves of hatred and confusion are fostered by the rhetoric of those in power, those responsible for policies and laws, spiritual guidance and religious protection. Therefore, my overall response will focus on the marginalization of lesbians, gays, bisexuals, transgender, intersex and queer (LGBTIQ) Christians.

The relationship between sexual diversity and the Church is one made in heaven and therefore fulfilled on earth. Let me begin by breaking into your comfort zone. My theological theory is that God did not just create one man and one woman. He actually made multiple men and women of diverse race, colour, sexual orientation and gender identity. If that makes you uncomfortable, I believe we have a dialogue.

Liberal theologians argue that Creation enabled all manner of people and species to be created in six days. God made them male and female, but this should not lead to the conclusion that humans are to be heterosexual only. This erroneous conclusion in a world dominated by faith has caused great trauma to those facing the challenge of having to deal with different sexual orientations.

I will show that sexuality and spirituality can be reconciled for the queer community and other marginalized people. In order to reconcile spirituality and sexuality for LGBTIQ Christians, we need to understand the biblical scriptural interpretation from a queer theological perspective. What does the Bible say about homosexuality? The quick answer is: nothing. Can we safely argue that God made gays and lesbians? Yes.

Psalm 139:13–14: *For it was you* [God] *who formed my inward parts* [the parts of me I have no control of, such as my senses, feelings, my thoughts, etc]; *you knit* [made, formed, moulded, constructed] *me together in my mother's womb. I praise you, for I am fearfully and wonderfully made. Wonderful are your works* [Creation including me].

Jeremiah 1:4–5: *Now the word of the Lord came to me saying, Before I formed you in the womb I knew you, and before you were born I consecrated you; I appointed you a prophet to the nations.*

Human Culture

We can begin by asking what culture is and what is right by human standards. How does homosexuality intrinsically affect the culture or faith of another person? How does the life of a homosexual person affect the basic life of another person, and indeed their religious beliefs?

These questions have been asked in many other places and situations but it is important that we raise them here.

Homosexuality does not belong to any culture. It is naturally part of the human race. We may not agree, but historically in many places there were never disputes about same-sex relationships. There are clear examples in history and the Bible of pederasty.

There is a clear understanding of cultures and basic hindrance within traditions that has enabled the hatred to rise against homosexuality. I look to literature to help debunk and demystify these anomalies.

A list of hindrances:

* Lack of understanding of homosexuality
* The myths about homosexuality
* Why people reject homosexuality
* The religious views and interpretation
* The history of homosexuality and the age of Christianity – which comes first

In many cultures, same-sex relationships are viewed as contrary to nature. But the anomalies associated with their level of discrimination are equally strange. These are often born out of a frustrated patriarchal and oppressive people.

Culture is part of everything. It is renewed with changed understanding and reasoning, an enlightenment and openness to reason. In biblical times, culture determined attitude. Modern culture and its structures make for a very different environment.

There are debates about the acceptance of or non-violence towards same-sex relationships in the first century. We also need to understand that the changes we experience in the twenty-first century mimic the extremity of peoples' response to matters that are controversial, both in politics and religion.

The media and religion are largely responsible for shaping culture; there is no such thing as a Christian culture. Nonetheless, we find the adoption of Christianity and other religions across many cultures.

The extreme absence of positive depictions of homosexuality in television and popular media deprives the gay and lesbian communities of heroes. Similarly, in the biblical argument, the denial and offensive repression and acknowledgement of same-sex heroes makes the interpretation and acceptance of LGBTIQ people more difficult. There is acrimony within religious communities to the point of physical assault.

We are called to introduce a new offering of Christian acceptance and inclusion. It is a chance to review what we think about a culture that would celebrate and affirm same-sex relationships in all religions.

Here are a few thoughts.

The resistance to homosexuality in many parts of the world is propagated by religion. This comes from the belief that we live in a religious world and the unreasonable fear that the so-called 'homosexual agenda' could hijack our heritage.

The reality is that Christianity without the inclusion of LGBTIQ people is dangerous. We cannot pretend that there are no gays and lesbians in the leadership and pews of our churches. That would be a very delusive attitude. To deny that the gay culture is part of human culture is ludicrous. Perhaps, the Christian reaction is fuelled by fear that public approval of homosexuality will predicate our global decline and bad things are sure to result.

Homosexual marriage was once a foregone conclusion. Recently, debates about gay marriage in civil society have been renewed, as have those about same-sex marriages and blessings in the Church. The writing has been on the wall for over a decade. Realistically, there is a greater urgency for the Church to rethink.

Keith Sharpe writes of 'texts of terror'.[1] The reference is to biblical passages such as Genesis 19:5; Leviticus 18:22; 20:13; Judges 19:22, Romans 1:21–28, 1 Corinthians 6:9–10; 1 Timothy 1:10 and Jude 7. They are invariably quoted to condemn homosexuality and used to justify punitive, discriminatory and unjust laws. Yet they are referred to with no understanding of their cultural context in terms of same-sex desires and behaviour.

With the prospect that homosexual marriage is here to stay, it is difficult to submit that culture is static. So, it would be appropriate to bring a new reflection on the issues and flood with light the dark parts of the human heart.

How do we talk about these things openly and clearly? What are the critical political and religious issues? How do we engage with both those who hold strongly to a homosexual, political or religious position – indeed, any combination of the three – and those who are in different phases of dealing with their own homosexual desires?

Some argue that there is an attempt to make homosexuality mainstream culture. This is not the case. Statistically there are 10 per cent or less of the world population that is same-gender loving. It would be impossible to achieve a monolithic gay culture that supersedes the mainstream heterosexual culture. There is, however, a need for a full understanding and acceptance of homosexuality. Extremist views and unprovoked attacks on gay people must end. Of course, making racism illegal has not effectively ended related attacks but we have moved a long way forward from slavery.

Homosexuals often struggle between their faith and sexuality, not with their cultural heritage. But when a particular heritage, such as African, becomes violent towards its own, then all too often gays and lesbians switch cultures due to the harsh realities of their lives. The many African gays and lesbians in Europe are more likely to abandon and reject association with their cultural heritage. But this comes at a cost. They invariably live in extreme denial, which often affects their well-being and health.

Ugandan scientists reported to the president in 2014, 'In every society, there are a small number of people with homosexual tendencies.' This was disregarded for the sake of political popularity. The president signed the notorious anti-gay law that advocates the death sentence for gay people.

It was a turning point for the campaign in Africa to analyse the prejudice against gay people in the culture and heritage of the continent.

In order to decide whether or not homosexuality is part of any culture, we must first examine the historical context. When the decision was made that homosexuality is wrong and not part of the Ugandan culture, it was time for this to be challenged. We then have to ask ourselves the question: what makes homosexuality unacceptable as part of any culture?

A few factors come to mind:

- Authoritarianism
- Religious interpretation and understanding
- Colonialism and new laws
- Change in attitude or corrupted cultural responses

The rejection of homosexuality as legitimate is linked to what I will call 'a new reasoning'. It involves the rejection of the truth and freedom of same-sex relationships, which existed in many cultures. This is evident in many religious and spiritual practices, and is linked with authoritarianism – a power-based attitude of society, institutions and religious communities.

'New reasoning' denies factual evidence. A good example is the argument used by the Ugandan politicians. They claimed that criminalizing homosexuality was a way to protect the future of the country and family values, to save children from molestation and other forms of recruitment.

As I wrote in Witness.org: Not only does legislation prohibit homosexuality in many African countries but its very existence is also denied as prevailing within the culture. There is a continual attempt to deny that gays and lesbians make up a significant part of the population. 'Gay culture' virtually does not exist from an African point of view. The subject of homosexuality is a huge taboo. Many Africans are in same-sex relationships but very few will be open about their sexuality to their families.[2]

4.3 It's Not Natural, It's Not Scriptural

It's not natural

There are two aspects to the debate on the legitimacy of homosexuality or homosexuals. The misunderstanding and misconception of its place in nature or outside of nature is often part of acrimonious debates. What do we mean when we say, 'It's not natural'?

Many believe that homosexuality is a choice, influenced consciously or subconsciously by a person's lifestyle. One argument for unnaturalness is the inability to reproduce the species because that is only possible between a fertile male and female. Another argument for unnaturalness uses the authority of the Bible. What exactly is that authority, and how has this been challenged by liberal theological interpretation?

It is relatively easy to accept the existence of a same-sex relationship as a 'lifestyle choice'. Indeed, it is acceptable in many cultures and seen as a valid way of life. But then the question of childbearing rises. Scientifically and biologically, it is impossible for a person to procreate without a person of the opposite sex. But what is absent in the fertility and procreation narrative is the need for the opposite sex for a relationship (and not simply for childbearing). This is very much a matter of the heart, mind and body. If a person is attracted to his or her own gender, this doesn't make them infertile and resistant towards childbearing. What is important is to find alternative ways of achieving fertilization.

Sometimes, the notion of unnaturalness depends on the environment. There is a historical argument in the understanding of established variations in homosexuality. These are linked to differing behaviour that may offer an explanation for homoeroticism, such as the Greeks' pederasty. In the Melanesian model, men pass through three compulsory stages. These are passive exclusive homosexuality, active exclusive homosexuality, and exclusive adult heterosexuality.

Research into cultures practising such behaviour was undertaken in Papua New Guinea. In the case of pederasty, society often dictates such behaviour: it would have been an expectation or part of the culture.

In some communities a same-sex relationship is considered to be natural as long as it is devoid of sex. It has been proven that it deepens communal bonding within families and tribes.

Even men describing themselves as heterosexual have often participated in acts considered to be homosexual. It is suggested that up to 85 per cent of the population might have experienced same-sex attraction.

Homophobia is driven by a general population of the species exhibiting evolutionary behaviour with regulatory actions. It is no surprise that this is found in political and religious conservatism. It is an attempt to force the overtly homosexual to reproduce in order that the tribe can be strengthened in numbers, thereby increasing everyone's odds of evolutionary success.

Homosexuality is natural. It occurs within nature and there are enough scientific studies to support this claim. To quote the project leader of an exhibition at the Oslo Natural History Museum documenting homosexual behaviour among animals: 'Homosexuality has been observed for more than 1,500 animal species and is well documented for 500 of them.' Based on these findings, the museum concludes that 'human homosexuality cannot be viewed as "unnatural" or a "crime against nature".'

Those who are not gay have very little experience of same-sex desire. If you are comfortable with your natural sexuality and perceived sexual orientation, those who are different are not a threat. That said, there are many heterosexuals who support the human and religious rights of homosexuals.

It's not scriptural

The rejection of homosexuality is often based on religious interpretations and teaching that seek to alienate those who are in the minority and on the edge of society. The dialogue on homosexuality is also an issue of justice. Micah 6:8: *God has told you, O mortal, what is good; and what does the Lord require of you but to do justice, and to love kindness, and to walk humbly with your God?*

The Bible asks Christians to *do justice* and *love kindness*. Yet the Church has, for centuries, been unkind and unjust towards same-gender loving people and others in overlapping areas: for example, those who are black or ethnic minority and gay, disabled and gay, a woman and gay, and transgender and intersex people.

A matter of much debate is if Jesus had anything to say about homosexuality, with many conclusions and increasing tension. The LGBTIQ people have largely walked away from such discussions.

However, where a theological approach has been used, there has been gain. It is fair to say that some of the views have been moderated and become more acceptable.

Many biblical scholars claim that Jesus met a gay man, who had a gay partner. These include the Reverend Jeff Miner and John Tyler Connoley who, in their *The Children Are Free*, quote Matthew 19:10–12: *His disciples said to him, 'If such is the case of a man with his wife, it is better not to marry.' But he said to them, 'Not everyone can accept this teaching, but only those to whom it is given. For there are eunuchs who have been so from birth,[3] and there are eunuchs who have been made eunuchs by others, and there are eunuchs who have made themselves eunuchs for the sake of the kingdom of heaven. Let anyone accept this who can.*

In that culture, if you were a gay man who wanted a male 'spouse', you, like your heterosexual counterparts, achieved this through a commercial transaction. A servant purchased to serve this purpose was often called a *pais*.

In the Gospel of Matthew we the instance of the centurion who wants his servant (pais) to be healed. Apparently, he was afraid of what people would say about his sexuality. But the centurion had no hesitation in asking Jesus to heal his male lover. It seemed the right thing to do. And Jesus did not make any comments about the centurion's sexual inclinations. For Jesus, the centurion was a man of courage and faith.

In Matthew 19 Jesus affirms that many others like this gay centurion, those who come from beyond the assumed boundaries of God's grace, will be admitted to the kingdom of heaven. He also warns that many who think of themselves as most likely to be admitted will be left out. *Let anyone accept this who can* – this is the most difficult, as many seek to deny the truth and often reject what they are unable to fathom.

Jeff Miner and John Tyler Connoley concluded, 'In this story, Jesus restores a gay relationship by a miracle of healing and then holds up a gay man as an example of faith for all to follow. So, consider carefully: Who is Lord? Jesus or cultural prejudice?'

We don't need fundamentalists to accept us. They need us because they are trapped in an understanding of God based on fear. They are frightened because they have never heard the message of hope. Moreover, there are young people and young families who are sexually different who need the message of hope.

The emphasis should be on sharing the message of hope in love. In order not to allow God to be disappointed it is important to carry the message even if we are persecuted.

Modern LGBTI people, especially many that I am connected with, want nothing to do with the Church. Between December 2013 and January 2014, I met approximately forty self-identified LGBTIQ people over the festive season. Conversation around the birth of Christ brought up many issues. Nearly 70 per cent are no longer connected with the Church. The remaining 30 per cent was seriously considering ending their relationship with it. The majority who no longer participate in the Church blame it on Christianity as it is practised today.

Anxious to wrestle with the dissent, I wrote the following article:

Over the years I have had many discussions and debate, in private and in public about the relevance of homosexuality, faith and Christianity. I have had many interesting discussions about the woes of religion, particularly Christianity. No surprises, but what aggravates me is that many still believe that Christians are awful people and whoever embraces Christianity must be a bunch of lunatics.

We cannot agree on every doctrine and interpretation of the Bible and other religious text.

As a black African gay man who embraces Christianity, I have had my share of discrimination and often violent anger towards me for the choice of being a Christian.

I have been told, 'If you are gay, lesbian, bisexual, trans, intersex or allied to LGBTI you cannot be a Christian. If you are a Christian you have to reject homosexuality; homosexuals will rot in hell; you have given your life to the devil.'

Was Christianity a choice? Or was it forced on me by my parents? ...

In my understanding, God is love and Jesus is the saviour of the world. I want to send out a message to everyone that there is nothing wrong with Christianity. We may find that many, who teach and promote hatred, don't understand the invaluable presence of God in the lives of ALL people. Christians don't hate. Christians are not homophobic. Christians are people who live their lives according to the teachings of Christ. 'God is love, love your neighbour, love your enemies.'

May I remind that Christianity is not the reason you left the church. You did not become an outsider because you no longer believe. You left because you were unable to reconcile Church with the ineffable love of God. You left depleted and feeling outnumbered.

Christianity is not responsible for the hate and abusive sermons that flowed from the pulpit. These are people who are ill-judged and lack the understanding of the mysteries of God. They failed to renew their theology of humanity in the understanding of the mystical God. Because we don't understand the stories of the Bible such as Noah's Ark and Creation does not make Christianity a farce.

You can find a home in a church that is all inclusive and welcoming to ALL people.

Galatians 5:22–23 says: *But the fruit of the Spirit is love, joy, peace, forbearance, kindness, goodness, faithfulness, gentleness and self-control. Against such things there is no law.*

There are many LGBTIQ people who feel unable to reconcile their Christian faith with the attitude of the Church. The Church of England is a classic example. In 2013, it was able to ensure that a legal clause was included in the Marriage (Same Sex Couples) Act to allow the Church to legally discriminate against and disallow same-sex weddings. Yet, there are many homosexuals who still wish to find a place in the Church.

There are continuous debates about Christian ethics and contemporary issues particularly with regard to homosexuality. I will examine if Christian ethics mean that sexual relationships should only take place in a marriage between a man and a woman. If there are unbiased benefits from sexual relations within marriage, why can this not be extended to homosexuals?

Let me start with a definition of Christian ethics: 'a way of thinking about human characteristics and conduct in the light of God's characteristics and conduct and above all as revealed in Jesus Christ'.[4] This is open to different interpretations. Theologians such as Karl Barth say that ethics and high theology ought to be closely related. Anthropologists of religion such as Clifford Geertz tell us similar things about ethics and worldview or social and intellectual practices. Yet rarely do Christian ethicists connect doctrines like incarnation, election and resurrection with race, gender and sexual orientation.

I will argue that the response of Christians should be tolerance of other forms of human sexuality and relations. Matters such as sexual relations outside of marriage can be alien to the Christian doctrine and cause conflict between liberals and conservatives. The resulting avalanche of issues and conclusion may make it difficult to stay within the expectations of a traditional Christian.

The definition of marriage is the formal union between a man and a woman recognized by law in which they become husband and wife. This is a civil marriage or contract. Marriage is defined and viewed differently in various customs and traditions, which may allow polygamy, polyandry and homosexuality. The biblical terminology of marriage does not apply to homosexuality. But civil and human rights campaigns for equality have enabled a better understanding of same-sex relations.

Twelve countries have redefined marriage to include same-sex relations. They are Argentina, Belgium, Canada, Denmark, Iceland, Ireland, Netherlands, Norway, Portugal, Spain, South Africa and Sweden. This has no doubt created a challenge for the traditional definition of marriage and, indeed, the application endorsed by Christian ethics.

The dynamics and relative response to the teaching on a union between couples change when we understand the restrictive laws relating to the definition of marriage. We can think about the countries listed above that provide a legal framework for same-sex marriage. Will Christian ethics on full sexual relations apply Rogers's definition to homosexuals or will this be hampered by apathy?

Liberals have accused conservatives of misreading biblical narratives about the rape of visiting angels at Sodom and Gomorrah. Biblical authors may not agree that the sex of the parties is immaterial. Some conservatives accept that the point of the story is as in Ezekiel 16:49–50: *This was the guilt of your sister Sodom: she and her daughters had pride, excess of food, and prosperous ease, but did not aid the poor and needy. They were haughty, and did abominable things before me; therefore, I removed them when I saw it.*

But the conservatives are shocked by the liberal interpretation of passages, which they see as being about same-sex homoerotic relationship. Take, for example, 2 Samuel 1:26: *I am distressed for you, my brother Jonathan; greatly beloved were you to me; your love to me was wonderful, passing the love of women.* Conservatives view the sexual interpretation of this passage as a misreading. They also see liberals as interpreting such passages too literally and ignoring the importance of the context of the text.

Rogers argues that the Bible is at stake and so are the principles of Christian ethics. 'Conservatives admonish rivals [who] prefer the hermeneutics of charity to the hermeneutics of suspicion.'[5] The question often raised in these arguments is whether or not Christian ethics demand that sexual relationships can only take place in a marriage. If sex within marriage is to be encouraged, this can be extended to homosexuality.

Dr Rowan Williams, former Anglican Archbishop of Canterbury, wrote, 'Sexual union is not delivered from moral danger and ambiguity by satisfying a formal socio-religious criterion.'[6] People may seek to build their marriage on the ideals of Scripture: *it is not good for the man to live alone* and the creation of a woman who is *bone of my bone and flesh of my flesh* and then beyond companionship to reproduction to be *fruitful and multiply*. (Genesis 1:22)

But, Williams added, the greatest blessing of human sexuality does not come in the form of childbearing alone; there is also committed love. Eve was created to be a companion and helper, first and foremost. Reproduction was a secondary reason. So, if companionship and committed love are the primary points of marriage, then same-sex relations can fulfil that objective.

Rogers was concerned with the morals of human sexuality, and not sexual relations, which for many provide stability, security, longevity and, above all, love. Human sexuality gives people the capacity to develop erotic feelings, experiences and responses. Sexuality has the capacity to characterize the sexual orientation or preference of the individual.

4.4 What the Bible Says

What does the Bible say about homosexuality? Nothing.

Sodom and Gomorrah

It is said that Genesis condemned homosexuality, which led to the destruction of Sodom and Gomorrah. The people of Sodom were violent, they threatened Lot and his guests. They attempted to destroy his door. The evidence is in Ezekiel 16:49–50. They behaved with callous indifference towards the weak and vulnerable, the poor, orphans, widows and strangers.

Whilst Lot's offer of giving his daughters to be abused is inexcusable, it was in line with the patriarchal behaviour of the time. If he had no daughters would he have given his sons?

Leviticus was directed at homosexual temple prostitution and that is how it should be applied. Leviticus 20:10, 11: *If a man commits adultery with the wife of his neighbour, both the adulterer and the adulteress shall be put to death. If a man lies with a male as with a woman, both of them have committed an abomination; they shall be put to death; their blood is upon them.*

The punishment for these two is the death. Today there are no ruthless advocates for the former, yet religious leaders in Uganda, Nigeria and Botswana ruthlessly demand the death penalty for homosexuals.

Going after strange flesh

Sodom and Gomorrah and the cities about them in like manner, giving themselves over to fornication and going after strange flesh, are set forth for an example, suffering the vengeance of eternal fire. (Jude 1:7)

At the time Jude wrote this text, many believed some of the women of Sodom had engaged in intercourse with male angels. This was what Jude was referring to when he talks about 'going after strange flesh'. He was referring to heterosexual sex between male angels and human women, not homosexual sex between humans.

Trading natural relations for unnatural

Romans 1: 21–32: *For although they knew God, they neither glorified him as God nor gave thanks to him, but their thinking became futile and their foolish hearts were darkened. Although they claimed to be wise, they became fools and exchanged the glory of the immortal God for images made to look like a mortal human being and birds and animals and reptiles.*

Therefore, God gave them over, in the sinful desires of their hearts, to sexual impurity for the degrading of their bodies with one another. They exchanged the truth about God for a lie, and worshiped and served created things rather than the Creator—who is forever praised. Amen.

Because of this, God gave them over to shameful lusts. Even their women exchanged natural sexual relations for unnatural ones. In the same way the men also abandoned natural relations with women and were inflamed with lust for one another. Men committed shameful acts with other men, and received in themselves the due penalty for their error.

This was not about homosexuality, but about people who:

- Refused to acknowledge and glorify God
- Worshipped idols
- Were more interested in earthly pursuits than spirituality
- Gave up their natural passion for the opposite sex in an unbounded search for pleasure
- Lived lives full of malice, envy, strife, slander, disrespect for parents, pride and hatred of God

The model of homosexual behaviour is explicitly associated with idol worship and gay relationships that are not loving, giving up what is natural in the process.

1 Corinthians 6:9–11: *Do you not know that wrongdoers will not inherit the kingdom of God? Do not be deceived! Fornicators, idolaters, adulterers, male prostitutes, sodomites, thieves, the greedy, drunkards, revilers, robbers – none of these will inherit the kingdom of God. And this is what some of you used to be. But you were washed, you were sanctified, you were justified in the name of the Lord Jesus Christ and in the Spirit of our God.*

In the urge to discriminate against effeminate men, most interpretations often leave out the key connector to verses 9 and 10 which is verse 11: ... *And this is what some of you used to be. But you were washed, you were sanctified, you were justified in the name of the Lord Jesus Christ and in the spirit of our God.*

If we take the word 'effeminate' literarily, then those who are effeminate and not same gender would also be criminalized by this interpretation. I submit that such an interpretation is driven by anti-gay prejudice. None of the evidence suggests that a loving homosexual relationship is a sin as it is understood today. Another modern-day interpretation uses the alternative 'homosexual offender'[7] instead of homosexual.

- Samuel 1:23, 26–27: David and Jonathan – loved each other more than they loved women = gay
- Ruth 1:16–17: Ruth and Naomi – Ruth said to Naomi, your people shall be my people, where you go I will go and where you die I will die[8] = lesbian

Behold, I Make All Things New

- Matthew 8:5–13 and Luke 7:1–10: The centurion and his male lover – the centurion cared so much for his young lover, but was worried about what the people would say, but he believed that Jesus could and would heal him.

Ecclesiastics 4:9–11: *Two are better than one, because they have a good reward for their toil. For if they fall, one will lift up the other; but woe to one who is alone and falls and does not have another to help. Again, if two lie together, they keep warm; but how can one keep warm alone?*

There is no mention of gender, just two people sleeping together.

There are a number of things that puzzle me. It started with a question that one of our members asked me in a Bible class in Nigeria: 'How old was Adam when he was created?' In general terms and with the basic literal Bible study, we assume that Adam was created as an adult of marriageable age. This would be an issue for many cultures. He could have been fourteen years old or forty years old. No one cares. The literal indication was that he was old enough to have a wife or a partner that was fit.

In my curiosity I looked at the question in light of other issues such as the race. Was Adam black or white? I have since understood more about the biology of the human race. We could all be related but it is likely that we are millions of years apart.

Next, I turned to my father, a leading theologian. I was not amused when he replied that Adam's age was a mystery. I had expected a better defence. Whilst I still don't have the answer, this suggests that there is much about the biblical accounts that we don't know: *Now Jesus did many other signs in the presence of his disciples, which are not written in this book. But these are written so that you may come to believe that Jesus is the Messiah, the Son of God, and that through believing you may have life in his name.* (John 20:30–31)

On the question of race, my father informed me that after the forty days and nights of the flood in Noah's story, his three sons became the ancestors of Europeans, Asians and Africans! I needed to find answers close enough and worthy of debate.

I believe in the creation of the earth and all that is in it by God. A concept enhanced under the tutorage of Professor Mary Tolbert at the Pacific School of Religion. Whilst she allowed me to understand the farce between the two versions of Creation stories, she insisted that it was important that I developed my own response and thoughts.

This is what I have to say.

I thought about animals and asked the participants in my workshops, 'If you saw a lion in Kenya and you saw a lion in the United Kingdom, what would you call it?' This was not a trick question; it is as simple as it appears. The overwhelming answer was 'a lion'. It may be called different names in different languages and dialects but it is still a lion.

Now, what do we call people, either in the United Kingdom or in Kenya? Same approach: they are called people, with the exception that we have names; (though animals may also be given names). But when I related this to biblical analogy, particularly the Creation, it seemed that the Bible scholars had introduced us to only one of the many humans created whom they called Adam. He was, in my view, identified as the one that would be the ancestor of the Saviour.

Therefore, just as sin came into the world through one man, and death came through sin, and so death spread to all because all have sinned – sin was indeed in the world before the law, but sin is not reckoned when there is no law. Yet death exercised dominion from Adam to Moses, even over those whose sins were not like the transgression of Adam, who is a type of the one who was to come. But the free gift is not like the trespass. For if the many died through the one man's trespass, much more surely have the grace of God and the free gift in the grace of the one man, Jesus Christ, abounded for the many. (Romans 5:12–15)

If this is the case and an admissible theory, it is possible that God created many men and women of diverse races at Creation. It is also possible that God determined every sexual orientation that we know or experience today.

The story of Noah and the flood is also not conclusive. The ark was not big enough to hold those who inhabited Earth after the flood. I have concluded that God wisely only flooded an area of human delinquency, not the entire world as we are expected to believe.

I also found that Christian condemnation of all manifestations of same-sex relationships was synonymous with colonialism and the introduction of the penal code in many of the colonial territories. There is a close relationship with the arrival of colonial rule, the Christian missionary and the denunciation of same-sex relationships.

Clearly what was slated as offensive over many centuries was indeed natural.

If homosexuality was a punishment, what was the original crime? The lack of understanding of this context makes things more difficult both for those who object to homosexuality and for those who are homosexuals.

The crime, as stated in the letter to the Romans, was idolatry. We can therefore assume, both by Paul's indictment and further conservative interpretation, that the punishment for idolatry is homosexuality. This is not in line with the teaching of Jesus. He made room and ways for societal outcasts and sinners who are welcomed into the Kingdom of God.

What was clear in the Romans chapter is the hedonistic lifestyle of the people. If this is the case, then every violation, particularly idolatry, ought to be punished by making the people homosexuals. This cannot be the correct interpretation. Why did God choose to punish the Romans with homosexuality? This is not the first or only case of idolatry in the Bible. Idolatry has nothing to do with homosexuality, nor homosexuality with idolatry. There are millions of gay people, who are devout Christians and lead exemplary lives.

There are, therefore, theological grounds for seriously doubting the authenticity of St Paul's position on homosexuality, and indeed further teaching and interpretation that seek to penalize gays and lesbians.

Later on, in the same chapter (Romans 1:28–32), Paul lists other things that must not be done. There is no mention of homosexuality. Hence the likelihood that the previous text could have been misinterpreted.

So, we need to come to a sensible conclusion about what is likely to provoke God's wrath, making death the only befitting penalty. If homosexuality is about love between two persons of the same sex, it cannot be categorized as an offence worthy of execution. Taking a literal approach is equally dangerous. In the same text we find that those who gossip and children who are disobedient to their parents are not sentenced to death. That gives us a reasonable perception of the inaccuracies of the translation that condemns homosexuals. Paul believes the acts listed in the text to be harmful, but does not include a loving same-sex relationship amongst them.

A thing or action may bring you contempt and ridicule but it doesn't define you as evil. The same would be a transgression, as in the case of idolatry.

4.5 Spotlight on Africa

In my work with LGBTI asylum seekers in the UK and many other places I often ask if they attend church. In many cases they do. Yet, they have never considered asking their minister for a pastoral letter of support in their asylum claim as a gay person. Clearly many people, particularly those of ethnic origin, join church communities as an extension of their country of origin. They enjoy the music, are able to speak the language, and participate culturally. But they cannot reveal their sexuality. So, in order to reconcile their sexuality and Christian faith, there must be a sacrifice, a serious and large price to pay.

Political homophobia

Over the past ten years, the question of equal rights, law reforms, community cohesion, diversity, families and migrations for LGBTI Africans has gone from bad to worse. The possibility for legal liberation on the grounds of sexual orientation and gender identity looks dismal. This assessment is a universal representation of the lives of LGBTI people in Africa, including South Africa, notwithstanding its enviable Constitution vis-à-vis same-sex rights.

Human rights defenders across the continent have faced serious threats to their lives. Many have fled to safety in Europe and America. Those who represent 'the face of the faceless and the voice of the voiceless' are scattered abroad. This has painful consequences for activism in Africa and for the diaspora.

Thirty-six countries in Africa have laws criminalizing homosexuality, some with death penalty, and many more with harsh jail sentences. It is by far the continent with the worst laws when it comes to homosexuals and other sexual minorities. This phenomenon is rooted in bad colonial-era laws and political situations. Other factors include religious autonomy, strong negative belief in cultural and family values, and the evil of patriarchy.

More than half the African governments have taken steps to formally criminalize same-sex unions. There is an increased homophobia with the media adding to the furore. However, anti-gay laws in Uganda at least are now weakened due to opposition from human rights groups. Malawi has witnessed the presidential pardon of a gay couple.

In March 2011, there was a second recall at the United Nations Assembly on the joint declaration to decriminalize homosexuality. The number of African signatory countries increased from six to eleven. These included Gabon, Sao Tome and Principe, Mauritius, Central Africa Republic, Cape Verde, Guinea Bissau, Angola, South Africa, Seychelles, Rwanda and Sierra Leone. Thirteen countries abstained and twenty-eight opposed the Joint Statement on Sexual Orientation and Gender Identity (SOGI).

The popularity of gay rights and advocacy for the social status of same-sex relationships has provoked politicians and governments in Africa to react. The number of cases of criminalization of same-sex relationships has increased in recent times. It is a situation already characterized by harassment, humiliation, extortion, arbitrary arrests, judicial violence, imprisonment, torture, hate crimes and honour killing – all on the grounds of sexual orientation and gender identity. These abuses are happening whether we like it or not, whether we admit it or not. Every year, there are numerous cases of hate crimes against LGBTI people and the advocates seeking justice for LGBTI people. The abuse is escalating.

LGBTI asylum seekers

In the past ten years, there has been a sharp increase and major concerns for many fleeing from persecution in their own countries. These include Nigeria, Gambia, Liberia, Sierra Leone, Uganda and Tanzania, to mention just a few. This is due to political leaders; the forceful introduction of anti-gay legislation, and the failure to repeal discriminatory laws. The number of LGBTI migrants fleeing to foreign countries has increased. We are dealing with cases of African LGBTI seeking asylum as far as Australia, Canada, North America and western Europe.

The attitude towards asylum seekers based on SOGI has in some cases been shameful. The challenges are many. The outcomes are horrendous. We believe that the International Organization for Migration could foster a better reception under international law. It could give credence to the cases driven by discrimination based on SOGI.

Religious homophobia

In 2003, the American Episcopal Diocese appointed its first openly gay bishop, Gene Robinson, in New Hampshire. Archbishop Peter Akinola, former primate of the All Nigeria Anglican Communion, was extremely vocal in his criticism: 'Anglican Orthodox members are poised to do the mission of the church and those who say that gay is their concern, woe unto them.'

The Nigerian anti-gay bill had his blessings and that of his church, along with President Olusegun Obasanjo, who declared that homosexual practice 'is clearly unbiblical, unnatural and definitely unAfrican'.

Popular religious communities, especially Christian and Islamic, have failed in many ways to embody and recognize the humanity of same-gender loving people. They have increasingly added to the furore of scepticism by using religious platforms and podiums to stigmatize, victimize and alienate homosexuals.

Inclusive and Affirming Ministries (IAM) hosted the first Dialogue on Homosexuality and Christianity in South Africa in November 2009. It was attended by nearly 100 delegates from more than thirty African countries. They included clergy and LGBTI people.

African LGBTI people need to decide on their own interpretation of religious text, basing this on the principle of understanding God within the context of culture and tradition. Historically, Africa has always been the most friendly and tolerant continent. Homosexuality and same-gender behaviour date back to before colonialism and the intervention of Western religion.

Colonialism contributed to the mass hatred against homosexuals. The influence of religious fundamentalism has also contributed to homophobia. Christianity teaches: 'Love thy neighbour as thyself.' Sadly, this concept has been abandoned because of the hate mission propelled by religious leaders. Examples can be found in Botswana, Uganda, Nigeria and Malawi where the churches, mosques and other popular religious communities are aiding and abetting their governments in the passing of laws that criminalize homosexuality, some going as far as to propose death penalty.

Religion is a beautiful concept that makes sense only when it is a place of sanctuary for the marginalized. Homophobic religion is not integral to the original concepts of Judaism, Christianity and Islam. Sad to say, gay and lesbian people today avoid the churches and the mosques, which are losing out on the opportunity to welcome all of God's children. Until the last colonial penal code is removed from the laws of African nations, and governments are empowered to understand the rights of sexual minorities, homosexuals in Africa will not experience peace.

4.6 Justice, Bible and LGBTI Matters

We cannot have a complete exegesis without talking about human rights and justice for LGBTI people. Over the decades the churches, and other religious institutions and communities, have persistently sought to ostracize and demonize LGBTI people. Many thousands have been jailed, dehumanized, abused and subjected to religious rituals of degrading humiliation.

So far as justice and LGBTI matters are concerned, it is encouraging that the constitutions of many countries give the right and freedom to the expression of faith. *Unspoken Rights*, a publication of the Initiative for Equal Rights published in Nigeria, seeks to align the country's Constitution with the Yogyakarta Principles developed in 2006 by notable lawyers in Indonesia.

Human rights and religion

There have been many advocates for LGBTI human rights and freedom of religious expression. People and organizations continue to seek to address violations against LGBTI people, often disguised under faith or religious impunity. This extends to punishment and ostracism of LGBTI against a background of hate and vicious incitement of violence.

We find that many LGBTI people struggle to reconcile sexuality with spirituality. Influenced by fundamentalist views, they often see being lesbian, gay, bisexual, transgender or intersex as an abomination, with a drastic impact on the rise of HIV transmission. We are hoping that this Church of Sweden and Global Interfaith Network initiative will change attitudes towards oneself. That it will shift LGBTIs from destructive behaviour towards a better self-understanding; self-hatred to self-love and improvement in self-esteem and assertiveness.

Principle 21 of the Yogyakarta Principles: The Right to Freedom of Thought, Conscience and Religion

I believe that the faith of LGBTI people is linked to the protection of their lives, respect and dignity. They can only survive and rise when the entire faith community fully understands the need of a safe place for them. The legislative process needs to consider their welfare, and churches must seek to provide refuge for LGBTI people, their families and friends.

Implications for sexuality, HIV/AIDS and health

The struggle against HIV/AIDS is undermined by criminalization of same-sex relationships. The United Nations Human Rights Committee has noted that driving marginalized communities underground runs counter to the implementation of effective education programmes in respect of HIV/AIDS prevention.

This finding is supported by UNAIDS. The former president of Botswana, Festus Mogae, and UN Special Envoy for HIV/AIDS in Africa, Elizabeth Mataka, have spoken out firmly and forcefully against criminalization of homosexuality in Africa. LGBTI people are struggling for access to public health services, with double discrimination being fuelled by state-sponsored homophobia.

Over the past twenty years, there has been a growing recognition of the relativity of sexual norms and of the difficulties of accepting Western conceptions of sexuality in Africa. This includes gay rights and public recognition of same-sex families.

The implications include:

- Homophobia that is deep-rooted in culture, religion, music and law. Expressions of homosexuality are repressed by condemning homosexuals, their families and friends.
- Shame, ostracism, scorn, violence, mocking and prayers for salvation are the reported means of keeping homosexuals in the closet or making them 'normal'. Some homosexuals respond to this stigmatization by moving away from their countries, communities, families. Others build supportive networks outside their communities. Still others struggle to keep it a secret by pretending to be heterosexuals.

- Same-sex loving people often lead multiple, secretive lives. They are men or women on the 'down low', also known as DL. Men who have sex with men (MSM) often do not admit they are gay or bisexual. These are mostly married men.
- Homosexuality is often associated with occultism.
- Many African governments have no mandate or projected plans to include LGBTI in sexual health provisions and services.
- There are inaccurate publications, unethical reporting, dubious and negative publicity on matters of HIV and homosexuality in Africa, which need to be addressed in order to change attitudes.

House of Rainbow

House of Rainbow Nigeria, founded in 2006, is a mission by the queer community to address the misgivings of mainstream religion about LGBTI people. Its focus is to guide and assist reconciliation for queer Africans. It takes a rare, liberal and deliberate view of Scripture. 'Queering' of the holy book poignantly is an act to retrieve the shattered bodies and souls of queer African people – the shattered vessels thrown out by religious communities. It is safe to say that this mission doesn't rob nor compete. It simply picks up the broken vessels to mend, reshape and remould.

Romans 9:19–20: *You will say to me then, 'Why then does he still find fault? For who can resist his will?' But who indeed are you, a human being, to argue with God? Will what is moulded say to the one who moulds it, 'Why have you made me like this?'*

Our work in spiritual activism and radical inclusive theology has continued to ruffle the feathers of the legislators in our home country, Nigeria. We have created a movement that reaches out to thousands of people in Nigeria and more worldwide. News of our mission is gaining ground in Africa and we are developing a scheme called 'Voluntary Local Leaders' now present in Burundi, Nigeria, South Africa, Malawi, Botswana, Zambia, Ghana, Lesotho and the United Kingdom. We are currently working on strategies and guidelines to replicate the new format across Africa and, indeed, around the world.

Our job is not to find fault or resist the will of God for sexual minorities, never to argue with God, the one who moulded us. Micah 6:8 sums it up nicely: *God has told you, O mortal, what is good; and what does the Lord require of you but to do justice, and to love kindness, and to walk humbly with your God?*

Self-esteem, confidence in your God and also in your faith are the key to reconciliation. Finally, GAY means God Adores You; God Accepts You; God Affirms You.

At House of Rainbow, we surveyed more than 600 people, including delegates from South Africa, Brazil, Mexico, Kenya, Ghana and Nigeria. The results:

- How many people were born or experienced religion/ faith as a child before becoming aware they were LGBTI?
  —96 per cent

- How many people have experienced homophobia/transphobia by their faith community or have been directly affected by religious hatred/messages?
  —100 per cent
- How many people would like to experience freedom of expression within their faith community?
  —84 per cent

4.7 Summing Up

We have been criticized for our inclusive and liberal interpretation of the Bible, but in doing so we have helped many people understand the love of God. How can we be assured of the ineffable love of God?

For many Christians it begins with the love of God for the world: *For God so loved the world that he gave his only Son, so that everyone who believes in him may not perish but may have eternal life. Indeed, God did not send the Son into the world to condemn the world, but in order that the world might be saved through him.* (John 3:16–17)

The tools for the journey towards reconciliation include:

- Understand that God made you.
- Accept the challenges of being a minority in a vengeful society.
- Recognize that you are not alone with the burden of survival in a hostile nation.

- Find a supportive network of people and create a web of friends who understand your issues.

Genesis 1:31 says: *God saw everything that he had made and, indeed, it was very good.* Of course, that includes LGBTI. It also includes healthy and very ill people, all races, all sizes and religions, from every part of the earth.

LGBTIs can be people of faith, proud of their cultures and traditions, enlivened by their celebration of human sexuality. I believe that a reconciliation of human sexuality and spirituality is possible only if families, lawmakers and wider civil society are willing to listen and act for the common good.

Can the Church live and or survive without LGBTI people? The immediate answer is NO. We are found from the priesthood to the pews. We are servers at the altar, music directors and choirmasters and in the choir. We are the most giving and yet most hated and misunderstood.

Roman 9:25–26: *Those who were not my people I will call my people, and her who was not beloved I will call beloved. And in the very place where it was said to them, 'You are not my people', there they shall be called children of the living God.*

Why did God create sex? The most popular reason is for childbearing and pleasure. At Creation, God said to Adam and Eve: *be fruitful and multiply.* (Genesis 1:28) This does not necessarily mean sex and childbearing alone. Galatians 5:22–23 defines fruitfulness when it says *the fruit of the Spirit is love, joy, peace, patience, kindness, generosity, faithfulness, gentleness, and self-control.* This is a singular construct for heterosexuals but it also deserves consideration for other sexualities, for companionship that embraces intimacy.

I agree that conservative views of Christian ethics around sexual relations have waned. They are now considered archaic, bearing in mind that Jesus did not say anything about homosexuality in particular or about sexual relations in general. The Church and Christian ethicists have, over the centuries, struggled with sexuality and become irrational about homosexuality. God may have made marriage primarily for companionship, not procreation. But if homosexuality is an abomination it could be an abomination, in or out of marriage — and thus still forbidden by consistent and logical Christian doctrine.

Christian ethics argue that a man and a woman enter into an intimate, faithful and lasting relationship, which includes sexual relations. The same argument can be used for homosexual relationships. The fact that sexual orientation has a part to play does not mean that sexual relations for homosexuals cannot be intimate. Archbishop Williams has stated: 'It is impossible, when we're trying to reflect on sexuality, not to ask just where the massive cultural and religious anxiety about same-sex relationships that is so prevalent comes from.'[9]

The House of Bishops explained:
Some would argue that a deeper understanding of God's will would show these difficulties to be unfounded. The Church, they would say, needs to undergo a profound and radical transformation of its attitude to, and understanding

of, the whole of human sexuality, including homophile relationships. Homophile couples, according to this view, are simply witnessing part of a truth which the Church will eventually come to accept, and ought to be allowed freedom for that witness.[10]

Williams in his conclusion said: 'It is surely time to give time to this, especially when so much public Christian comment on these matters is not only non-theological but positively anti-theological.'[11]

Some Bible scholars argue about the powerful nature of sex. They view it as the only intimacy sanctioned by God to keep the desire between male and female couples enlivened. This argument remains inconclusive. Take, for example, the Bible story of a woman who married seven brothers and at death remained childless, the subject of a debate between Jesus and the Sadducees. They asked him which of the seven brothers would be her husband in heaven. Jesus replied: *You are wrong, because you know neither the scriptures nor the power of God. For in the resurrection they neither marry nor are given in marriage, but are like angels in heaven.* (Matthew 22:29–30) To exert the rule of sexual relations within marriage renders the response redundant.

Clearly the defence of the traditional definition of marriage is losing weight in the light of twenty-first-century thinking and knowledge. This includes evidence of fidelity among homosexuals – a relationship based on mutual support. Yet Christian ethics for homosexuality are far removed from the realities and understanding of same-sex relationships today. It cannot have the final say on sexual relations in the face of growing evidence and evolution of diverse patterns of sexual relations. Times and knowledge are changing and so must the application of Christian ethics. The fact is that we are forced to think about same-sex relations in a way that is neither socially nor religiously required for heterosexual relations.

Expected outcome

- Homophobia exists in all faiths and religious text is manipulated to engender this.
- LGBTI groups and people exist (and are to some extent tolerated) in all faiths.
- Queer groups can come together across faiths to challenge homophobia and provide support to each other.
- Religious text should be read and interpreted through your own understanding, resisting the narrow-minded interpretation.
- The ethos of spirituality, rather than religious doctrines and rituals, needs to be followed.
- It is possible to be gay and have a faith.
- Some religions, and aspects of organized religion, are welcoming of gay people.
- There are resources for LGBTI people, and their friends and parents.

The way forward

- Legal and policy reform is urgently needed on many fronts to enforce the legal status of same-sex love and ensure the full protection of human rights in the context of HIV/AIDS.
- Underlying prejudices and discrimination could be addressed through education programmes in schools and community dialogue to help create a more supportive environment for same-sex unions.
- Media training that is explicitly designed to discourage attitudes of discrimination and stigmatization towards sexual reproductive health and rights and same-sex relationships, especially with regard to HIV/AIDS, needs to be promoted. The media should be encouraged to adopt ethical rules of conduct that prohibit disclosure of confidential patient information.

We hope that, in sharing this brief overview, we give a clear understanding of the issues of same-sex relationships, LGBTI human rights in Africa, and their implications for sexuality and HIV/AIDS. We strive for an inclusive church, the absence of pain for LGBTI people; we hope that the harmony expressed by Isaiah 11 will soon be a reality.

The way churches and people inflict pain on LGBTI people is short-sighted as well as unjust. Reasonable thought has not been given to future damage and exclusion. The church should be in the business of winning souls, but many LGBTI souls have been lost. They are not willing to return to the place where they have lost their dignity and felt ashamed.

Bibliography

Boswell, J., 1980. *Christianity, Social Tolerance and Homosexuality*. Chicago: University Press.

House of Bishops, 'Issues in Human Sexuality', Church House Publishing (CHP), 1991; follow-up report 'Some Issues in Human Sexuality: A Guide to the Debate', CHP, 2003.

Rogers, E.F. (ed.), 1999. *Sexuality and the Christian Body*. Oxford: Blackwell Publishers.

Williams, R., 1996. 'The Body's Grace'. In C. Hefling, ed. *Our Selves, Our Souls and Bodies: Sexuality and the Household of God*. Cambridge: Cowley Publications, 1996, pp. 58–68.

Holy Bible, New International Version

Rev'd Jeff Milner and John Conolley, 2002. *The Children Are Free*. Indianapolis: Life Journey Press.

Rev'd Rowland Jide Macaulay, 2005. *Pocket Devotional for LGBT Christians*. Philadelphia: RBM Consulting (Publishing).

———, 2010. *I Say A Little Prayer for You*. Philadelphia: RBM Consulting (Publishing).

Guest, Goss, West and Bohache (eds), 2015. *The Queer Bible Commentary*. London: SCM Press.

Marcella Althaus-Reid, 2003. *The Queer God*. Oxfordshire: Routledge.

Marcella Althaus-Reid, 2001. *Indecent Theology*. Oxfordshire: Routledge.

Goss & West (eds), 2000. *Take Back the Word*. Cleveland; Pilgrim Press.

Robert L. Brawley, 1996. *Biblical Ethics and Homosexuality*. Westminster: John Knox Press.

Gene Robinson, 2008. *In the Eye of the Storm*. New York: Seabury Books.

Howard Bess, 1995. *Pastor, I Am Gay*. New York: Palmer Publishing Co.

Terry Brown (ed.), 2006. *Other Voices Other Worlds*. New York: Church Publishing Inc.

Michael Ford, 2004. *Disclosures: Conversations Gay and Spiritual*. London: Darton Longman & Todd.

Internet sources

http://www.ridley.cam.ac.uk/about/life-at-ridley/training/ethics (accessed on 15 February 2013)

http://abcnews.go.com/blogs/politics/2012/05/obama-comes-out-i-think-same-sex-couples-should-be-able-to-get-married/ (accessed on 15 February 2013).

Web Links

religioustolerance.org

wouldjesusdiscriminate.org

hrc.org/scripture/soulforce.org mcchurch.org

jesusmcc.org/resource/notasin.html

jesusmcc.org/resource/rev_james.html imaan.org.uk

jglg.org.uk

http://www.houseofrainbow.org

http://www.revrowlandjidemacaulay.blogspot.com

http://www.houseofrainbowfellowship.blogspot.com

http://www.youtube.com/houseofrainbow

http://www.facebook.com/rowlandjidemacaulay

http://www.twitter.com/revjide

http://www.youtube.com/houseofrainbow

Inclusive and Affirming Ministries; http://www.iam.co.za

Inner Circle; http://www.innercircle.co.za

Documentaries/Films

Jihad for Love
Gay Muslims
Prayers for Bobby
Dangerous Living
For the Bible Tells Me So
Call Me Troy
Rag Tag
All of God's Children
Missionaries of Hate
Fitrah: Negotiating Sexual Orientation, Gender Identity and Islam

5

A Muslim Perspective

By Imam Ludovic-Mohamed Zahed

- Introduction: Nature and Islamic Tawheed
- Same-sex Unions and Marriage
- Universal Islamic Humanism and Individual Well-being
- Alternative Islamic Liberation Theologies
- Testimonials

*B*ismil-laah ir Rahmaan ir Raheem (In the Name of God, the most merciful and gracious, the most compassionate and the dispenser of grace)

5.1 Introduction: Nature and Islamic Tawheed

O mankind! Lo! We have created you male and female, and have made nations and tribes that ye may know one another. Lo! The noblest of you, in the sight of Allah, is the best in conduct. Lo! Allah is Knower, Aware.

Islam, in Arabic, means to be at peace. It is a grammatical form that implies a process of being while still evolving. This is theoretically based on the knowledge of the self, the knowledge of others, and a proactive respect for diversity. Thus, we ask, how can the knowledge of Islam help combat homophobia, lesbophobia, biphobia and transphobia peacefully? How can knowledge of the Islamic theology of liberation add value to human consciousness, particularly the contribution of LGBT and feminist intellectuals or activists?

Simply put, how can the Islamic doctrine of Tawheed – literally, uniqueness – enable individuals, belonging de facto to a sexual minority, live better and empower themselves?

Tawheed must be understood as the apex of a humanity able to transcend differences. According to the Qur'anic verse quoted at the beginning of this chapter, the diversity of human cultures is the fertile ground in which our human consciousness is rooted. This is based on knowledge of the self and others, and makes us more valorous than angels of light.

The Qur'an says: *And when thy Lord said unto the angels: Lo! I am about to place a viceroy in the earth, they said: wilt Thou place therein one who will do harm therein and will shed blood, while we, we hymn Thy praise and sanctify Thee? He said: Surely, I know that which ye know not. He taught Adam all the names, then showed them to the angels, saying: Inform me of the names of these, if ye are truthful. They said: Be glorified! We have no knowledge saving that which Thou hast taught us. Lo! Thou, only Thou, art the Knower, the Wise. And when We said unto the angels: Prostrate yourselves before Adam, they fell prostrate, all save Iblis. He demurred through pride, and so became a disbeliever.*

Only the devil – the most destructive part of our humanity, 'the momentum of death'– refused to recognize the universality of God's gift. What argument did Iblis – the 'devil' – use to not kneel before the Divine? It was: *I am better than him. Thou createdst me of fire, whilst him Thou didst create of clay.*

The devil used the argument of nature that Adam was made of clay, the momentum of life, while he himself was made of fire, the momentum of destruction. It is a symbol also of regeneration among Zoroastrians, in Japanese philosophy, and for Christians during the Middle Ages. However, one element is complementary to the other. No so-called human 'nature' shall be considered better than another.

The Qur'an uses another parable to illustrate this. The djeen – a spirit, repeatedly cited – would be a reference to the duality of the human caught in the microcosm of his or her existence, the macrocosm of his or her universality. Our dogmatic brothers and sisters come to us saying that we are gay or transgender, because a djeen – a term used in this case to describe an 'evil spirit' – possesses us. The djeen, who is repeatedly described as blinded by its pride, even after eons of worship of the Lord, also refers generally to 'what is inside [the psyche of] the human being'.

Recall also the pride of what God in the Qur'an called Shaitan, saying: *I am better than him...* Pride is, therefore, to think that some of us are inherently, by nature, better than others. It is fuelled by regenerator fire. Thus, the fire, one of 'the higher elements' according to the Akbarian mysticism, leads to pride – a kind of pride, so far not attributed to any particular object during the creation of human beings, that leads the djeen, the inner part of ourselves, to rebellion. It turns some human tendencies into those of demons – *shayaateen*.

Our pride should be in the regeneration of postmodern Islamic sciences, not in the exclusion of the weakest or the minority among us. Is it not exactly that regeneration of the Islamic sciences that feminists, LGBT Muslim activists and intellectuals have been trying to achieve for decades?

These questions about the true meaning of the messages that believers consider to be revealed are not inherently exclusive to Islam. According to the Bible, *The Lord says: 'These people come near me with their mouth and honour me with their lips, but their hearts are far from me. Their worship of me is based on merely human rules they have been taught. Therefore, once more I will astound these people with wonder upon wonder; the wisdom of the wise will perish, the intelligence of the intelligent will vanish.'*

Similarly, it is said in the Qur'an: *Allah knoweth that which every female beareth and that which the wombs absorb and that which they grow. And everything with Him is measured. He is the Knower of the invisible and the visible, the Great, the Nigh Exalted. Alike of you is he who hideth the saying and he who noiseth it abroad, he who lurketh in the night and he who goeth freely in the daytime. For him are angels ranged before him and behind him who guard him by Allah's command. Lo! Allah changeth not the condition of a folk until they (first) change that which is inside of them.*

These verses illustrate very clearly a theology truly adapted to human beings, truly liberating, transcendent and immanent. It is based on the love of God and of our humanity, rather than fear and intellectual dogmatism. As did the books that preceded it, the Qur'an teaches that it is up to us to free ourselves from our fears, to transcend this difference respectfully – and thereby to become fully aware of what 'human being' can mean. This verse speaking of the prophet Isaiah shows that religion should be seen as a manifestation of our human spirituality. It transcends temporal and cultural particularities.

Abraham disrupted the social idols that allowed the wealthiest to oppress the weakest. Another verse that speaks about his pure *Tawheed* ends with: *Abraham, the upright, who was no idolater, certainly points to the fact that Abraham was a monotheist. But more than that, Abraham was in favour of a united humanity, one and indivisible.*

Mohamed Iqbal says:

… the Qur'an often communicates through these stories the teaching of a value or philosophical content rather than providing a historical account. It does this by removing the names of characters and locations likely to set the story in a historical context, and also by removing specific details … This method is not unusual; it is more often used in non-religious literature, for example, the story of Faust, to which the genius of Goethe gave an entirely new meaning.

Thus, as Imam Daayiee Abdullah said: 'Islam is a living religion, it must breathe.' It reveals diversity as sacred, unified yet differentiated human nature. It is the 'social contract' that the Qur'an has offered for fourteen centuries. The Arab-Islamic civilization, known until recently for its tolerance, was to some extent its vivid illustration.

One unique human dignity

Thus, the metaphor of 'shirk' – literally translated as 'polytheism'– is the worst social evil. It can be understood as a profusion of humanities and would mean, for example, that one would consider some people not fully human, or inferior to a so-called elite – just because of the colour of their skin, their beliefs (their atheism) or the fact that they belong to a sexual minority.

In Tawheed, however, we are all, according to the Qur'an and by divine decree, equal before the Eternal, our Lord. We are all subject to a single divine law, that of knowledge, diversity and self-definition, which makes us all different but also all equal. It is the basic concept of an Islam that is 'the purest monotheism'. As Maimonides said, primarily because there is no intermediary between God and humans, it implies that the individual is placed at the centre of axiological values and systems of belief. Some Muslim philosophers go further. They view Tawheed as the spiritual union of all in a single Creator.

The uniqueness of Tawheed is, therefore, the symbol of the universal union – the symbol of the potentially divine identity in every part of our humanity! On this point, many thinkers and Sufi ascetics have postulated that the major religious axiologies are likely to converge, by different routes. They will move towards a unified view of the diversity of the divine plan. To quote Mansur al-Hallaj, known as the Christ or the martyr of Islam: 'at the end of my flight, which exceeded all limits, I wandered the plains of proximity, then looked in the mirror of water, and thus could not see beyond my face.' Others include Bayazid Bastami and Shaqeeq Blake.

Ibn 'Arabi, the master of masters of Sufism, teaches us that it is from ourselves that we conclude to Him; we ascribe in Him no quality without embodying ourselves that capacity, excepting the principled autonomy. Since we know Him by us and from us, we attribute to Him all that we attribute to ourselves and that is why, secondly, the revelation was given to us by the mouth of the interpreters [prophets], and why Allah describes Himself to us through us. Contemplating Him, He contemplates Himself, although we are evidently numerous regarding individuals and genders; we are united, indeed, in a single essential reality, but there is a distinction between individuals, otherwise, by the way, there would be no diversity in uniqueness.

Thus, we might call this path, which leads to the transcendence of our difference and the unconditional love of diversity desired by Allah, incarnation, or *houloul*: Jnana Yoga and nirvana, or Tawheed and *fana*. As the Indian mystic Ramakrishna Paramahamsa said: 'All paths lead to God, but all paths are not God.' Of course, all these conceptions of the relationship to God are not to be confused. But it is plausible to think of them like the branches of one tree of faith and knowledge, which makes us move towards the Universal.

This convergence of the diversity represented by our humanity is one of the fundamental Islamic values that not so long ago was recognized and praised. We find this even among some European thinkers such as Edgar Quinet: 'The Mohammedans [Muslims] reached religious and social unity before us; before we offer to deprive them from it and to enter with us into contradiction. How would they accept the exchange?'

Indeed, how?

Being deprived of the blessing that the Qur'an enjoins us to follow is to forget the spirit of Islam. It is to retain only the institutionalized dogma of a politico-religious elite, formed on the basis of racial, ethnic, sexual and religious prejudices. In the Qur'an, God addresses the Prophet of Islam: *We narrate unto thee* (Muhammad) *the best of narratives in that We have inspired in thee Qur'an, though aforetime thou wast of the heedless.* And also: *In their history verily there is a lesson for men of understanding. It is no invented story but a confirmation of the existing* (Scripture) *and a detailed explanation of everything, and a guidance and a mercy for folk who believe.*

If God has made us incarnate, these prophetic stories are there for us to extract the metaphorical sense. They certainly do not have one unique possible interpretation. Some Sufis, the greatest thinkers of what some considered to be 'the golden age' of Islam, boasted of being able to find up to 7,000 interpretations of a single verse.

So, the position of Islam seems to have been a metaphysical position of vanguard spirituality, such as it was in the context of the seventh century revelation. This is the ideal posture of a Muslim who is submissive to the internal and social peace of his Lord, using the spirit, as well as the examples offered by the spiritual tradition, to differentiate between good and evil, with no intermediaries between himself/herself and God!

The stories of Abraham and other prophets allow us to place the debate about homophobia and Islam at the heart of a debate that is much broader and quite real. It is about respect. Even more, it proactively promotes respect for individual freedom and inalienable human rights. This is no doubt a new representation, enlivened, ecumenical, egalitarian, universal and thus secular. It is a representation of Islam that we believe is opposed to 'soft fundamentalism', which some traditionalist Arab-Muslims are trying to import into Europe and across the Arab and Asian Muslim world.

It is our responsibility, as believers, to bring our stone to the human spiritual building, in this era of globalization and 'global community' that we hear so much about. Is it not also the deeper meaning of the Hadith of the Prophet of Islam, which is proactively committed to respecting all forms of gender identities and religious diversity? *My position in relation to the prophets who came before me can be explained by the following example: A man erected a building and adorned this edifice with great beauty, but he left an empty niche, in the corner where just one brick was missing. People looked around the building and marvelled at its beauty, but wondered why a brick was missing from that niche? I am like unto that one missing brick and I am the last in the line of the Prophets.*

You will notice he did not say he was sent to eradicate any other form of religion on earth, or to enclose the entire world in a rigid, predefined mould. This would go against the very nature that has been assigned to every one of us. And a significant part of this nature lies in everyone's gender identity and sexual orientation. On the contrary, our Prophet taught us that Islam is here to fit harmoniously into a building of pre-existing human metaphysical beliefs, in agreement with a diversity of human genders and identities that could be seen as sanctified by the Qur'an.

This is the essence of Rumi's wonderful poem: 'Lit in one place, are ten lamps. They all have different shapes, but when you see the light they shed together, it is impossible to say what light comes from this or that particular lamp. Regarding the area of the spirit, there is no partitioning, not the least individualization.'

Only the evolution of our consciousness of Tawheed, the cognitive representation of uniqueness of faith that each of us has built, individually and in relation to our human community, will allow us to change our concept of human dignity – that which some are quick to assume we do not have, therefore reducing human beings to their sexuality or gender identity only. Thus, only the reform of the representation we have of Islam will allow us to proactively accept and sustain the complexity of our human identities, far from any form of axiological dysphoria.

5.2 Same-sex Unions and Marriage

Indeed, the issue of reforming the representation we have of our own heritage of worship, the main cause of dysphoria, is no doubt included in a necessary axiological revolution. The term in Arabic is *tajdid wa Islah*.[1] It is a conciliatory, inclusive and appeased reform. And it is achieved by a constant and dynamic renewal of the representation we have of ourselves as Muslims and the relationship we have with the 'other', our co-religionists, as well as all the rest of our sisters and brothers.

The reform of Islam is clearly a process of reclaiming Islamic texts. On this particular point, the most progressive as well as the most dogmatic seem to almost all agree.[2]

Shortly before the monopolization of Islamic interpretation carried out by highly politicized Islamic sects, some Sufi mystics of the Middle Ages found founts of knowledge and inspiration in Far Eastern mysticism. They also looked at ancient Mediterranean philosophy. Today it seems difficult to envisage that sources held sacred by the majority of Muslims – the Qur'an and Sunna, or prophetic tradition – are there primarily as examples, to protect the innocent against injustice and prejudice, especially minorities. They were not meant for the establishment of a rigid, patriarchal, dogmatic and hegemonic social order.

As the most sublime Averroes said, the use of reason is a 'speculation about the universe as it does teach us about the Artisan'.[3] He encouraged the study of philosophy as it seeks to make the Creator known:

The fact of philosophy consists in nothing else than the rational consideration of beings. In fact, thinking on them reflects that they are proof of the existence of the Artisan ... Thus it is clear that the act referred to under this name [of philosophy] is, under the revealed law, either *mandatory* or recommended.[4]

The study of science and the use of reason – called *ijtihad* in Arabic – are crucial for an understanding of what Islam is, i.e., without excess one way or the other. As the Qur'an (29.41) reminds us, reason is more complex but at the same time more fragile than the spider's house, the frailest of all houses.

Rumi speaks of being constantly worried and tormented by the thought, effort and attempts to seize the God Almighty, although He is elusive.[5] 'The reason is like the moth and the Beloved is the candle. As the moth flies into the flame, it burns and is emptied. But the moth is the one who, while being burned and tortured, cannot bear to be away from the flame [of the wisdom of God].'[6]

Like any monotheistic religion, since the earliest days of Islam, the problem of the dynamic and the reform of the relationship we maintain with our heritage of worship has been defined by two reefs. Islam keeps manoeuvring between excessive innovation and a total lack of dynamic and continuous reform of the relationship we entertain with our spirituality. The former is especially achieved through the use of reason and *ijtihad*.[7] The latter, the *bid'a*,[8] leads us to create a wealth of liturgy. This makes Islam no longer a tradition, an example, *a path to enlightenment*, but a real axiologico-liturgical cabinet of curiosities.

In the pre-Islamic context, for example, the condemnation of idolatry by the Prophet Mohammed Peace Be Upon Him (PBUH) was considered an innovation, a real threat to the social tribal order of Arabia. The Prophet took the opposite side of his accusers – the conservative notables of Mecca in particular – by turning the controversy about the *bid'a* on its head. In this case, he did it by saying that Abraham (PBUH) was a patriarch and the monotheistic Arabs had deviated from his practice. Thus the Prophet Muhammad (PBUH) cleverly used the concept of *bid'a* for his own benefit. With the advent of Islam, the term Sunna came to be closely linked to the normative education and conduct of the Prophet Muhammad (PBUH); previously it had referred to the customs and practices of tribes. Later, after the Prophet's death (PBUH) *bid'a* came to be defined in contrast to the Sunna.

Today we see how the Muslim community has taken to extremes. Either you follow the strict Sunna or you make a *bid'a*: the golden path of our beloved Prophet (PBUH). The middle way is difficult to follow. Yet the Qur'an reminds us: *Thus, We have appointed you a middle nation, that ye may be witnesses against mankind, and that the messenger may be a witness for you.* (Qur'an 2.143) We cannot say that everything is a *bid'a* in the literal sense; otherwise we should question everything that came into effect after the Prophet Muhammad (PBUH) died.

Marriage and coming out

In a rational use of *ijtihad*, independent reasoning, the question is not whether all Muslims should get married. It is an issue on which traditionalist Muslim scholars do not agree.[9] Moreover, our main goal is always the well-being and empowerment of LGBT Muslims or those LGBT individuals who are from a Muslim background. The quest is rather to discover how equal rights for all, especially allowing the marriage of same-sex couples, can enable LGBT Muslims to better empower themselves,[10] and better express their gender identity and sexual orientation.

Accordingly, the availability of an 'inclusive marriage' to all,[11] particularly to same-sex partners, is an 'excellent *bid'a*'![12] Or should we state, as some extremely dogmatic Muslims do, that every innovation is misguidance, and leads to the fire?[13]

Ibn Abd al-Barr, a famous Andalusian Maliki scholar of the eleventh century, says the *bid'a* is strictly ritual: 'When we are dealing with innovations in the practical operation of this world, there is no restriction and no fault.'[14] In other words, technological progress, architecture, urban development and interpersonal relationships, called *mu'amalat* in Arabic,[15] do not constitute *bid'a*. The criterion, therefore, imposes a restrictive framework for creative ideas. This ensures continuity with the spiritual path and Islamic tradition, as well as conformity with the spirit of the law – thus avoiding any form of excessive liturgical innovation.

This concept of *bid'a* is reinforced in Islam by that of *ijtihad*, which is defined by Dr Umar Faruq Abdallah as 'critical legal thinking in search for answers to new problems'.[16] In this, the opening of marriage to all is simply a way to move beyond all forms of homophobic, misogynistic prejudice. It is a pragmatic response to 'new problems' and a way for true equality between all citizens.

Moreover, to quote Ibn 'Arabi:

We are not saying that *ijtihad* is what the scientists call esoteric. *Ijtihad* for us is the effort that achieves the interior disposition by which one becomes able to host this particular inspiration that no prophet or messenger could accommodate at the time of the prophecy – provided that this revelation may not undermine legal status firmly established by Envoy (PBUH).[17]

This also suggests that 'what the law is silent about is no less fortuitous than what it says. If each word in the shari'a has a sense so too does the absence of a word. Man [human beings] should not transgress the Word of God, should also not fill the silences of God. The "holes" in the Law are part of its fullness.'[18] It implies that one cannot add requirements, much less bans, which are not clearly mentioned in principal

Islamic texts: namely the Qur'an and the Sunna of the Prophet (PBUH) *Ijtihad* is, therefore, an intellectual process – fair, pragmatic and measured. Al-Baji, another Andalusian jurist and a contemporary of Ibn Hazm, defined it as expending one's fullest [intellectual] capacity in search of the right ruling.

Dr Fazlur Rahman speaks of *ijtihad* as the effort to understand the meaning of a relevant text or precedent containing a rule. It is also to alter that rule by extending or restricting or otherwise modifying it in such a manner that a new situation can be subsumed under it by a new solution.[19] George Makdisi, professor emeritus of Arabic and Islamic studies at the University of Pennsylvania, notes that *ijtihad* is obviously related to the existence of the classical schools of Islamic thought. It was the imperative to perform it that led to the formation of the classical schools of Islamic law, many decades after the death of the Prophet (PBUH).[20]

Finally, Abu Zayd al-Dabusi, a prominent Sunni jurist who died 430 years after the Hegira, noted that what may be allowable in one time or place may become prohibited in another because of changing circumstances, just as what was prohibited may become allowable by the same criterion. He added that changing times and places are not the only considerations. There are others, such as the particular realities of a person's social group. What is beneficial for one segment of society may be harmful for another.

These are all designs of Islamic religious dialectic between the spirit of the law and human societies that embody them – an Islamic dialectic that seems in total agreement with the valorization of the dynamic evolution of a humanity guided, not enslaved, by the spirit of divine law. Since one of the Hadiths of the Prophet (PBUH) of Islam encourages critical thinking by saying, 'If a judge passes judgment and makes *ijtihad* and he is right then he will have two rewards. If he makes a mistake he will have one.'[21]

Those who refuse to recognize our love, simply because we embody a form of Creation's diversity, cannot understand that *ijtihad* is not only good, it is obligatory. Those who do not practise it are poor scholars, who apply the jurisprudence of the Islamic schools of the past without thinking. The renowned Egyptian jurist of the thirteenth century, Abu Abbas al-Ahmad al Sanhaji Qarafi, said there was scholarly consensus – *ijma'* – about the hardness of the reprimand vis-à-vis the religious scholars who make a decision mechanically, without performing legal *ijtihad*, and simply following the ancient texts in their books, literally, without regard to the new realities. The absence of such lawyers was inexcusable and was disobedience to God.[22]

The famous lawyer of the following generation, Ibn Al-Qiyyam, said, 'this is pure understanding of the law.'[23] And the Qur'an bids us to use reason and expertise in ethics: *ask people of science if ye know not.* (Qur'an 21.7) The French contemporary Imam, Tarek Oubrou, talking about postmodern Muslim scholars: says 'although some claim to be modern, they stop at the popularization of a work more on the form and literary aesthetics than on the substance.'[24]

We could go even further. Some only follow their own prejudices and those of their fathers before them. Yet, does not God put us on guard against unjust traditions and false idols? *They are but names which ye have named, ye and your fathers, for which Allah hath revealed no warrant. They follow but a guess and that which (they) themselves desire. And now the guidance from their Lord hath come unto them.* (Qur'an 53.23) People of this ilk usually respond: *'We found our fathers following a religion, and we are guided by their footprints.'* (Qur'an 43.22) *What! Even though the devil were inviting them unto the doom of flame?* (Qur'an 31.21)

Some Muslim jurists today and Islamophobic individuals or political organizations would do well to first ask what the experts in human sciences think of individuals belonging to a sexual minority or of marriage between same-sex partners. In this, let us not forget the Prophet Muhammad's (PBUH) pearl of wisdom: *A Muslim is a brother to a Muslim. He should neither deceive him nor lie to him, nor leave him without assistance. Everything belonging to a Muslim is inviolable for a Muslim; his honour, his blood and property. Piety is here (and he pointed out to his chest thrice). It is enough for a Muslim to commit evil by despising his Muslim brother.*[25]

5.3 Universal Islamic Humanism and Individual Well-being

To claim the legacy of the prophets, that of Abraham and Mohammed (PBUH) is above all to use reason and enjoy freedom of choice, with respect for human diversity. Yet it is clear that the Arab-Islamic dogma has tremendous work to do.

Abdenour Bidar explains that it is not possible to continue to base our axiological choices on a traditional Islamic ethic that defines and recognizes a person as a slave creature, whose rights are limited to 'submission' set by God. It is a contradiction between dogmatic Islamic and human rights that Muslims should have the courage to address in an open dialogue with the world.[26] Clearly, Arab-Islamic civilization is walking slowly out of the 'Janus' phase, described by Victor Segesvary.[27] This is the European society of the fifteenth century, still beset by wars of religion, yet also being reformed, that we have inherited.

We must insist on Islam leaving the fifteenth century as found in the schedule of the Hegira. It seems to be the model of a civilization before the reform, which causes us to look too often to the past. A model, however, already carrying many hopes for the future largely because the Arab peoples are now developing their own version of Islamic humanism.[28]

Similarly, in Europe, the humanism of the Enlightenment would have participated in the initiation of religious and political reform. This was mainly through the emancipation of the individual at the time, of *res publica christiana* which was based on the feudal concept of a European Christian nation. In the sixteenth century, the power of the clergy was surpassed by the inevitable changes of the era. This heralded the advent of modernity. No doubt, to some extent, European religious and political reform was also sustained by the Protestant Reformation.[29] Notwithstanding the free will of the majority of Protestant thinkers, they refrained from a critique of the sacred text.

Finally, this reform would have been mainly the result of a return to the axiological sources. This is always a form of rebirth. Some think it was also the expression of a Europe in crisis as it faced the strong power of a threatening Ottoman Empire at the gates of Venice, Vienna and Buda (modern day Budapest) – an Ottoman Empire 'infidel' to the Christ, yet carrying a form of Qur'anic truth. Was this especially through the metaphysical posture of Mohammed (PBUH) carrying another form of message, for a human being fundamentally conscious of his freedom? In peace?

Most of the Protestant reformers condemned Islamic heresy – some even called Muhammad (PBUH) the Antichrist – yet everyone seemed to praise the unique righteousness of Islam. The Lutheran in particular but also the Calvinistic critics of the Catholic Church said it had moved far from Christ's concept of universal humanity. At any rate, if Muslims cannot find a way to return to the roots – the Islam of France, Europe and the Arab-Islamic civilization in general – it will postpone for a long time its postmodern 'renaissance'. We will all suffer the consequences. Muslims in particular will be unable to participate at the concert of nations and will be condemned to reproduce the position of Janus, the Roman god, with one face turned towards the past of humanity, full of events and ideas, and another towards the future of the human species, both beautiful and dantesque.[30]

The Islamic contribution to universal humanism must reconnect with the seeds of its founding texts to re-establish its humanism in one form or another. This, in turn, will be far from any religious extremism or nationalist political exclusivity, and close to a *tselem elohim* or *capax dei*, representations of a kind of universal and ecumenical, Jewish or Christian humanism.[31] A form of metaphysical concept that corresponds to one of the possible exegesis of the verse of the Qur'an where the Lord said to the angels: *I will establish a caliphate on earth*. Elsewhere in the Qur'an that term is interpreted as 'successor', but here the traditionalist exegetes did not dare interpret this term as accurately. They translated it as 'regent under the authority of God'.

As if, says Abdenour Bidar, exegetes did not dare to attribute such freedom to humans. Human knowledge establishes the human being as a creator with God: 'All that human being represents ... all these are things inseparable from himself, inseparable from his essential self!'[32] Therefore, inalienable freedom given by God seems to be the cornerstone of humanism proposed by the Qur'an. This is stronger and truer than the *houloul* incarnation of God in man.

Islam teaches us, indirectly, that the noble purpose of spirituality is to help to learn. It is also to fully own our love and human potential for compassion rather than to 'normalize' our behaviour according to prejudices and pride. Islam is there to purify us through its dynamics, such as water movements, as the great master Rumi says.[33] This understanding of Islam, the only one that could last, tells us, therefore, that it is up to us to decide what we want to be and what kind of world we want to live in.[34] Besides, modern neuroscience and philosophy teach us that human beings have been endowed with extraordinary minds which are truly 'creators of possibilities'.[35]

Power, domination and vanity

Rumi says the cousins, Jesus and John the Baptist, laughed a lot. The latter asked Jesus: Are you insured against the powerful and subtle tricks (of the devil) that you laugh so? Jesus answered: Have you forgotten the graces and subtle, pleasant, extraordinary, powerful blessings of God that you cry so much? A saint [wali] present asked God, 'which one is greater?' God replied, He who has the better vision of me. That is to say, I'm here where the thoughts of my servant are. What he imagines about me, that's where I am. Purify, O my creatures, your imagination, since it is my home and my residence. [86]

Yet, this concept is far removed from the dogmatic representation that all sides impose without valid reasons and irrespective of the suffering of our brothers and sisters. Indeed, this research on the path leading to the Omega, the Lord our God, should be based on a total freedom of thought coupled with the freedom of voluntary action. It is the only bulwark against holocaust: the indifference to the suffering of the 'other' that would mean the end of any justification for the existence of humanity.

It is the only way our human caliphate could make us a true creator of possible realities, when we shall fully assimilate that knowledge, and thinking shall take precedence over power and strength. As evidence we can look to the history of the illustrious prophet and king, Solomon, when he asked his servants to bring him the throne, a symbol of power, of the Queen of Sheba. The dark spirit of the human being, *al-djeen,*[37] proposed in a wink, the time it takes the nervous system to transmit from one neuron to another, to bring the power of Sheba into his hands. Yet it was the man of science, embodying knowledge and reason, and not the djeen, the symbol of fire, the force of unfettered power, who was more than ready to satisfy the desire of his master.

O chiefs! Which of you will bring me her throne before they come unto me, surrendering? A stalwart of the Djeen said: I will bring it thee before thou canst rise from thy place. Lo! I verily am strong and trusty for such work. One with whom was knowledge of the Scripture said: I will bring it thee before thy gaze returneth unto thee. And when he saw it set in his presence, (Solomon said:) This is of the bounty of my Lord, that He may try me whether I give thanks or am ungrateful. Whosoever giveth thanks he only giveth thanks for (the good of) his own soul: and whosoever is ungrateful (is ungrateful only to his own soul's hurt). For lo! My Lord is Absolute in independence, Bountiful. He said: Disguise her throne for her that we may see whether she will go aright or be of those not rightly guided. So, when she came, it was said (unto her): Is thy throne like this? She said: (It is) as though it were the very one. And (Solomon said): We were given the knowledge before her and we had surrendered (to Allah) [in peace?]. (Qur'an 27.38–42)

True knowledge of the reality of this world, can offer us potentially much more power over our fears and ignorance than the political compromises and manipulations used for purposes of conquest and power. Truly, understanding reality provides the power of immanent enlightenment. Political power and physical strength may seem heady: 'Vanity of vanities, all is vanity.'[38]

The illusion is that the real power of the Almighty is a brutal force. Like slaves of our own fears and illusions in the cave of Plato's republic, we must look beyond what our senses seem to tell us.[39] In the verse quoted above, is it the throne that the Queen of Sheba refers to when she says *as though it were the very one?* Yet it was an illusion. At the end of the sentence in Arabic is 'hu', which is also the syllable from the testimony of the oneness of Tawheed that every Muslim has to say: *la ilaha illa hu* – 'there is no God but Allah'. A syllable almost 'magical'. A symbol of absolute creation, from the divine power of the Almighty. It turns out that it has been used for centuries by many Sufi brotherhoods in their mystic trances. Some have also made the connection between the Muslim 'hu' and Om, the Hindu and Buddhist symbols that state the supreme enlightenment of the human being,[40] according to the prayer: *Om Mani Padmé Hum.*[41] And the Qur'an says, *we knew this before her because we were at peace* [*muslimoum*], while it describes the celestial journey of the Prophet Muhammad (PBUH), who was taken during his night journey to the confines of 'paradise', where the glory of God appeared to him under the aspect of the tree of life called *the lotus of the outcome.* (Qur'an 53.14)

In other words, as the archetypal human being is the articulation of the divine attributes, according to the Qur'an, the true nature of humans is not guilty. It is the opposite! We humans are, metaphorically, pillars of the universe. We are the reason for all creation, a reflection of the compassion of God on Earth, the only kind of creature potentially able to apprehend the infinite gentleness of our Creator. *Vision comprehendeth Him not, but He comprehendeth (all) vision. He is the Subtle, the Aware'* (Qur'an 6.103); *nothing could be compared to Him* (Qur'an 42.11); or the words of the Bible: *To whom will you compare me and make me equal? To whom will you compare me so that we can be alike?* (Isaiah 46.5)

This is called the incognoscibility of God, which the human mind is simply unable to conceive,[42] just as most of us are unable to understand the reason for the diversity of gender identities and sexual orientations. However, in the words of Ibn 'Arabi in his *Treaty on Love*: 'The celestial sphere makes its journey through the breaths of human beings, we will even say, through the breath of every creature that breathes ... This is why the world continues to be intimately associated with humans.' He adds that the Word of God is understood by Him alone ('*the essence of my being is the form*').[43] God has made us his caliphates and successors, the pillars of creation. Why did he create us as such diverse beings and not otherwise? Only God knows precisely. We have to fully accept it with joy, even if we do not always understand His plan in detail. That is the *mithak* – pact – which God establishes with humans[44]; it is *al-Amanat* – the deposit of faith – God has sealed in us,[45] and that only humans are capable of beholding.

The precise reason God created such diversity of genders and sexualities is unknown. It may be seen as a test of our compassion and love for others. This is the type of disclosure that is accessible, according to Sufi mysticism, only to some elected saints that God blessed with the *kashf* – the unveiling of the truth.[46] It does not matter whether we believe or don't believe in such concepts. The key is that the heart of Islamic mysticism enjoins us to trust in the projects of the Almighty.

Ibn 'Arabi called this *al' ilm al-ladouni* – immanent knowledge – that God grants 'head-to-head on the mat of contemplation'. It is the theophany,[47] when ego and human reason collapse against the infinite lordship of God. Just as Moses gave up duality on Mount Sinai: *And when Moses came to Our appointed time and his Lord spoke to him, he said, 'Lord! Show yourself to me so I can see you.' God said, 'You will not see Me, but look at the mountain, if it remains in its place, then you will see Me.' But when his Lord manifested (His) glory to the mountain, it collapsed and Moses fell unconscious. When he came to himself he said: 'Glory unto Thee! I turn unto Thee repentant, and I am the first of (true) believers.'* (Qur'an 7.143) Thus 'God alone knows the Tawheed that is worthy of Him'.[48] Only God knows the uniqueness that is worthy of our humanity.

The poet Rumi tells us that 'as the copper astrolabe is the mirror of the spheres, so are human beings the astrolabe.' God says in the Qur'an: *Verily We have honoured the children of Adam.*[49] When the Almighty has revealed Himself to the human being and made him aware of His existence, this human, in his own astrolabe sees all the time, at every moment, the influence of God and His beauty like no other. And this beauty is never absent from the mirror.

After that Rumi adds to this wonderful and hopeful imagery, lines for a truly immanent serenity: 'O thou who is a copy of the divine archetype, O thou who are the mirror of the royal beauty, apart from thou nothing exists outside in the world: what you want, seek it in yourself, for you are everything.'[50]

Islamic ethics of unconditional love of diversity

Knowledge of the self and others is the key to the freedom that makes us creators of possible realities, true caliphates of God on Earth, peaceful, united by the Tawheed of the universal. This is despite or through the diversity of humanity. According to Ibn 'Arabi, it is not enough for the lieutenant – caliphate – to avail himself of the divine essence. He was assigned to Adam, to the exclusion of other creatures of the universe, because God created him according to His own shape. A lieutenant must have the attributes of the person he represents, otherwise he is not strictly a lieutenant.[51]

Ibn 'Arabi teaches us that only an exemplary character, free of jealousy, anger, all forms of violence, prejudice, discrimination towards others, can recover, here and now, the human being in his/her original theomorphism, *in divinis*. This is mainly by dedicating himself/herself to the prophetic tradition of tolerance and openness, for the well-being of the greatest number of lives consecrated to God.[52]

It is now clear to us that the illusion driving power into the hands of those who give free rein to their passions, their prejudices, their thirst for domination, is vanity. A more just human order was never released and never shall be *biithni'Allah* from the discrimination of the minority among us. An immanent human transcendence, here and now, is our responsibility. Thus, it is an Islamic ethic of unconditional love of diversity brought by the 'other' that we must develop – a truly Islamic theology of equality and liberation.

The Qur'an enjoins us many times to respect all humans as our brothers, our sisters, our equals, created by God.[53] Ibn 'Arabi believed that the message of peace in Islam, issued by the Prophet Muhammad (PBUH) 'embraces all human beings without exception and His mercy, by which he [the Prophet] was sent, embraces the whole universe towards which he was commissioned; they believe in him or not, all beings are part of His mercy'.[54] It is the great Jili[55] who said that, among all the attributes of God, it is that of mercy that encompasses them all. This is according to the Word of God in the Qur'an: *Say* (unto mankind): *Cry unto Allah, or cry unto the Beneficent, unto whichever Name ye cry* (it is the same). *His are the most beautiful names.* (Qur'an 17.110)

Isn't it in the name of this universal humanity, inspired by Islam, that Spain in the eighth century became one of the most prestigious academic centres in the world? This was especially in Cordoba and Granada, which attracted many students from Europe, including some Jewish students, both in arts and sciences.

And when the Muslims were expelled from Spain in 1492 Jews had to leave too. Majid Tehranian tells us that the 'lesson of this episode is clear: diversity is a source of strength, conformism leads to cultural stagnation.'[56] Thus Auschwitz has demonstrated the validity of the philosophical proposition that mere uniformity is death.[57] Indeed, at the time of al-Andalusia,

Jews fleeing the pogroms that followed in Europe found refuge at the heart of the Ottoman Empire. There, many of their descendants occupied the highest offices of state, especially in the fifteenth and sixteenth centuries.[58]

In sum, I would like to stress the fact that the representation of universal humanism, which Islam can claim to be a part of, must be re-founded in part on the primacy of temporal rule of the human law in order to support the development of a fair social dynamic. On the other hand, under the divine impulse (if you believe in God), there is an axiological superiority of the divine 'laws' over dogmatic traditions. 'This does not imply that God simply does not care anymore', as denounced Malcolm Edwards.[59] We mean rather that God is the ultimate goal of the journey of our humanity in this world, as 'the union of the soul with God'.[60]

The other pitfall of this bilateral representation of our axiological development would be to jump headlong into a backward-looking nostalgia, a rejection of postmodernism, and a literal adherence to the creation myths. That would lead us to throw ourselves headlong into misogyny and homophobia, which according to some is the 'natural' order of Creation. On the contrary, we firmly believe that God wanted to create rich diversity, always maintaining the potential of Tawheed and causing us to constantly evolve towards greater humanity.

In other words, according to refined techniques of teaching, God in His infinite wisdom would have shown us the voice to be followed by examples – those offered by our prophets and others – while leaving us to find our balance in a society that has to remain free, submissive only to universal equality and fraternity. Thus, if we want to sustain the emergence of a renewed form of Islamic spirituality, we must return to the roots of Islam to realize God's plan for our generation. That is, without doubt, to sustain a dynamic development of new Islamic theologies which take into account the views, experiences, aspirations and welfare of every minority.

Misogyny and homophobia are not Islam – because nowhere in the Qur'an nor in the Sunna is homosexuality condemned.[61] Inter-religious dialogue is a duty. So then, the acceptance and the unconditional love of all humans should be brought to the pinnacle of our Islamic values. We must not divide ourselves in vain quarrels, reproducing or internalizing dehumanizing standards. No matter if our human sisters and brothers are gays or lesbians, bisexuals, transgenders, Jews, Buddhists, Christians, atheists, rich, poor, powerful or weak: to love unconditionally is a duty for every Muslim.

Since that love proactively sustains diversity, we are, according to the Qur'an, potentially better than the angels described as the *highest Synod*. (Qur'an 38.69) *He taught Adam all the names.* (Qur'an 2.30–32) Knowledge is what makes our humanity a *caliphate* and it is nothing without diversity! (Qur'an 49.13) Only the acceptance of diversity could allow us to empower a de facto sexual minority. Thus we have no choice but to be, just like the Muslim feminist, at the vanguard of reform. We must unite for the well-being of all our human brothers and sisters, since *Allah loveth those who battle for His cause in ranks, as if they were a solid structure.* (Qur'an 61.4.)

How do we do that, from an inclusive Muslim perspective? The next section will address this.

5.4 Alternative Islamic Liberation Theologies

The problem of de facto sexual minorities must be reassessed by taking into account Christian liberation theology.[62] Identity shaping is seen nowadays as organized from diffuse influence centres. They are not localized within particular communities and are in strong political evolution.[63] The grammar – sociological representation – related to sameness is changing very fast.[64]

In *Precarious Life*, Judith Butler defines vulnerable bodies as dependent on an unstable and sometimes violent social and political environments. They exist but their value and dignity is not recognized. Butler argues that we have to 'rethink the body ontology' through progressive politics and by questioning 'cultural modes of regulating affective and ethical dispositions through a selective and differential framing of violence'.[65]

Prior to the modern era, after the eighteenth century, the attitude to gender, corporality and homoeroticism did not pose as much of a problem as it does now in Arab-Muslims' public spheres and amongst diaspora communities. Then, in less than a century, the unfriendly attitude towards homosexual love attributed to the French was adopted by the advanced classes of Arab society.[66] The beginning of the twentieth century has seen the emergence of the modern social category of 'abnormal', as described by Foucault.[67]

How do these individuals, considered a sexual minority, position themselves against these postmodern sociological discriminatory mechanisms? What are the important figures of this reformed and alternative social grammar with regard to corporality, gender and religiosity?

In response to these dehumanizing representations,[68] a new generation of engaged intellectuals is brainstorming at the foremost sources of Islamic tradition. They also fall in line with women's liberation movements – those which sometimes appear to be paradoxical, appropriating the veil and not forcing to unveil, as was the case at the time of French Algeria.[69] The bodies of women are often associated with the body of the nation, whose honour must be defended, sometimes by revealing it and other times by covering it – yet too often oppressing it.[70] Raewyn Connell, who coined the term 'hegemonic masculinity', defines this 'conventional or idealized'[71] masculinity as a gender practice that embodies the currently accepted answer to the problem of the legitimacy of patriarchy. This guarantees the dominant position of men and the subordination of women.[72]

Thus, from a theological perspective and over twenty years, women and individuals belonging to sexual minorities have been at the forefront of mutations through the elaboration of a postmodern, post-identity and inclusive Islamic theology of liberation. It was not until the early eighties, with the introduction of gender studies in the field of Islam, that intellectuals increasingly questioned the most dogmatic, homophobic, transphobic and misogynist interpretations of Islamic heritage.

There was Fatima Mernissi with her *Women and Islam* followed by authors such as Everett Rowson who spoke of the *Effeminates of Early Medina*.[73] They were the *mukhanathun* – effeminate men, perhaps even transgenders – that the Prophet of Islam would have defended and welcomed in his very home, among his wives and children. These studies would pave the way to an avant-garde appropriation of Islamic heritage – this more than 1,400 years after the first Muslims. They would proceed firstly by Qur'anic exegetical reformulation of verses related to the people of Lot in Sodom and Gomorrah, by putting forward the context of the verses and the primary reason for the revelation (known as *al-'Ilat* in Arabic) as well as the ethical lessons which have nothing to do with 'homosexuality' as defined since the nineteenth century.

Scott Kugle[74] considers, in his 'systematic' study of the entire theological corpus related to the issue of homoeroticism, both the Qur'an and the tradition of Hadith. In his analysis, Islamic condemnation of same-sex intercourse would more accurately apply to punitive tribal traditions. These would have been implemented by men considered to be reckless by their own social group, virile and embodying a valued all-mighty masculinity. They engaged in violent homosexual relations, such as in Syria until the nineteenth century.[75]

Samar Habib,[76] a Palestinian refugee of Christian origin in Australia, views it as the link between the performative[77] grammar of human sexuality, modern puritanism and the need to break free from the legacy of contemporary postcolonialism. Just like Kecia Ali and her renewed 'sexual ethics',[78] Habib thinks that a 'queer-friendly' Islam is possible, primarily by rejecting the inauthentic Prophetic traditions – apocryphal hadiths – on which the first Muslim scholars developed their dogmas. They would then have to 'de-programme' homophobic interpretations of some verses from the Qur'an, and develop an entirely new 'Islamic theology of liberation'.

Finally, Joseph Massad, a Christian intellectual of Palestinian background, refused to be included in the LGBT-affirming acronym, saying it was too simplistic and inherited by the Arab-Muslim world after Western colonization.[79]

Queer dis-identification

From a more general perspective, the paradigm of Islamic queer dis-identification is inherently linked to Christian liberation theology, itself related to naturalistic theology – a theology focused on the attributes of the Universe's study. This, in turn, had replaced the 'dependency theory' based on centres of power.[80] Notably, liberation theologies grant a preferential option to the poorest, the weakest,[81] minorities at the periphery of traditional power grammars,[82] through spiritual transformation.[83] Contrarily, some radical dogmatic Muslims who talk about power sharing[84] with the 'white'[85] majority in Europe are afraid to be inclusive towards women and LGBT within their own community. They fear having to share their decision-making and negotiation[86] within the public sphere concerning their community identity with LGBT and women as well as Western Muslims.

Unlike the dogmatic intelligentsia within particular religious communities, alternative theologians emphasize the context and what the message follows from – just as in the sixties when Christian liberation theologians like Gustavo Gutiérrez[87] and many others, defined their religiosity as a 'critical reflection of historical practice under the light of faith'.[88] With regard to the particular Muslim context, for Ali Shariati[89] – historical figure of the Islamic liberation theology – tackling injustice and inequality in the world is a religious duty. He roots his understanding of faith in the Islamic Tawheed, which put forward that all human beings are fundamentally, by essence, equal in front of the uniqueness of their Creator.[90] According to Asma Lamrabet,[91] one of the most illustrious figures of the contemporary Moroccan Islamic feminism, this is the mission of the *khalifat*,[92] of human beings on Earth.[93] Farid Esack views it a key to redefining within Islam a 'hermeneutic of Liberation'.[94]

Associations and citizen networks are inspired by gender studies applied to Islam, Christian liberation theology and Islamic feminists such as Amina Wadud's 'gender jihad'.[95] These alternative Muslims are developing an approach described by some as a 'Tawheed paradigm'. It places at the pinnacle the uniqueness of our humanity. In the plurality and respect for diversity they mirror what they see as the oneness of God.[96]

In a book dedicated to the work of *Wadud*, the American essayist Michael Muhammad Knight describes how his

Behold, I Make All Things New

generative ethics of Tawheed destroy sexual hierarchies and all imaginations of difference in Muslim and non-Muslim communities. *Wadud*, he says, achieves this through the extraordinary humility of equal service to God.[97] That paradigm conforms to what Muños calls 'dis-identification' from prejudices and stereotypes.[98]

This alternative grammar about religiosity always goes through a form of symbolic negotiation among peripheral ritual actors, and is adapted to social reality. It is a long process, littered with political resistance and more than 500 years of resistance from indigenous people to, for instance, colonialism and repression of identity diversity.[99] The alternative Muslims use religion as a factor of emancipation whereas it was used against them as a factor of political oppression.

The challenge of these liberation theologies is to focus on the spiritual praxis and well-being of each human being rather than on dogmatic and bourgeois conservatism. They must continue to embody a holistic vision of the spiritual and axiological ethics in the world, without being the traditional clone of either political or ideological partisan paradigms. They need to articulate and strengthen all struggles against all forms of oppression instead of weakening humanistic struggles by opposing one another.

Alternative theologians had to choose the renewed theoretical grammar closest to their axiological and political struggles. They first focused on adapted practices, while maintaining the axiological superiority of faith in God. This would be at the heart of the political arena and of their understanding of faith and human societies.[100] Therein lay the danger for the majority in power because it was about the deconstruction of their elitist, bourgeois, non-egalitarian dogma, and rejection of the 'infallibility' of religious institutions. Those first liberated Christians thought that Marxism – or, in any case, anti-capitalism, against the exploitation of the poorest – would be the best grammar in the world to explain oppression and address the relevant theologies rooted within our faith traditions.

For Muslims, it was also through the identification with other anti-capitalist struggles that their liberation was initiated. More precisely, it was on the basis of an economical and geopolitical critique of postcolonialism. It is a liberation vis-à-vis imperialism and westernisation at an external level. At an internal level, these alternative Muslims struggled for the emancipation of women, LGBTIQ individuals and religious minorities in Arab-Muslim societies.[101] No doubt, their struggles also sent a loud message into the public sphere, within particular Arab-Muslim societies, and into Muslim diaspora communities. They provide complex axiological reflection pathways. Unfortunately, these are not always accessible to the broader religious audience.[102]

5.5 Testimonials

Having highlighted the tremendous ground-breaking work undertaken by intellectuals and activists, we would like to share selected testimonies of LGBT and queer Muslims so that the importance of those achievements may be better understood.

Azzah, a transgender Muslimah – Amsterdam

A devout Muslim 'trapped' in the wrong body, Azzah Hari-Wonmaly (forty) has chosen to live as a Muslimah. At first glance she is no different from thousands of Muslim women in the city of Amsterdam in the Netherlands. A pair of eyes peek from a tight black headscarf. Dressed in a skirt, overalls and matching stockings, she is holding a trendy iPad bag as she introduces herself, 'Hello, I am Azzah.'

Speaking at a seminar on homosexuality and Islam in 2011, she spoke of how her sex change surgery at the OLVG Hospital in Amsterdam was handled by a Muslim surgeon, R.B. Karim, and an assistant of Iranian descent. 'I was allowed to wear my headscarf in the operating room and after the surgery doctors put a Qur'an in the palm of my hand. I deliberately chose a Muslim surgeon. It feels more comfortable entrusting my body and post-operative care to people of faith,' she explained.

The seminar was targeted at lesbian, bisexual, gay and transgender Muslims faced with the dilemma of choosing between faith and love. A problem Azzah understood too well. While still an androgynous man, she was the manager at a leading Dutch telecommunications company. For a long time, she was in a relationship with a man from Morocco. 'We loved each other, but did not live under one roof,' explained Azzah. 'He grew up among Muslim fanatics and his family began to suspect my identity. Our relationship would have brought disgrace if recognized,' she continued. Azzah does not talk much about her own family. 'What is clear is that it is still hard for them to accept my decision to change sex.'

Azzah, who is of Indonesian descent, spent her childhood in social institutions. She was thirty years old when she decided to become a Muslim. Today, she accomplishes her five prayers a day, eats halal products, and wants to marry a Muslim. However, so that patients at the clinic where she works don't feel awkward, she sometimes takes her veil off.

Before surgery, Azzah stopped over in Egypt. There, Islamic courts pronounced a fatwa stating that her male sex was not in line with the heart, soul and body. Shortly thereafter she underwent gender identity disorder treatment at the VU Hospital in Amsterdam. Thereafter, she began her anthropological odyssey to find an identity.

She explained, 'Actually, Muslims are quite open about sexuality … I always emphasize that my decision is about reconciling my femininity and not a gender identity crisis. I had never demanded of anyone that they acknowledge my gender. I know many married men who have intimate male friends secretly.'

According to Azzah, immigrants in the Netherlands were more accepting of her. 'There was a local nurse who refused to touch me, saying she preferred to help people with broken bones. Yet some Muslim cleaners were very enthusiastic and asked me to pray with them. We sobbed together as our prayer ended.'

At the seminar, Azzah outlined her plan to form a transgender community of Muslims in Amsterdam. 'Sort of a vehicle to

Behold, I Make All Things New

exchange thoughts and information among Muslim brothers. We want to convey that we are not sinners or apostates,' she explained.

At time of writing this she was working as a psychotherapist at a clinic.

Salif*, gay visual arts student – Cairo

I grew up in a middle-class family, typically conservative and religious. My mother is illiterate; my father comes from the countryside. In fact, I did not even know if what I felt was right or wrong. I started surfing blogs in English. It was during a chat that a user told me Allah would send me to hell. So, I inquired about what Islam said. I prayed and read the Qur'an to stop thinking about men. I was in a terrible state of confusion, overwhelmed by the idea that God hated me. But after three days, I realized that I was doing nothing wrong. Today, I feel perfectly comfortable with who I am.

Besides, being heterosexual in Egypt is not that great either.

All this suffering because we do not feel the same as others … It's very difficult to have a relationship of any kind, to find people who accept you as you are. If you hide those things, you feel lonely and uncomfortable. And if they find out, you could lose everything: friends, family, work … perhaps even life. And this is not because you're gay: it's like friendship, but more than that, you need to like them and share things such as: 'Did you come out? Are you an atheist?

In general, I do not speak out unless I'm really confident. I think the uprising has opened the eyes of some gays to the fact that there is much to do and it's not just about sleeping around. I have seen many gays on Tahrir Square. But for now, we must join the fight for freedom. The rest may come. Maybe, writers and film directors could refer to the suffering of gays.

[*Pseudonym; testimony available in the article of Albertine Bourget on 360°: https://360.ch/monde/14398-le-printemps-homo-devra-attendre/, translation, L. Zahed.]

Sahar*, gay and married with two children – Amsterdam and Iraq

Sahar belongs to Secret Garden, a foundation for LGBT Muslims. It was established in Amsterdam in December 1994, with the intention of reaching out to and drawing together young Muslims who are transgender, or have homosexual or bisexual feelings.

My name is Sahar (pseudonym), I am thirty-six years old and I am a gay. I am very gay, but in secret. I cannot tell anyone that I am attracted to men, and I cannot share my experiences and feelings with anyone. It is not easy growing up with the feeling that everything you do with your sexuality is wrong and prohibited.

I am the son of my mother and I still do not know who my father is. My mother went out with lots of men, particularly influential men in government such as army generals and men from the secret service. When I was small, I remember many men coming to our house, and there was always lots of food and drinks.

It is very difficult to grow up in the Muslim community, because when your mother is not married and entertains men at home, she is considered a whore. I think my mother lived her life in her own way and was just trying to survive during Saddam Hussein's government. That wasn't easy for a woman, who got pregnant before marriage and did not stay with the man who was responsible. She got a bad reputation in the neighbourhood and her family never spoke with her again, because she damaged their honour. That is how women, who have chosen their own freedom and their own happiness are looked upon.

Growing up in such an environment is not easy. It is a very hard life. People who don't like the way you live will not respect you, and will abuse you and sometimes even rape you. When I was very young I already knew I was gay. My mother knew it as well but we never talked about it, as long as I could keep it a secret and was careful in how I handled it.

When I was between thirteen and fifteen years old, I had sex with many young guys but also with men who visited our house. Sometimes men would come to our house while my mother was away. They would take me and give me money for it, but I had to promise them never to tell my mother.

I met my first love when I was sixteen years old. That was also the year my mother passed away. I was very depressed, was left alone with my sister, who is older than me. My three brothers wanted nothing to do with me. They all moved somewhere else, where they could escape the intolerance and misunderstanding of their surroundings, and where they could start a new life.

My new friend Jihan was three years older than me and the man of my dreams. He went to the same school as me, and he saw how alone and depressed I was. In the beginning it was just a story of two young guys at the same school, taking the same courses and often hanging out together in school and out. He was always there for me, for whatever I wanted or needed.

I became so used to his presence that I could not do anything without him. He meant everything to me, and if I had to spend a day without him I was always in a bad mood. My love for him grew every day and he began to treat me as his possession or his 'girlfriend'. He wouldn't allow me to talk to anyone, especially not to other boys. If he caught me with a boy he would get very angry and yell at me. But still I felt happy with him. Like Romeo and Juliet. I say that because I do not know of any tale of two men in love with each other.

Jihan was my friend, my brother, my father and my biggest love. I remember our first intimate contact. It happened at his parents' house. During the summer holidays his parents had to go to Amman, Jordan, with the entire family, but he stayed behind. Everything was planned so that we had the whole house to ourselves. We made jokes and we laughed so hard. We were teasing each other and were running in the house.

We were cooking dinner together when he told me that he wanted to live like that: together with me, in our house, two guys who love each other. Then he hugged me and held me for several minutes. His hands started moving around my shaking body, and we started breathing faster. I couldn't resist any more.

Behold, I Make All Things New

But everything comes to an end. When he became an adult, his mother wanted him to get married. After six years of love, he had to get married, and so did I. But I could not fall in love with another boy, because he was still everything to me.

Sahar did indeed get married, to a woman, and now has two children: a boy and a girl. In 2003, he fell in love again with a boy, but it was not easy for them to be together. One day, Sahar decided to rent an apartment. The owner of the apartment called him and got his wife on the phone. He told her that he had arranged for everything and that Sahar could use the apartment when he wanted. His wife was surprised; she did not understand why her husband wanted a second home.

When he came home, she asked him to explain. He couldn't say anything, but his wife thought he was taking a second wife, and she was very angry. The fight about that grew and at some point, the whole family knew about it. They threatened to kill him if he took a second wife. So, his plan failed and he could only be with his lover in secret. He was even more careful after that because the family suspected something.

Sahar still lives with his family and he keeps seeing his lover in secret. Thousands of gay and lesbian youth lead double lives like that. The majority of them are married and have children while still living out their homosexuality in secret. This double life brings many challenges, and often leads to psychological problems. But can it really be different? Can homosexuals one day choose their own happiness, or will they keep choosing what family and society expects from them?

[*Pseudonym]

Hussam*, from Secret Garden – Amsterdam and Morocco

Every second Wednesday of the month Secret Garden has a movie night, showing a documentary followed by a discussion. Last year there were a series of documentaries about homo- and bisexuality, but also transgenderism and transsexuality. Films such as *Hob Al Nisa, I cannot think straight, Me and Nuri Bala, Silent Stories, Sex Change in Iran* and more. There were many visitors. The evenings started with a meal together; then there was some time to get to know each other, followed by the documentary and a discussion.

On Wednesday, 14 December 2011 the *Dancing Boys of Afghanistan* was shown, and a few Afghan boys were invited to participate in a panel discussion: Amin Sadat (eighteen), Jafar Haidari (fifteen), Reza Haidari (sixteen) and their (straight) older brother Ali Haidari. They talked about the situation of homosexuals in Afghanistan. It was a very special evening.

That evening there was a new visitor and he was very impressed with the whole event. He later told us the following story:

My name is Hussam and I am twenty-three years old, of Moroccan descent. I have heard a lot about Secret Garden, but I never thought I would visit. I live in Amsterdam and so does my family, which makes hanging out in the gay scene very dangerous for me. I have no contact with other Arab gay youth. I am hiding my homosexuality, because I am afraid that my family might find out and then all kinds of terrible things will happen.

I do receive information about Secret Garden activities through email. I have tried several times to go to an event, but I didn't dare. I really wanted to do that, but I just could not. Early December 2011, I heard that the Secret Garden was organizing a movie night with *The Dancing Boys of Afghanistan*. That's when I decided that I would go.

On 14 December, around six in the evening, I went to the building of Secret Garden. I did not just go to see the movie, but also to meet new people. I stood at the door, but still hesitated to enter. It was nerve-wracking. I did not dare to press the doorbell, but then unexpectedly this guy opened the door. He said hello to me and asked me to enter.

I went inside and saw about twenty people of different ages. It was easy to make contact and I heard many different languages: Arabic, Farsi, French and Dutch. A few minutes later someone announced that dinner was ready. Iranian food was served and the cook talked about the dishes. I think he did that to make it clear to the attendees who are Muslims that only halaal food was served. I too eat halaal and I liked the fact that he explained how he had prepared the dinner.

I also met Emir, the event organizer, for the first time. I knew his face; I had seen him a few times on the street. He is gay and well known in Amsterdam. Apparently, he has no problems with his homosexuality. I cannot be open about it myself. I think I have not accepted myself yet. I try to do my best, but I feel that I cannot do that yet, because if my parents found out I would get nothing but trouble.

An hour later all of us were asked to go to the second floor for the film and discussion. We all went upstairs and after a few minutes the documentary started. Everyone watched the fifty-minute documentary, subtitled in English, intently. After the movie Emir came forward and talked about homosexuality in Afghanistan. He welcomed three Afghan brothers, two of them gay, and said how special it was that they were there.

They stepped forward and Emir began asking them questions about their sexual orientation while an interpreter translated from Farsi into Dutch.

The two brothers talked about their feelings and the problems they had experienced in Iran and Afghanistan. Their straight brother talked about the government and social control in Afghanistan, and the fact that being gay is very difficult. He said that when he lived in Afghanistan, he also hated homosexuality. But when he came to the Netherlands and met a few people who were also gay, he began to consider it more normal, and that is why he now supports his two brothers.

When I heard that, I could not believe it: three brothers who were here together. I would really like to be able to talk to my brother about my feelings, but I'm too scared to do that. I am convinced that if I mention anything to any of my relatives, I will definitely have problems because it is not allowed and not possible.

Later I talked to one of the brothers, he was very nice. I got his phone number and he said I could call him whenever I want. I have also spoken with a few other guys and got their phone numbers as well. I will definitely call them. I think it is important to keep in touch. Maybe, I will get the courage to make a choice for my own happiness and tell my parents about my sexual feelings; who knows?

[*Pseudonym; testimonies available on the Secret Garden's January 2012 newsletter; a huge thank to Emir Belatoui for his cooperation; http://www.stichtingsecretgarden.nl/; info@ stichtingsecretgarden.nl.]

Saffiya*, bisexual Muslimah – USA (East Coast)

When was the first time I realized I was not heterosexual?

I was eighteen when I got really close to one of my friends and realized it was different for me and I told her. Some of my friends know, but it is not public. I don't want to complicate things. I am fine with the way I'm living. I am married and pretty happy with my family. My friends who know are supportive and do not have any problem with who I am. They respect my decisions and what I have done in my life and how I choose to live. Most of the people I have told I knew I would not have a negative reaction from. They have been neutral and non-judgemental. They have just let me talk about my problems/relationships like any other issues in my life.

I have friends who are bisexual and Muslim. They are not, in social terms, 'practising' Muslims, but they are Muslim and we talk about our lives. I have not gone out and tried to connect specifically with these people, they were already my friends and we talk. I have a very good friend, who told me she was bisexual way before I even figured it out about myself. She was the first person I went to talk about my relationship. It really helps to have people like yourself to talk to because they can understand what you're going through. I have been with a Muslim girl. We have been together on an emotional and physical level.

Do I foresee my relationships evolving from casual to a more sacred bond like marriage?

No, I don't. I am married to a guy whom I love and I am content with this relationship. Perhaps, in another world it would be okay to have that kind of bond. For now, all I can say is I wouldn't feel comfortable in an open relationship with a girl – maybe because I feel like it's wrong.

How do I reconcile my faith and my sexual orientation?

I keep them very, very, very separate. I block out my faith and religion if I am with a girl. I completely ignore its existence. And when I pray and try to practise my faith, I ignore my homoerotic desires. I have a lot of internal conflicts as a result.

If someone reading this is struggling with their sexual identity, what advice would I provide to them?

I honestly do not know what to say. I myself struggle with it, but I have chosen to ignore it for the most part because I am married and do not want to compromise my marriage or my family. Go with what your heart desires.

What message would I like to convey to Muslims about Muslims from the LGBTIQ community?

There are worse things a person can do, and there are worse problems [facing] the Muslim community. We need to get rid of this taboo. Lying is bad; cheating is bad; oppression is bad; rape is bad, but being a gay/lesbian is a personal choice. What's the point if you're straight and a horrible person? Why should people like that be allowed to be Muslim, but a person who is not straight is seen as a heathen? We need to check our priorities.

[*Pseudonym]

Mohsin*, gay Muslim – London

When was the first time I realized I was not heterosexual?

I couldn't have been more than eleven or twelve years old. I had this friend called Umran. Like me, he too had shifted to Lahore, Pakistan, from London the previous year and we had a lot in common. We used to hang out after school and spend our summer holidays together. Puberty hit and he developed an insane crush on this girl, whom I instantly took an intense dislike to. It wasn't just him, but all the boys around him as well.

A few weeks later Umran and the girl started 'going out' and I was insanely jealous. I remember being devastated, crying at times. Whenever a group of boys would get together, the topic of discussion would ultimately turn to girls, rating them on a

1–10 scale. Although I took part, I never really had any interest whatsoever. And that was my first inkling.

Who did I inform?

No one. Even though I had no idea what gay meant, I definitely knew I wasn't supposed to be liking other guys, the way they liked girls. That, quite frankly, scared the heck out of me. I've only very recently started coming out. I've told my closest friends, two of my sisters, and one of my nephews. I am not out to the community at large. My nephew had the best response I could ever hope for: 'You're still my uncle, and I still love you.' I nearly started crying.

Sister 1: 'Eww, I don't want to talk about it.' I think she's okay with it, as long as she knows nothing more. Sister 2 was the disappointment. She used to tell me everything about her life, how things were with her husband, the problems she was having, real heart-to-heart talks. She often remarked that I never shared anything with her, and she was right, I wasn't out to her, so I couldn't tell half the stuff that I wanted to without coming out to her. She accepts me, but doesn't want me to tell anyone else (the rest of the family, mother, etc). This forces me to lead a double life, which makes me miserable. It is why I want to come out to the rest of the family.

How have Muslims reacted when I revealed my sexual orientation?

To be honest, it has not come up in conversation. I don't go about telling everyone I meet, and when it does come up, I bite my tongue, take deep breaths, and walk away.

Have I connected with other Muslims from the LGBTIQ community? If so, how do I connect?

Once, I went to a meet-up group for LGBT Muslims, when one of the guest speakers they had was Imam Daayiee, a self-styled gay imam and scholar.[103] He was quite inspiring and I liked him, having found him really well read and an all-round nice person.

The others in the group were, however, a bit cliquey as they all knew each other and weren't inclusive at all of me. Let's just say I didn't fit in – different values, opinions, insights – and they were a lot more conservative than me. Whilst I was beginning to feel more comfortable with my sexuality, they seemed to be struggling. And I didn't need that, especially since I had just reconciled myself.

I would eventually like to meet someone that I could spend the rest of my life with, but frankly, I feel as if I'd be asking too much. I know I'd have to choose either family or love and I don't know how I'm going to do it. The problem has caused me endless anxiety. When I do come out to them, will they still want to know me? Will they throw me out? Cut me off? I'm extremely close to my entire family.

How do I reconcile my faith and my sexual orientation?

I'm working on that bit. I've been very angry for a very long time at Islam, Muslims and God for making me feel how I feel – why couldn't He just have made me 'normal'? I actually used to pray to be straight in my late teens and when that failed, I lost faith. But, recently, I've started to come around because you know what? He's my God too. Not just the God of the people, who want to condemn me to hell. In particular, one verse of the Qur'an gives me strength from time to time: *On no soul doth Allah place a burden greater than it can bear.* [Qur'an 2:286] It feels hopeless at times, but I try to be a good person, keep my intentions pure, and my heart at ease.

Let me live my life as I let you live yours. I'm responsible for my actions and you are responsible for yours. No amount of praying will make you straight. It's neither an illness nor a disease.

Does safety ever concern me in terms of retaliations from the Muslim community? Have I been threatened?

Personally no, but I've heard plenty of horror stories. It gets better. Stay strong. Breathe. To all those who think we don't exist: We do. I could be your brother, your uncle, your cousin, your nephew. I am a caring brother, a doting uncle, a dutiful son. I'd like nothing more than to see you happy – in fact, what makes you happy makes me happy.

To my family: I'll need you. Do you have any idea how terrifying it is? The idea of facing it without you?

[*Pseudonym]

Hamid*, gay Muslim – Canada

When was the first time I realized I was not heterosexual?

I think I realized I wasn't 'normal' from childhood but I only accepted it a year ago. My family in general is conservative especially with this issue. I hope they will not disown me in shame, but at this point I am scared to take the chance. I know my parents will be disappointed and feel it's their fault. I pray that one day I can be completely honest with them, but I never want to risk losing their love and support.

I have never interacted with any Muslims from the LGBT community offline, but have read about their experiences online. It was both touching and informative. It did provide me with peace of mind to know there are people like me out there.

Do I foresee my relationships evolving from casual to a more sacred bond like marriage?

This topic scares me, no lie. Whenever I hear my parents talking about marriage and finding me a bride, I get sick. It's one thing to not come out, but to pretend to love someone you have no attraction to is something I cannot bring myself to do. As for marriage with a man, I have given it thought. At the end of the day, I think everyone wants to find someone they can spend their life with and share love.

How do I reconcile my faith and my sexual orientation?

For a long time, I just told myself this is a phase and I will change one day. I began to hate a big part of myself and was angry for being different/unusual. It took me a long time to come to the conclusion that a just God would not want someone to live a lie!

I, like many other gay Muslims, have probably read a tonne of blog posts, articles and fatwas saying it's unnatural, disgusting, immoral and a deviation. It is very easy to say what is natural and what is not when you are not affected by the issue. That is all I can say because at this point I have heard it all, and all I want is to find peace within myself and hope everyone can respect that.

If someone reading this is struggling with their sexual identity, what advice would I provide to them?

At the end of the day, you need to be true to yourself.

Does safety ever concern me in terms of retaliations from the Muslim community? Have I been threatened?

Thankfully, living in Canada, I can say no, but that is not the case for many gay Muslims around the world.

Lukman*, gay Muslim – USA

My faith?

I really do not have one yet! I am on the fence between Islam and Judaism, and attend a Unitarian Universalist church.

When was the first time I realized I was not heterosexual?

I realized in kindergarten when I had a crush on my best friend, and after I told him how much I liked him he made it really clear that it was not 'normal'. I did not fully come out until I was a junior in high school around 1993–1994. I told my absolute best friend Patty. She cried with me and became my strongest support and biggest advocate despite being a preacher's daughter.

Everyone knows now. I have been with the same man for twelve years and married for almost seven! I did not tell my parents until I was around twenty-one. They handled it far better than I know they would have if I were open in high school. Though they knew back then, we did not discuss it. When I came out in high school I was rejected, harassed and pushed so far that I was suicidal. I lost my best friend and a few supposedly good friends. My real friends kept me from doing anything to myself, and did all they could to never leave me alone or get upset.

Over the past twelve years I have become very interested in Islam, but have been terrified to become a Muslim because of attitudes towards gay people. I recently reached out to a local imam, asking if he would help. His response was:

'From my position as imam my heart and my intention is to help people in following the *deen* of Islam. This position includes encouraging people to do what Allah asks of us and to stay away from those things that he has asked us to stay away from.

'Now you have said a couple of times in your email that you want to learn about Islam. And I say to you that I do not think that is entirely true. It is quite possible that you want to learn about Islam those things with which you already agree. Finding justification for one's beliefs in a religious tradition, and rejecting those things about that religious tradition which one does not believe in is not that uncommon.'

This was entirely unfair of him and it only got worse. It is hard for me to recount as it has happened a couple of times when I reached out to Muslims. The reason why I do reach out is that I feel Islam is a communal religion. Your prayers are meant to be said in unison with your community, the wider the ummah. Though I know I can technically say the *Shahadah* by myself, I keep reading that you should repeat it in front of a community of Muslims in order to make it more 'authentic'.

The imam also said:

'Certain things are allowed and certain things are not allowed. One of the areas in Islam in which there are fairly clearly laid out restrictions has to do with sex. Sex between men and sex between women is simply not allowed. So, in my mind, the performance of that is detrimental to your deen and puts all else in doubt.

'The second problem for me is the idea that two men or two women can marry. This is also not allowed in Islam. Actually, it is so far removed from what marriage means in Islam that it is not even considered. As an Imam, I am asked to wed people according to Islamic law as found in the Qur'an and Hadith. There is nowhere in those laws and traditions (believe me I have looked), which could even be used to design a wedding ceremony for a same-sex couple, much less a marriage.'

For about the eighth time in my life my hope of being taught about Islam and becoming a believer was destroyed.

How do I reconcile my faith and my sexual orientation?

Despite everything I keep reading, I feel a deep connection to God, Allah or however you want to label the Divine. Having read the Hebrew Bible and the Qur'an, I do not see what people throw in my face about my sexuality. I feel comfortable with my sexuality and Islam or even Judaism.

A lot of the condemnations I hear are more cultural or translation dependent, some from a time when science was only beginning and not nearly as advanced as it is now. Yet Islam's message is above and beyond all cultures or time periods! ... Safety is a concern for me, I have never been threatened but I am terrified after reading many stories of others who are like me. There is nothing to fear from us. We just want to be treated like the brothers and sisters we are! I think a lot of the fear comes from a misconception and misunderstanding of what it means to be LGBT.

With the rampant Islamophobia around the world, members of the LGBT community would be powerful allies in the fight against the lies and deceit. We have dealt with it, and still do unfortunately, and many of us do stand up and fight against Islamophobia. It would be amazing to be able to stand side-by-side and fight for equality and respectful treatment of all of us, united.

[*Pseudonym; these testimonies are available on Organica: the story of an Arab American girl; http://organicmuslimah. blogspot.com/. A huge thanks to the author, Cindy Abdelaziz.]

Louisa and Clara – Islamophobia, anti-Semitism and homophobia

I met Louisa in front of Gustave Courbet's famous painting *L'origine du monde* at the Orsay Museum in Paris. Seeing a beautiful girl, who looked North African, admiring it, I was intrigued and decided to approach her. We hit it off. She had a little time and we decided to get acquainted over a cup of tea. Three quarters of an hour later we found ourselves in a friendly, cosy place.

Louisa described herself as a very shy woman. She was twenty-eight, a practising Muslim and a lesbian. She worked in IT and had a two-year-old boy from an arranged marriage. Life was not very easy since she hid her sexuality from everyone, especially from herself.

Of her marriage she said little but confessed that, torn between two worlds, she did not have the strength to say no to her parents. In Algeria her husband's family treated her like a puppet. There was much bitterness and regret in her voice, but she was an optimist and found in her son and in Allah all the comfort that allowed her to live.

Divorced from her husband, she was in a happy relationship with a young Jewish woman. But there was sadness because she could not to share this with her family. Although she yearned to tell them everything, she knew deep inside that her parents would reject her. Moreover, they would take her child away.

She entertained only superficial relations with them and saw them during religious feasts and holidays in Caen. I asked if I could meet her Jewish friend one day, because so much religious strength opens my respect and tickles my curiosity. And I have to say that this couple is very beautiful, very rare, and it was my pleasure to enter their world.

She invited me to visit her home the following day to meet Clara.

I was greatly surprised by their apartment which gave the impression of being a single person's flat. Nothing indicated that a lesbian couple with a child lived there. No pictures of them together. No personal effects, only common and ordinary utensils. And Louisa revealed that mistrust prevents them from behaving as a family. They prefer to live like that, hidden even in their most intimate place. Clara confirmed that they preferred to live in secret.

May our Lord Allah and Yahvé stay beside them with His love.

Notes

2. In the Name of God: A Letter to Muslims, Jews and Christians

1   *The Message of the Qur'an*

2   E.g. 23:6; 25:6–7; 31:7; 36:5; 37:26; 40:11–12; 51:1–2; 52:8; 57:9–11; 86:5; 86:5; 100:5; 103:8–12; 106:1; 107:1; 109:26–27; 115:1; 118:1–4 and 29; 119:64; 130:7; 136:1; 145:8–9, as well as in other texts in the Hebrew Bible (e.g. Exodus 34:6–7; Numbers 14:18; Deuteronomy 4:31; 1 Kings 8:23; Nehemiah 9:27; 1 Chronicles 16:34; 2 Chronicles 30:9; Isaiah 30:18, 49:13, and 54:8; Jeremiah 3:12; Lamentations 3:22–23 and 32; Daniel 9:9; Hosea 2:23; Joel 2:12–13; and Micah 7:18).

3   E.g. 23:6; 25:6–7; 31:7; 36:5; 37:26; 40:11–12; 51:1–2; 52:8; 57:9–11; 86:5; 86:5; 100:5; 103:8–12; 106:1; 107:1; 109:26–27; 115:1; 118:1–4 and 29; 119:64; 130:7; 136:1; 145:8–9, as well as in other texts in the Hebrew Bible (e.g. Exodus 34:6–7; Numbers 14:18; Deuteronomy 4:31; 1 Kings 8:23; Nehemiah 9:27; 1 Chronicles 16:34; 2 Chronicles 30:9; Isaiah 30:18, 49:13, and 54:8; Jeremiah 3:12; Lamentations 3:22–23 and 32; Daniel 9:9; Hosea 2:23; Joel 2:12–13; and Micah 7:18).

4   For instance, to Matthew 5:7; Luke 1:50 and 78; The Acts of the Apostles 20:24; Romans 5:8 and 15, 6:15, 9:22–24, and 12:1; 1 Corinthians 10:13; 2 Corinthians 1:3; Ephesians 2:4–7; Colossians

3:12–13; 2 Timothy 1:9; Titus 2:11, and 3:5; Hebrews 4:16; James 2:13; 1 Peter 1:3, and 5:10; and 2 Peter 3:9.

5   'Not-so-holy matrimony', *The Guardian*, 29 June 2003.

6   *Making Wise the Simple: The Torah in Christian Faith and Practice*, Grand Rapids, Michigan: William B. Eerdmans Publishing Co, 2005.

7   Karen Armstrong, *The Spiral Staircase: My Climb Out of Darkness*, New York: Knopf Publishing Group, 2004.

8   Scott Siraj Al-Haqq Kugle, *Homosexuality in Islam*, London: Oneworld Publications, 2013.

9   Report of the Ad Hoc Committee on Homosexuality and the Rabbinate comprising official representatives of several institutions affiliated with Reform Judaism, 1990.

10   William Stacy Johnson, *A Time to Embrace Same Gender Relationships in Religion, Law, and Politics*, Grand Rapids, Michigan: William B. Eerdmans Publishing Co, 2006.

11   David Von Drehle, 'Gay Marriage and the Law of the Land', *Time*, 22 January 2015.

12   Quoted in Annemarie Schimmel, *Gabriel's* Wing, Leiden: E.J. Brill, 1963.

13   Arthur J. Arberry (tr), The mysteries of selflessness: a philosophical poem ('Rumuz-e-Bekhudi') by Sir Muhammad Iqbal, London: J. Murray, 1953.

14   Halide Edib, *Inside India*, London: Allen & Unwin, 1937.

15   Ibid.

16   From Coleman Barks (tr.) *Essential Rumi*, New York: HarperOne, 2004, first published 1273.

3. A Jewish Perspective

1   Simon LeVay, *Sexual Brain*, Cambridge, Massachusetts: MIT Press, Bradford Books, 1994, pp. 16–17. See Judith Plaskow, 'Sexual

Orientation and Human Rights: A Progressive Jewish Perspective',
in Saul M. Olyan and Martha C. Nussbaum (eds), *Sexual Orientation
and Human Rights in American Religious Discourse*, New York: Oxford
University Press, 1998, pp. 30–34; Andrew Sullivan, *Virtually
Normal*, London: Picador, 1995, pp. 16–17, 170–71.

2   Adrienne Rich, 'Compulsory Heterosexuality and Lesbian
Existence', in *Signs: Journal of Women in Culture and Society* 5
(Summer 1980): 631–60, reprinted in Adrienne Rich, *Blood, Bread,
and Poetry*, New York: W.W. Norton & Company, 1994.

3   Lillian Faderman, *Surpassing the Love of Men: Romantic Friendship
and Love Between Women from the Renaissance to the Present*, New York:
Harper Paperbacks, 1998, pp. 15–20. On the form of the 'Boston
marriage,' in which two women would live with one another, see
ibid., pp. 190–203.

4   Shakespeare, 'Merchant of Venice', Act I, scene 3.

5   Basil Hume, *The Mystery of Love*, Brewster, Massachusetts:
Paraclete Books, 2001, p. 20

6   Gareth Moore, *A Question of Truth*, New York: Continuum, 2003,
p. 9.

7   See Alicia Ostriker, *For the Love of God*, New Brunswick, New
Jersey: Rutgers University Press, 2009, pp. 9–33; David Carr, *The
Erotic Word: Sexuality, Spirituality, and the Bible*, London: Oxford
University Press, 2005, pp. 109–51.

8   Ibid., 117.

9   See Christopher King, 'A Love as Fierce as Death', in *Take Back
the Word*, pp. 126–42; Gary Comstock, *Gay Theology without Apology*,
Eugene, Oregon: Wipf & Stock, 2009, pp. 27–48.

10 The comments appeared on Andrew Sullivan's blog, The Daily
Dish, 5 November 2006. Quoted in http:// ericedberg.wordpress.
com/2006/11/05/bearing-false-witness/.

11 For an application of this teaching to gay ethics, see Rebecca T. Alpert, 'Do Justice, Love Mercy, Walk Humbly: Reflections on Micah and Gay Ethics', in *Take Back the Word*, pp. 170–78.

12 http://www.youtube.com/watch?v=O0h5Vtke3OA; Advocate. com editors, 'Barney Frank Reveals Gay Agenda', *Advocate*, 22 December 2010.

13 See Nicholas Wade, 'Depth of the Kindness Hormone Appears to Know Some Bounds', *New York Times*, 10 January 201.

14 See Steven Greenberg, *Wrestling with God and Men*, Madison, Wisconsin: University of Wisconsin Press, 2005, pp. 192–214. Rabbi Greenberg offers several possible rationales for the Levitical prohibition, including concerns about reproduction and category confusion. See also pp. 147–52, 175–91.

15 See Rebecca Alpert, *Like Bread on the Seder Plate*, New York: Columbia University Press, 1998, pp. 29–35; Greenberg, *Wrestling with God and Men*, pp. 86–95. The original source of the prohibition is the Sifra's commentary on Leviticus 18:3, which says that in Egypt, men would marry men and women would marry women. Interestingly, this may have been true historically at the time the Sifra was compiled. See Bernadette J. Brooten, *Love Between women*, Chicago: University of Chicago Press, 1996, pp. 65–66.

16 Saul M. Olyan, 'And with a Man You Shall Not Lie the Lying Down of a Woman: On the Meaning and Significance of Leviticus 18:22 and 20:13', Vol. 5, No. 2 (October 1994), pp. 179-206. In Numbers 31:17–18, the term *mishkav zachar* is used in connection with whether a woman is a virgin or not. If she has known as *mishkav zachar*, she is not.

17 Robin Bell, 'Homosexual Men and Women', *British Medical Journal* 318.7181 (13 February 1999), pp 452–455.

18 See Rebecca Alpert, *Like Bread on the Seder Plate*, p. 28 (quoting Orthodox rabbi Norman Lamm).

19 See Saul Olyan, 'And with a Man You Shall Not Lie the Lying Down of a Woman': On the Meaning and Significance of Leviticus 18:22 and 20:13', *Journal of History of Sexuality* 5 (1994): pp. 179–206, reprinted in Gary David Comstock and Susan E. Henking (eds), *Que(e)rying Religion*, London, New York: Continuum, 1977, pp. 398–414. Olyan calls *toevah* a 'socially constructed boundary'. To be clear, Olyan disagrees with the reading of Leviticus that I provide here. His view is that the purpose of the prohibition is not to guard against idolatry, but to prevent defiling emissions from mixing with one another.

20 Deuteronomy 12:31, 13:14, 17:4, 20:18, 27:15, and 32:16.

21 1 Kings 14:24 (general); 2 Kings 16:3 (child sacrifice); 2 Kings 21:2 and 2 Kings 21:11 (idolatry); 2 Chronicles 28:3 (child sacrifice); 2 Chronicles 33:2 (idolatry); 2 Chronicles 34:33, 36:8, and 36:14 (general).

22 Ezekiel 5:11, 6:9, 6:11, 7:20, 14:6, 20:7–8, 22:2, 44:6–7, 44:13.

23 Ezekiel 18:13.

24 Ezekiel 16:47–50.

25 Ezekiel 22:11, 33:26.

26 Ezekiel 33:26.

27 Ezekiel 5:9, 7:3–4, 7:8–9, 9:4, 11:18, 11:21, 12:16, 16:2, 16:43, 16:51, 18:24, 20:4, 33:29, 36:31.

28 Ezekiel 16:22, 16:36, 16:58, 23:26, 43:8.

29 Jeremiah 2:7, 7:10, 32:35.

30 Jeremiah 6:15, 8:12, 44:22.

31 Isaiah 1:13, 44:19

32 Isaiah 41:14

33 Isaiah 66:3

34 Proverbs 3:32, 13:19, 15:8–9, 15:26, 16:12, 21:27, 28:9, 29:2

35 Proverbs 6:16, 16:5

36 Proverbs 8:7

37 Proverbs 11:1, 20:10, 20:23

38 Proverbs 11:20

39 Proverbs 12:22, 26:25

40 Proverbs 24:9

41 Proverbs 17:15

42 Matthew 24:15, Mark 13:14, Luke 16:15, and Revelation 17:4–5, 21:27

43 Olyan denies significance to this juxtaposition, since he believes the Levitical text may have been redacted prior to the form in which it appears today. Olyan, 'And with a Male', p. 408.

44 Olyan adds that other prohibitions, such as against adultery and incest, are found in numerous places in the Bible, but the ban on male anal sex is only found in these two Levitical passages. 'There is no reason to assume any necessary association between the prohibitions of male couplings … and the various incest, adultery, and bestiality interdictions.' Olyan, 'And with a Male', p. 399.

45 I Kings 15:12.

46 II Kings 23:7.

47 *The History of Herodotus*, translated by George Rawlinson, edited by E.H. Blakeney, in 2 vols, London and New York: Everyman's Library, first published 1910 Vol. I, p. 58.

48 See David Greenberg, *Construction of Homosexuality*, Chicago: University of Chicago Press, 1988, pp. 94–100; George Edwards, *Gay/Lesbian Liberation: A Biblical Perspective*, Cleveland, Ohio: Pilgrim Press, 1984, pp. 51–64.

49 See Ken Stone, *Practicing Safer Texts*, London and New York: T&T International, 2005, pp. 46–67; Brooten, p. 298; Jay Michaelson,

'Chaos, Law and God: The Religious Meanings of Homosexuality', *Michigan Journal of Gender & Law,* Vol. 15, No. 41, 2008; Christie Davis, 'Religious Boundaries and Sexual Morality', in Gary David Comstock and Susan E. Henking (eds), *Que(e)rying Religion,* pp. 39–60. I return to the question of boundary in chapter 6.

50 See Jay Michaelson, 'It's the Purity, Stupid: Reading Leviticus in Context: Parashat Metzora', in *Torah Queries,* pp. 145–50; Daniel A Helminiak, *Sex and The Sacred: Gay Identity and Spiritual Growth,* Abingdon, UK and New York: Routledge., 2006, pp. 51–67.

51 For excellent treatments of the Sodom story and its misinterpretation, see Michael Carden, *Sodomy: A History of a Christian Myth,* Abingdon, UK and New York: Routledge, 2014; Mark Jordan, *The Invention of Sodomy in Christian Theology,* Chicago: University of Chicago Press, 1998; Ed Noort and Eibert Tigchelaar, eds., *Sodom's Sin: Genesis 18–19 and Its Interpretations,* Leiden/Boston: Brill, 2004.

52 Some scholars maintain that to 'know' does not necessarily have a sexual connotation. See e.g. Scott Morchauser, 'Hospitality, Hostiles and Hostages: On the Legal Background to Genesis 19.1–9', *Journal for the Study of the Old Testament,* Vol. 27, No.4, 2003, pp. 461–85.

53 Christian readings of the Sodom story that focus on these elements include John McNeill, *The Church and the Homosexual,* Boston, Mass.: Beacon Press, 1993, pp. 42–50; Rick Brentlinger, *Gay Christian 101: Spiritual Self-Defense for Gay Christians,* Salient Press, 2007, pp. 33–40; Michael S. Piazza, *Gay by God: How to be Lesbian or Gay and Christian,* Carol Stream, Ill.: Hope Publishing, 2008, pp. 38–41; Daniel A Helminiak, *Sex and The Sacred: Gay Identity and Spiritual Growth,* pp. 43–50; George R. Edwards, *Gay/ Lesbian Liberation: A Biblical Perspective,* Cleveland, Ohio: Pilgrim

Press, 1984, pp. 24–50; White, pp. 37–40. McNeill notes that there are similar ancient near eastern stories, all of which are about hospitality and the abuse of strangers. McNeill, p. 44. See also Victor H. Matthews, 'Hospitality and Hostility in Genesis 19 and Judges 19', *Biblical Theology Bulletin: A Journal of Bible and Theology* 22.1 (February 1992): 3–11.

54 For parallel readings of this story with that of Sodom, see Carden, 'Sodomy', pp. 14–41; Rogers, pp. 67–68; Dwyer, 'Those 7 References', pp. 12–20; John McNeill, *The Church and the Homosexual*, Boston, Mass.: Beacon Press, 1976, pp. 47–48; Raymond de Hoop, 'Saul the Sodomite', in Ed Noort and Eibert Tigchelaar, (eds) *Sodom's Sin: Genesis 18–19 and Its Interpretations*, Leiden, Brill, 2004, pp. 17–28.

55 This analogy was suggested by Miner and Connoley, *The Children Are Free*, Life Journey Press, 2002, p. 4. Even anti-gay writer Robert Gagnon has said that the story of Sodom is 'not ideal' because it is about non-consensual activity. Gagnon, *The Bible and Homosexual Practice*, Nashville, Tennessee: Abingdon Press, 2002, p. 71.

56 See Carden, *Sodomy: A History of a Christian Myth*, pp. 44–48.

57 Deuteronomy 32:16–32.

58 Isaiah 1:9–10 (quoted in Rom. 9:29); Isaiah 3:9.

59 Isaiah 13:19, Jeremiah 49:18, Jeremiah 50:40, Lamentations 4:6, Amos 4:11, Zephaniah 2:9.

60 BT Sanhedrin 109a, BT Eruvin 49a, BT Ketubot 103a.

61 Greenberg, *Wrestling with God and Men*, pp. 64–69.

62 See Tom Horner, *Jonathan Loved David: Homosexuality in Biblical Times*, Philadelphia, Fortress Press, 1977, pp. 40–46; Theodore W. Jennings, Jr. *Jacob's Wound: Homoerotic Narrative in the Literature of Ancient Israel*, New York: Continuum, 2005, pp. 227–34;

Michael S. Piazza, *Gay by God: How to be Lesbian or Gay and Christian*, Carol Stream, Ill.: Hope Publishing, 2008, pp. 54–62. Mary Hunt, 'Lovingly Lesbian: Toward a Feminist Theology of Friendship', in James Nelson and Sandra Longfellow (eds), *Sexuality and the Sacred,* Westminster John Knox Press, 1994, pp. 172–78; Lillian Faderman, 'Surpassing the Love of Men', in *Sexuality and the Sacred*, pp. 179–81; Mary Rose D'Angelo, 'Women Partners in the New Testament', *Journal of Feminist Studies in Religion* 6.1 (1990). Other applications of Rich's 'lesbian continuum' include Micaela di Leonardo, 'Warrior Virgins and Boston Marriages: Spinsterhood in History and Culture', in *Que(e)rying Religion*, pp. 138–55.

63 Rev'd Jeff Miner and John Tyler Connoley, *The Children are Free*, p. 33. See also Celena M. Duncan, 'The Book of Ruth', in *Take Back the Word*, pp. 92–102.

64 Scholarly studies that locate the David and Jonathan story within the warrior love convention include Susan Ackerman, *When Heroes Love: The Ambiguity of Eros in the Stories of Gilgamesh and David*, New York: Columbia University Press, 2005; Theodore Jennings, *Jacob's Wound: Homoerotic Narrative in the Hebrew Bible*, pp. 3–80; David Halperin, *One Hundred Years of Homosexuality*, Abingdon, UK and New York: Routledge, 1990, pp. 75–87; Jean-Fabrice Nardelli, *Homosexuality and Liminality in the Gilgamesh and Samuel*, Amsterdam: Adolf M. Hakkert, 2007; Martti Nissinen, *Homoeroticism in the Biblical World*, Philadelphia: Fortress Press, 2004; and Tom Horner, *Jonathan Loved David: Homosexuality in Biblical Times*, Philadelphia, Fortress Press, 1977. My analysis here is indebted to these sources. Horner's book was a pioneering one in this genre, and he has a down-to-earth style that makes the book an easy read for laypeople. Ackerman and Jennings are

more academic. See also K.J. Dover, 'Greek Homosexuality and Initiation' in Comstock & Henking (eds), *Que(e)rying Religion: A Critical Anthology*, pp. 20–33.

65 See Crompton, pp. 262–69; Boswell, *Same-Sex Unions,* New York: Villard Books, 1994, p. 137–45; Tom Horner, *Jonathan Loved David*, p. 27.

66 Frederick S. Roden, 'What a Friend We Have in Jesus: Same-Sex Biblical Couples in Victorian Literature', in Raymond-Jean Frontain (ed.), *Reclaiming the Sacred: The Bible in Gay and Lesbian Culture*, Philadelphia: The Haworth Press, 1997, pp. 118–21.

67 Martti Nissinen, *Homoeroticism in the Biblical World*, pp. 53–56. See Horner, *Jonathan Loved David*, pp. 26–39; Greenberg, *Wrestling with God and Men*, pp. 99–105; Rick Brentlinger, *Gay Christian 101: Spiritual Self-Defense for Gay Christians*, Salient Press, 2007, pp. 140–91 (providing a thorough linguistic analysis).

68 Horner, *Jonathan Loved David*, pp. 27–28.

69 Comstock, *Gay Theology without Apology*, pp. 79–90.

70 See evidence collected in William N. Eskridge Jr. and Darren R. Spedale, *Gay Marriage: for Better or for Worse?: What We've Learned from the Evidence*, New York: Oxford University Press, 2006.

71 Charlotte L. Patterson, 'Children of Lesbian and Gay Parents', *Current Directions in Psychological Science* 15 (2006): 241. Online at http://cdp.sagepub.com/content/15/5/241 and http://www.apa.org/pi/lgbt/resources/parenting.aspx. Patterson's article cites dozens of studies. See also Bridget Fitzgerald, 'Children of Lesbian and Gay Parents: A Review of the Literature', in *Marriage and Family Review* 29 (1999): 57–75. No sociological study has ever shown that children do better with a mother and a father than with two fathers or two mothers.

72 Fitzgerald, 'Children of Lesbian and Gay Parents: A Review of the Literature', PsycINFO Database Record (c) 2016 American Psychological Association.

73 N. Gartrell, H. Bos and N. Goldberg, 'Adolescents of the U.S. National Longitudinal Lesbian Family Study: Sexual Orientation, Sexual Behaviour, and Sexual Risk Exposure', in *Archives of Sexual Behaviour* (2010), doi:10.1007/s10508-010-9692-210.1007/s. Online at http://www.nllfs.org/publications/.

74 H.M.W. Bos and T.G.M. Sandfort, 'Children's Gender Identity in Lesbian and Heterosexual Two-parent Families', in *Sex Roles* (2010), pp. 62, 114–12. The reported rate of exclusive homosexuality among these children is about 2.8 per cent.

75 Laura Langbein and Mark A. Yost, Jr, 'Same-Sex Marriage and Negative Externalities', '*90 Soc Sci Q 2*' (June 2009); Mary Virginia Lee Badgett, *When Gay People Get Married*, New York: NYU Press, 2010, pp. 64–85.

76 George Chauncey, *Why Marriage: The History Shaping Today's Debate Over Gay Equality*, New York: Basic Books, 2005, pp. 59–60.

77 See Marvin Ellison, *Same-Sex Marriage? A Christian Ethical Analysis*, Cleveland, Ohio: Pilgrim Press, 2004; Boswell, *Same-Sex Unions*, pp. 28–52; Mark Jordan, *Blessing Same-Sex Unions*, Chicago: University of Chicago Press, 2005, pp. 13–15.

78 Say and Kowalewski, pp. 19–82.

79 See e.g. James B. Nelson and Sandra Longfellow, (eds), *Sexuality and the Sacred: Sources for Theological Reflection*; James B. Nelson, *Between Two Gardens*, New York: Pilgrim Press, 1983, pp. 73–85; Letha Dawson Scanzoni, and Virginia Ramey Mollenkott, *Is the Homosexual My Neighbor*, New York: HarperOne, 1994, pp. 122–35; Davies and Haney, (eds), *Redefining Sexual Ethics*, Cleveland:

Pilgrim Press, 1991; Marvin Ellison, *Same Sex Marriage?*, pp. 139–46.

80 James B. Nelson, *Between Two Gardens: Reflections on Sexuality and Religious Experience*, p. 124.

81 Carter Heyward, *Touching our Strength: The Erotic As Power and the Love of God*, San Franciso: HarperSanFrancisco, 1989, pp .121, 125. Heyward proceeds to develop such an ethic in her book, pp. 124–55.

82 See, e.g., J. Michael Clark, *Doing the Work of Love: Men & Commitment in Same-Sex Couples*, Tennessee: Men's Studies Press, 1999.

83 See e.g. Robert Goss, *Jesus acted up: A gay and lesbian manifesto*, San Francisco: HarperSanFrancisco, 1993, pp. 165–68; Patrick Cheng, *Radical Love: An Introduction to Queer Theology*, New York: Seabury Books, 2011; Audre Lorde, *The Use of the Erotic: The Erotic as Power*, New York: Sage Publishing, 1978.

84 Iris Murdoch, 'The Moral Decision about Homosexuality', *The Ladder* (December 1964), Available online at http://www.asp6new.alexanderstreet.com/was2/was2.object.details.aspx?dorpid=1003347896.

85 'Anti-Gay Hate Crimes: Doing the Math', *Southern Poverty Law Center Intelligence Report* 140 (Winter 2010). http://www.splcenter.org/get-informed/intelligence-report/browse-all-issues/2010/winter/anti-gay-hate-crimes-doing-the-math# According to statistics kept by the FBI from 2005 to 2010, gays are 2.4 times more likely to suffer a violent hate crime attack than Jews, 2.6 times more than blacks, 13.8 times more than Latinos, and 41.5 times more than whites.

86 One Orthodox rabbi told another rabbi that it would be a 'mitzvah' (commandment, good deed) for gay kids to kill

themselves. Steven Greenberg, 'The Cost of Standing Idly By', *The Jewish Week*, 12 October 2010.

87 Carl Jung, Collected Works, Vol. 9, part 1, p. 87, quoted in McCleary, p. 20. On Jungian psychology and homosexuality, see Robert Hopcke, (ed), *Same-Sex Love and the Path to Wholeness*, Boulder, Colorado: Shambhala, 1993. On the idea of a special receptivity, see Andrew Harvey, *Essential Gay Mystics*, Book Sales, 1998.

88 For introductions to queer theology, see Gerald Loughlin (ed.), *Queer Theology: Rethinking the Western Body*, New Jersey: Wiley-Blackwell, 2008; Elizabeth Stuart, *Gay and Lesbian Theologies: Repetitions with Critical Difference*, Burlington, Vermont: Ashgate, 2003; Patrick Cheng, *Radical Love*. Some of the key names in queer theology have already been mentioned: Donald Boisvert, James B. Nelson, Elizabeth Stuart, Audre Lorde, Carter Heyward, Robert Goss, Gary Comstock, Patrick Cheng, Rebecca T. Alpert, Irene Monroe, George Edwards, Virginia Ramey Mollenkott, Marcella Althaus-Reid, Gerald Loughlin, Justin Tanis, Michael Kelly, Nancy Wilson, and on the (somewhat) more traditional side, John McNeill, Rev'd Candace Chellew-Hodge, J. Michael Clark, Michael S. Piazza, Chris Glaser, and Malcolm Boyd. Key queer biblical scholars include Ken Stone, Theodore Jennings, Stephen D. Moore, as well as many of the theologians listed above. Key writers in gay spirituality include Toby Johnson, Mark Thompson, Christian de la Huerta, Randy Connor, Joe Perez, and Andrew Ramer.

89 James B. Nelson, *Between Two Gardens*; Goss, *Jesus Acted Up*, pp. 69–72; Mollenkott, *Sensuous Spirituality*, New York: Crossroad Publishing Company, 1992, pp. 107–21; Donald Boisvert, *Out on Holy Ground*, Cleveland: Pilgrim Press. 2000, p. 45; See e.g., Marcella Althaus-Reid, *The Queer God*, London: Psychology Press, 2003, pp.

30–33; Marcella Althaus-Reid and Lisa Isherwood (eds), *The Sexual Theologian: Essays on Sex, God, and Politics*, London: T&T Clark, Bloomsbury, 2005. See www.irenemonroe.com; Spencer, *Gay and Gaia: Ethics, Ecology, and the Erotic*, Cleveland: Pilgrim Press, 1996, pp. 118–20; Rebecca Alpert, *Like Bread on the Seder Plate*, pp. 37–111.

90 See Randy Conner, *Blossom of Bone: Reclaiming the Connections Between Homoeroticism and the Sacred*, San Francisco: HarperSanFrancisco, 1993; Toby Johnston, *Gay Spirituality: The Role of Gay Identity in the Transformation of Human Consciousness*, Maple Shade, NJ: Lethe Press, 2004; Mark Thomspon, *Gay Spirit: Myth and Meaning*, New York: St Martin's, 1988; Christian de la Huerta, 'Coming Out Spiritually: The Next Step, New York: TarcherPerigee, Penguin Books, 1999, pp. 7–44; Harry Hay quoted in Mark Thompson, *Gay Soul*, New York: HarperOne, 1995, p. 20. See generally *Harry Hay, Radically Gay: Gay Liberation in the Words of its Founder*, Boston: Beacon Press, 1997.

91 See Marcella Althaus-Reid and Lisa Isherwood, *Trans/Formations (Controversies in Contextual Theology)*, London: Hymns Ancient & Modern Ltd, 2009; Justin Tanis, *Trans-Gendered: Theology, Ministry, and Communities of Faith*, Cleveland: Pilgrim Press, 2003; Noach Dzmura, *Balancing on the Mechitza: Transgender in the Jewish Community*, Berkeley, California: North Atlantic Books, 2010.

92 See Randy Connor, *Blossom of Bone: Reclaiming the Connections Between Homoeroticism and the Sacred*, New York: HarperCollins, 1993, pp. 40–43; Greenberg, *Construction of Homosexuality*, pp. 40–56.

4. A Christian Perspective

1 Keith Sharpe, *The Gay Gospels: Good News for Lesbian, Gay, Bisexual and Transgender People*, Christian Alternative, 2011, p. xx.

2 http://www.thewitness.org/agw/macauley121604.html.

3   The terminology 'born eunuchs' was used in the ancient world to
     refer to homosexual men.

4   Ethics lecture, Ridley Hall (Elizabeth Philips, 2012).

5   E.F. Rogers (ed.), *Sexuality and the Christian Body*, Oxford: Blackwell
     Publishers, 1999, p. 23.

6   'The Body's Grace' is a lecture and essay written by Archbishop
     Rowan Williams on the topic of Christian theology and sexuality.
     It was composed when he was Lady Margaret Professor of
     Divinity at the University of Oxford in 1989. His writings on
     the subject were perceived as quite liberal before he became the
     Archbishop of Canterbury. It is now part of a series of essays
     collected in Eugene Rogers (ed.), *Theology and Sexuality*, Oxford:
     Blackwell, 2002, first published1996, p. 64.

7   New International Version (NIV) 1984.

8   An ancient marriage covenant

9   Eugene Rogers (ed.), *Theology and Sexuality*, 1966, p. 66.

10   Ibid., 2002, p. 44.

11   Ibid., 1996, p. 68.

5. A Muslim Perspective

1   Renewing and conciliation of what we Muslims generally consider
     the Islamic 'law'.

2   T. Ramadan, *Radical Reform: Islamic Ethics and Liberation* (Oxford,
     UK: Oxford University Press, 2008.

3   A. Badawi, *Averroès, Ibn Rush*, Paris: Librairie philosophique J.
     Vrin, 1998, translated by L. Zahed.

4   Averroès, *Discours décisif*, Traduction de Marc Geoffroy, Paris:
     Flammarion, 1996, translated by L. Zahed.

5   Celaledin Rumi Mevlana (1207–73) was a thirteenth century
     Persian Muslim poet, jurist, theologian and Sufi mystic. Rumi is a

descriptive name meaning 'Roman' since he lived most of his life in an area called 'Rum' (then under the control of Seljuq dynasty) because it was once ruled by the Eastern Roman Empire.

6   Rumi and E. Vitray-Meyerovitch, *Discourses of Rumi (Or Fihi Ma Fihi)*. Based on the original translation by A.J. Arberry (Iowa: ACEND, 2011, translation by L. Zahed. These debates around the use and limitations of the reason are very old. From the early centuries of Islam, in fact, theologians have understood that they could not decouple the understanding of the religion from understanding the world. This is what we call in Islam *usul al-fiqh*: the foundations of understanding of the Law.

7   Using enlightened reason to reform the representation that each individual can develop towards the spirit of Islam.

8   From the radical *bid'* – begin a new action.

9   In the early days of Islam, the special practice of *zawadj mout'a* – a marriage of convenience – allowed two people to be married for a limited period of time, without consulting anyone else. Some Shia Muslims still practise this type of marriage, while the Sunni Muslims are generally fiercely opposed to it. To learn more: http://www.zawajalhalal.com/ fb_cb/89c837a62566d7add68851ae8b665909/video/cheikh-explique-et-justifie-pratique-islamique-al-zawaj-muta-mariage-temporaire.html. Eventually, remember that some authors point out rightly that *zawj* – 'spouse' in Arabic – is neutral. See A. Habib, *Arabo-Islamic Texts on Female Homosexuality, 850–1780 AD*, Londres: Teneo Press, 2009. And since nowhere does Islam condemn gender and sexual diversity as such, everyone would be free to develop his own choices, at peace with the nature that God has given him/her. See the article 'Homosexuality is not a sin by nature according to Islam': http://www.homosexuels-

musulmans.org/homosexuality-is-not-a-sin-perversion-according-to-islam.html.

10 Because they have been raised in Muslim families, where they were educated a certain way, they do give great importance to marriage, children and filiation matters. Not to mention the very positive psychological effects, on self-esteem and facilitating the projection in the future among others, regardless of the origin of the individuals concerned, that may have the simple freedom to choose: to choose to marry, or not, to conceive or adopt children, or not.

11 Recall that seven European countries, including Spain and Portugal, now allow marriage for same sex couples, while France is still debating about it. Learn more: http://www. touteleurope. eu/index.php?id=5560.

12 Caliph Omar has a dynamic representation of the spirit of Islam and was known to adapt the prophetic example – Sunna – to daily contingencies.

13 A prophetic tradition that seems to warn against excessive wealth in Islamic law – Abu Dawud: 4607; Tirmidhi: 2676; Ibn Majah: 43. Yusuf ibn 'Abd al-Barr 'Al-Tamhid li-Ma fi al-Muwatta' min al-Ma'ani wa al-Asanid', 18.4 (1999): 93–95, 100. Al-Faruq al-Haditha li-al-Tiba'a, Cairo.

14 Yusuf ibn 'Abd al-Barr, 'Al-Tamhid li-Ma al-Muwatta' min al-Ma'ani wa al-Asanid', 18.4 (1999): 93–95, 100. Al-Faruq al-Haditha li-al-Tiba'a, Cairo.

15 And all *mu'amalat* are allowed, according to all the main Muslim scholars from the early centuries of Islam, until Islamic 'law' – *fiqh*, or 'understanding' – says why exactly one of them should be prohibited for a precise, reasonable cause – or *'ilat*. See T. Ramadan, *Radical Reform: Islamic Ethics and Liberation*, chapter 1, Oxford, UK: Oxford University Press, 2008.

16 http://www.nawawi.org/downloads/article4.pdf. Dr Abdallah is
president of the American foundation Al-Nawawi, named after the
famous hadith scholar and commentator of the thirteenth century.

17 Ibn 'Arabi, *Meccan revelations*, translated by L. Zahed.

18 M. Chodkiewicz, 'Mystique, culture et société', organised at the
Sorbonne in 1983; acte du colloque, p. 30.

19 Fazlur Rahman, *Islam and Modernity: Transformation of an Intellectual
Tradition*, Chicago: University of Chicago Press, 1982, pp. 7–8.

20 Makdisi, *Rise of Colleges: Institutions of Learning in Islam and the West*
(Edinburgh: Edinburgh University Press, 1984, pp. 2, 66.

21 'Ali ibn al-Qassar, *Al-Muqaddima fi al-Usul*, (ed.) Muhammad ibn
al-Husayn al-Sulaymani, Beirut: Dar al-Gharb al-Islami, 1996,
pp. 114–15; Sulayman ibn Khalaf al-Baji, (ed.), *Abd al-Majid al-
Turki, Ihkam al-Fusul Ihkam fi Ahkam al-Usul*, Vol. 2, Beirut: Dar
al-Gharb al-Islami, 1995, pp. 714–16; 'Ubayd-Allah ibn 'Umar
al-Dabbusi, 'Al-Asrar fi al-Usul waal-Furu' fi Taqwim Adillat
al-Shar', (ed.) Mahmud Tawfiq al-Rifa'i, Vol. 3, pp. 114–16; Ibn
Amir al-Hajj, *Al-Taqrir wa al-Tahbir*, Vol. 3, Beirut: Dar al-Kutub
al-'Ilmiyya, 1983, p. 306.

22 'Adil 'Abd al-Qadir Quta, Al-'Urf: *Hujjiyyatuhu wa Atharuhu fi Fiqh
al-Mu'amalat al-Maliyya 'inda al-Hanabila*, Vol. 2, Mecca: al-Maktaba
al-Makkiyya, 1997, p. 64.

23 *I'lam al-Muwaqqi'in'*, in 'Adil Quta, '*Al-'Urf'*, 1:65. 26; Qur'an 21.7.

24 Tareq Oubrou, *L'Unicité de Dieu. Des Noms et des Attributs divins*
[opuscule n. 1], Bayane Editions, (translated by L. Zahed), 2006,
p. 25, n. 14.

25 Hadith reported by Tirmidhi, quoted by Imam al-Nawawi in his
very famous book *Ryadh al-Salihin*, hadith n. 234.

26 A. Bidar, *L'islam sans soumission: pour un existentialisme musulman*,
Paris: Albin Michel, 2008, p. 36 (translated by L. Zahed).

27 The question here is not about idealising the 'West' versus 'the Orient', especially when one considers the relative freedom in the Ottoman Empire, e.g., in connection with a Europe often described as puritanical until the modern era. See K. El-Rouayheb, *Before Homosexuality in the Arab-Islamic World, 1500–1800*, Chicago: University of Chicago Press, 2009; and W. Andrews and M. Kalpakli, *The Age of Beloveds: Love and The Beloved IinEarly-Modern Ottoman and European Culture And Society*, Durham, N. Carolina: Duke University Press, 2005.

28 Although both Islam and Arabic 'culture' are intrinsically linked, the Arab peoples undertook their societal revolutions many years ago, of which political revolutions are considered to be a consequence. See E. Todd, *Allah n'y est pour rien*, Paris: Le Publieur, 2011. We reject the essentialising of Arabic 'culture' (very diverse, not monolithic), just as we reject the essentialising of Islam as inherently misogynistic and homophobic.

29 See the principles of the Protestant Reformation, among which the 'universal', pp. 350–51 de «*Priesthood of All Believers*», L. Siegele-Wenschkewitz in *The Encyclopedia of Christianity*, Grand Rapids, Michigan: Eerdmans Publishing, 2005.

30 V. Segesvary, *L'islam et la réforme*, Lanham, Maryland: University Press of America, 1998, p. 26.

31 Bidar, *L'islam sans soumission*, p. 47.

32 S. Shirazi, cited in H. Cobrin, *Corps spirituel et Terre céleste, de l'Iran mazdéen à l'Iran shi'ite*, Paris: B. Chastel, Paris, 1979, p. 194.

33 Rumi, *Discourses of Rumi* (translation from the French version of the book by L. Zahed).

34 E. Geoffroy, *L'islam sera spirituel ou ne sera plus*, Paris: Seuil, 2009.

35 A. Berthoz, *La decision*, Paris: Odile Jacob, 2003.

36 Rumi, *Discourses of Rumi*.

37 Ibn 'Arabi, *Meccan Revelations*, p. 13; Qur'an 27.38–42.

38 Ecclesiastes: 1.2. Ibn 'Arabi gives us a great theophany: 'The divine order has spread within the existing as light propagates through the ether. So the causes, reasons and effective laws [of divine manifestation] appeared, while each existing, losing sight of its essential origin, its relativity and causality, proclaimed: "Me!" and swelled with importance. Beings have competed with pride, and hurt each other, forgetting from Which they derived their pride and claims, considering with pride their lustrous relationship with Him and their divine causality. Thus, appeared pride in the world, without the divine supremacy manifested in an appropriate way. For such an event, in fact, depends on who is filled with real pride, and that One is God, the August, the Most Wise. Ibn 'Arabi, *Le Livre des théophanies d'Ibn Arabi: Introduction philosophique, commentaire et traduction annotée du Kitâb al-tajalliyât* (The Book of Theophanies), Theophany n. 13, Cerf, 2000, (translated by L. Zahed).

39 Plato, *Republic*, New York: Oxford University Press, 2008.

40 R. Guénon, *L'homme et son devenir selon le Védânta*, Paris: Editions traditionnelles, 2000, chap. XI. According to Ibn 'Arabi, the science of letters is a secret science which is the privilege of insiders who have a pure heart, just as pure as prophets and saints'; a science that is the divine Breath and articulated elements of the Word. Ibn 'Arabi, *Le livre du Mîm, du Wâw et du Nûn*, Paris: Al-Bouraq, 2002.

41 Prayer known as the universal Compassion Buddha and meaning *'Peace be upon you, O jewel [hidden] in the lotus.'*

42 Ibn 'Arabi, *Le Livre des théophanies d'Ibn Arabi*, p. 239.

43 Ibn 'Arabi, *Traité de l'amour*, Paris: Albin Michel, 1986. According to Maurice Gloton, the idea is that the human being is the ultimate manifestation of the *'divine Eros'*.

44 Ibn 'Arabi, *Le Livre des théophanies d'Ibn Arabi*, n. 12.

45 *Lo! We offered the trust unto the heavens and the earth and the hills, but they shrank from bearing it and were afraid of it. And man assumed it. Lo! He hath proved a tyrant and a fool.* (Qur'an 33.72)

46 Particularly regarding the eschatological fact, dealing with the world of the afterlife and religious cosmogony – from the Greek *eschatos*, 'last', and logos, 'word'. This is a rather complex notion around which Ibn 'Arabi seems to turn; it is a category of the mind that seems to completely escape the 'categories' of Aristotle, but also the 'reason' of Descartes. This is the *hayra* – this perplexity which, in its accomplished stage, becomes stupor. This is what Ibn 'Arabi calls 'the Tawheed of contemplation' or the 'white light' of knowledge; a concept of the 'vision' of God close to that of the 'cloud of unknowing' of the anonymous Christian Platonist, or the discovery of 'emptiness' – *shunyata* – of Zen Buddhism produced by the discovery of enlightenment – *satori*. In short, human reason, according to Islamic Sufism, cannot understand the reason that God chose to create us as we are, yet we are, potentially, the 'apple of His eyes' according to Ibn 'Arabi. See Ibn 'Arabi, *Le Livre des théophanies d'Ibn Arabi*, pp. 85–92.

47 'Theophany (from the Ancient Greek (ἡ) θεοφάνεια theophaneia, meaning 'appearance of god') is the appearance of a deity to a human.' (Wikipedia)

48 Ibn 'Arabi, *Le Livre des théophanies d'Ibn Arabi*, n. 74.

49 *Verily We have honoured the children of Adam. We carry them on the land and the sea, and have made provision of good things for them, and have preferred them above many of those whom We created with a marked preferment.* (Qur'an 17.70)

50 Rumi, *Discourses of Rumi* (translated by L. Zahed).

51 Ibn 'Arabi, *Meccan Revelations.*

52 Ibn 'Arabi, *Meccan Revelations.*

53 Reza Shah-Kazemi, *Common Ground between Islam and Buddhism,* Louisville: Fons Vitae, 2011.

54 Ibn 'Arabi, *Meccan Revelations.*

55 Abd al-Karīm al-Jīlī, or Abdul Karim Jili, was a Muslim Sufi saint and mystic born in 1366 at Jil in Baghdad. He is famous in Muslim mysticism as the author of *Universal Man.* Abd al-Karîm al-Jīlî, *Universal Man,* Cheltenham, UK: Beshara Publications, 1995.

56 Majid Tehranian and Daisaku Ikeda, *Global Civilization: A Buddhist–Islamic Dialogue,* London: I.B. Tauris, Bloombury, 2003, p. 50.

57 T.W. Adorno, *Dialective negative,* Suisse: Payot, 1978.

58 J.S. Stanford, *The Jews of the Ottoman Empire and the Turkish Republic,* Londres: MacMillan, 1991, p. 25.

59 Malcolm Edwards; 'The queer Christ', in E. Stuart, *Religion is a Queer Thing,* Cleveland, Ohio: The Pilgrim Press, 1997, p. xx.

60 E. Stuart, 'Sex in Heaven', in Davies and Loughin, *Sex These Days* (Sheffield, UK: Sheffield Academic Press, 1997.

61 L. Zahed's article for HM2F: 'Homosexuality is not a sin by nature according to Islam, neither a crime, nor a perversion, nor a pathology', http://www.homosexuels-musulmans.org/ homosexuality-is-not-a-sin-perversion-according-to-islam.html.

62 S. Moscovici, *Psychologie sociale,* Paris: PUF, 2003.

63 E. Todd, *Allah n'y est pour rien,* Paris: Le Publieur, 2011.

64 L. Boltanski and L. Thevenot, *De la justification/les économies de la grandeur,* Paris: Gallimard, 1991; F. Zourabichvili, *Qu'est-ce qu'un devenir pour Gilles DeleuzeI,* Paris: Horlieu, 1997; F. Mernissi, *Comprendre pour se dépasser,* 'Lamalif, n 175, March 1986', pp. 58–59.

65 Judith Butler, *Precarious Life*, New York: Verso, 2006, http://humanities.wisc.edu/assets/misc/Butler.pdf, pp. 7, 8.

66 El-Rouayheb, *Before Homosexuality in the Arab-Islamic World, 1500–1800*, p. 241. See also Andrews and Kalpakli, *The Age of Beloveds*, Durham: Duke University Press, 2004.

67 M. Foucault, *La volonté de savoir*, Paris: Gallimard, 1976.

68 Belief that members of the in-group are more human than the out-group. J.P. Leyens, 'Retrospective and Prospective Thoughts About Infrahumanization', in *Group Processes and Intergroup Relations*, Vol. 12, No. 6, pp. 807–19.

69 F. Fanon, L'Algérie se dévoile, 'L'An V de la révolution algérienne', Paris: La Découverte, 2001. Amina Wadud, for instance, sees the headscarf as the sine qua non condition to penetrate the most conservative Islamic circles, and without which she said she would not be taken seriously by the majority of her opponents.

70 A. Najmabadi, *Women with Mustaches and Men without Beards: Gender and Sexual Anxieties of Iranian Modernity*, Berkeley: University of California Press, 2005.

71 D. Buchbinder, *Studying Men and Masculinities*, London: Routledge, 2012.

72 R.W. Connell, *Masculinities*, Berkeley: University of California Press, 1995, 2005.

73 Fatima Mernissi, *Women and Islam: An Historical and Theological Inquiry*, Oxford: Basil Blackwell, 1991; Everett Rowson, American Oriental Society, http://www.jstor.org/discover/10.2307/603399?uid=3738016&uid=2129&uid=2&uid=70&uid=4&sid=21102425325177.

74 Graduating in history of religions from Duke University, born in Hawaii, he is one of the organisers of the annual retreat of LGBT Muslims in Philadelphia.

75 Rouayheb, *Before Homosexuality in the Arab-Islamic World, 1500–1800*.

76 A graduate in literature from the University of Sydney, she is one of the experts on female homosexuality in Islam.

77 Judith Butler used that term, defined in the speech acts theory (part of the philosophy of language), to refer to politically oriented sentences which are not only passively describing a given reality – here, sexual orientation – but which are changing the (social) reality they are describing.

78 K. Ali, *Sexual Ethics and Islam: Feminist Reflections on Qur'an, Hadith, and Jurisprudence*, (New York: Oneworld, 2006.

79 Born in Jordan in 1963, Massad graduated in political science from Columbia University. He is sometimes considered to be the heir of Edward Said, fierce opponent to all forms of Orientalism.

80 K. Blaser, *La théologie au XXe siècle: histoire, défis, enjeux*, Suisse: L'Age d'homme, 1995.

81 Grand opening of Vatican II by Pope John the 23rd's speech, on 11 October 1962, integral texts available online.

82 G. Goldstein, *Kelines lexicon zur theologie der befreiung*, Dusseldorf: Patmos, 1991.

83 Introspection and first axioms, conversion, metacognition.

84 T. Ramadan, *Radical Reform: Islamic Ethics and Liberation* Newe York: Oxford University Press, 2008.

85 Houria Bouteldja, spokesperson of the anti-racist organisation Les indigènes de la République, has been accused of 'anti-white racism' before being relaxed. See the article in Rue89: http://www.rue89.com/2011/10/07/bouteldja-peut-dire-souchiens-le-racisme-anti-blancs-nest-rien-225122.

86 M. Warner, *The Trouble with Normal: Sex, Politics, and the Ethics of Queer Life*, New York: The Free Press, 1999.

87   Born on 8 June 1928 in Lima (Peru), he was a priest, philosopher and theologian. Considered to be the father of liberation theology, he became a Dominican monk in 1998.

88   I. Gebara, 'Théologie de la libération au féminin et théologie féministe', in *Théologies de la liberation*, Paris: L'Harmattan, 2000.

89   Sociologist, philosopher and Iranian political activist, he was born near Sabzevar in November 1933 and was assassinated in Southampton, 19 June 1977. He remains a prominent figure of what could be called the Islamic theology of liberation movement.

90   M. Amaladoss, *Vivre en liberté*, Bruxelles: Lumen Vitae, 1998.

91   Hematologist doctor at Children's Hospital in Rabat, Morocco, Lamrabet is a Muslim intellectual engaged in thinking about women in Islam.

92   Referring to one of the verses of the Qur'an – particularly liked by alternative progressive, inclusive Muslims – about the fact that human beings are the *khalif,* 'successors' of God on Earth, creators of possibles.

93   A. Lamrabet, *Islam – femmes – occident*, Paris: Séguier, 2011.

94   F. Esack, *Qur'an, Liberation and Pluralism: An Islamic Perspective of Interreligious Solidarity against Oppression*, New York: Oneworld, 1997.

95   A. Wadud, *Inside the Gender Jihad: Women's Reform in Islam* Londres: Oneworld Publications, 2006.

96   Contribution of Abdennur Prado (President of the Spanish Conference on Islamic Feminism, Barcelona, former president of the *Junta Islamica*) in K. Al, J. Hammer and J. Silvers (eds), *A Jihad for Justice: Honoring the Work and Life of Amina Wadud* (dir.), 48hrsbooks. com, United States, http:// www.bu.edu/religion/ files/2010/03/ A-Jihad-for-Justice-for-Amina-Wadud-2012–1.pdf.

97 Ibid., p. 33.

98 J.E. Muños, *Disidentifications: Queers of Color and the Performance of Politics, Cultural Studies of the Americas,* Minnesota: University of Minnesota Press, 1999.

99 J. Estermann et al, *Teologica Andina: el tejido diverso de la fe indígena. Tomo I,* Bolivia: Instituto Superior Ecuménico Andino de Teologia, 2009.

100 Praxis encompasses more than just actions; it includes changing societal representations and habits.

101 Often also today, after the 'Arab Spring', targeted by extremists from all sides.

102 See the article by Bernard Faure in *Sciences Humaines* about the evolution of the representation commonly shared about Buddhism as a tolerant religion: http://www.scienceshu- maines. com/le-bouddhisme-une-religion-tolerante_fr_12908.html.

103 Imam Daayiee Abdullah is a gay Muslim who aids in the fight against discrimination and hatred towards homosexuals and Muslims alike. Wikipedia.

Index

Note: figures in bold denote chapter numbers and verses of religious scriptures

Aarons, Leroy, 139
Abdallah, Umar Faruq, 220
Abdullah, Imam Daayiee, 211
Abimelech, King, 111
abomination, 102–4, 106, 178, 191, 197; Bible and, 102; homosexuality as, 197; sodomy as, 109
Abraham, Prophet, 7, 21, 50, 111, 116, 210, 214, 218, 223
Abrahamic faiths, 22
Ackerman, Susan, 118, 123
Acts **15:20**, 48
Adam, 7, 20, 31, 44, 79–81, 100, 181, 183, 208, 232, 235; children of, 31, 44, 231
adulterers, 178, 180
Africa, 151, 160, 185–90, 192, 194, 200; criminalization of homosexuality in, 186, 192; gay people in, 166, 187; homosexuality in, 159, 193; LGBTI people in, 186; sexual minorities in, 152, 190
al-Ahmad al Sanhaji Qarafi, Abu Abbas, 222
al-Barr, Ibn Abd, 219, 221
al-Dabusi, Abu Zayd, 221
al-djeen, 228
al-Hallaj, Mansur, 212
al-Haqq Kugle, Scott Siraj, 38, 45
Alpert, Rebecca, 143
al-Qaeda, 23
Alternative Islamic liberation theologies, 236–42
Althaus-Reid, Marcella, 143
Amos **4:1–11**, 112
anal sex, 100–101, 107
anti-gay prejudice, 180
anti-women laws, 19
armour-bearer relationship, 118–19, 121, *see also* Jonathan

Armstrong, Karen, 28, 35, 37, 48, 54
Asad, Muhammad, 16, 43, 47–48
Augustine, on celibacy and conversion, 29
Auschwitz, 233

Babylonian Talmud, 114
Bathsheba, 114
believers, 7, 18, 35, 44, 209, 214, 231, 262
Benjamites, 112
Bess, Howard H., 156
Bible, 48, 75, 77–78, 86–87, 96–97, 99–100, 102, 104, 107, 113–16, 125, 142, 154–55, 161–62, 176–77; against aloneness, 86; 'family values' in, 75; and homosexuality, 70; LGBTI lives in, 154; and values affirming sexual diversity, 80–109
Bidar, Abdenour, 224, 226
bisexual, 3, 68–70, 89, 154, 173, 191, 193, 235, 243, 253
Bismil-laah ir Rahmaan ir Raheem, 13, 16, 26, 57, 207
Boisvert, Donald, 143
Books of Kings, 104
Boswell, John, 123
Brooten, Bernadette, 76
Buddhism, 6, 8
Butler, Judith, 236

Calvin, 29

Carr, David, 84
celibacy, 29, 55, 88, 131, (*see also under* Augustine); Armstrong on, 28
Christ, Jesus, 5, 18, 21, 28, 55, 75, 108, 158–59, 170–73, 181–82, 184, 197–98, 212, 225, 227; as final prophet, 7; on love, 55; as Messiah, 182; as saviour, 173; as son of God, 7
Christian: ethics, 174–76, 197–99; gospel, as 'good news,' 153; liberation theology, 236, 239–40
Christianity, 6, 9, 13–15, 17–18, 21–23, 25, 28–37, 45–46, 48, 54, 56–57, 107–8, 153, 155–56, 160, 162–64, 172–74, 189; followers of, 7; idea of loving God in, 6; sub-groups in, 7
Chronicles, 104
Church, 49, 109, 153, 157–58, 160, 164, 170, 172, 174, 196–98
colonialism, 159–60, 166, 183, 189, 241
companionship, 78, 80–83, 130, 177, 197
compassion, 13, 15, 17–19, 32, 35, 43, 56, 65, 94–95, 226, 229–30
'compulsory heterosexuality,' 69
concubines, 75, 111–12, 114, 129
Connell, Raewyn, 237
Connoley, John Tyler, 170–71
conservatives, 128, 135, 175–76

1 Corinthians, 94, 100, 107; **6:9–10**, 164; **6:9–11**, 180; **7:4**, 129; **12:1–21**, 158; **13:11**, 138
Coward, Colin (Rev), 157
creation of human beings, 209; as sexual, 27
creation stories, 80, 182
criminalization: of homosexuality, 166, 186, 192; of same-sex relationships, 186–87, 191
cultic prostitution, 107–8
culture, 3–5, 67, 161–67

David, 114–26, 180; 'armour-bearer' for Saul, 117; faces Goliath, 119; marries Michal, 120; Saul plots against, 119
Day of Judgement, 32, 46
Defence of Marriage Act (DOMA), 41
Deuteronomy **6:5**, 87; **7:3**, 116; **7:25–26**, 102; **16:20**, 95; **17:1**, 105; **18:9–12**, 102; **19:19**, 105; **21:18–21**, 48; **22:5**, 105; **23:27**, 107; **24:1**, 28; **24:4**, 105; **25:16**, 105; **30:19**, 85; **32:16**, 103
Diary of a Gay Priest, 157
discrimination, 33, 42, 152, 154, 162, 173, 188, 200, 232
disobedience, 7, 222
diversity, 4–5, 8, 43, 77, 140, 207, 211–13, 215, 230, 232–35, 240; Qur'anic creation of, 45
djeen, 208–9, 228

doctrines, 7, 68, 175
double life, 249, 256
'down low' as DL, 193
Dzmura, Noach, 144

Ecclesiastics **4:9–11**, 181
ecstasy, 133–34
Edib, Halide, 52
Edward II and Piers Gaveston, 123
Edwards, Malcolm, 234
empathy (karuna), 8
Ephesians 6: 12, 156
eroticism, 125, 132
Esack, Farid, 240
ethics, 21, 23–24, 78, 106, 110–11, 127, 131–33, 152, 174–75, 222
Eve, 7, 80–82, 100, 130, 177, 196
Exodus **6:20** vs. Leviticus **18:12**, 116; **8:22**, 103; **22:21**, 96; **25:8**, 91
extremism, 13, 22
Ezekiel, 104, 113; sexual *toevah* and, 104; **8:1–18**, 104; **16:49–50**, 113, 176, 178
Ezra **9:1**, **9:11** and **9:14**, 104

Faderman, Lillian, 69
Fall, 29–30
family values, 29, 75, 129, 166, 186
feminine, 9, 143–44
feminist theology, 141; in Islam, 35

Festival of Theology, 25
fornication, 29, 178, 180, *see also*
    abomination
Four Fs, 37–38
Frank, Barney, 95
Fyzee, A.A., 15

Galatians **5:22– 23**, 174, 196
Garden of Eden, 29–30
Gaveston, Piers, 123
gay, 3, 65, 67–68, 70–71, 73,
    88–89, 91–92, 97, 100–101,
    122–23, 127–28, 135–37, 139,
    143–46, 156–57, 163–65,
    169–71, 188–89, 193–94,
    245–47, 251–52, (*see also*
    homosexuals); mob attack
    on, 155; parents, 97, 128;
    recognition, 40; relationships,
    171, 180
'gay sexual ethic,' 132
'gay spirituality,' 144
Geertz, Clifford, 175
gender: identity, 66, 91, 152,
    186–87, 215–16, 219, 230;
    minorities, 141–44, 146
'Gender complementarity,' 72
Genesis, 78, 81–82, 84–85, 93,
    103, 109–10, 116, 164, 178,
    196; **1:22**, 177; **1:28**, 196; **2:18**,
    78, 81, 84, 98; **2:18–25**, 78;
    18:8, 116; **19**, 109–10; **20:12**,
    116; **43:32**, 103; **45:1**, 93
Genesis Rabbah **42, 49**, 114
Gerar, 111

Global Interfaith Network
    (GIN), 191
God: attributes of, 14; capital
    letters for, 8; Fyzee on justice
    of, 15; grace of, 16, 171; as
    just, 16; as love, 83, 173;
    merciful and compassionate,
    14–18, 55; mercy of, 16–18,
    22, 27, 43, 56; as Rahmaan
    and Raheem, 13, 15, 22, 43,
    45, 49, 53–54; as word, 8, 86,
    94; as 'Word of God', 21
God-centred religions, 22, 46
'God versus Gay,' 65–66, 108–9
Goliath, 118–19
Gospel of Matthew, **5:44**, 55;
    8:5–13, 181; **19**, 171; **19:10–
    12**, 170; **22:29–30**, 198
Gospels, The Gay, 154
Gould, Josh, 35
grace, 13, 16–18, 43, 68, 79, 157,
    171, 183, 227
Greenberg, Rabbi Steven, 114,
    123
Griffith, Mary, 139
Gutiérrez, Gustavo, 240

Habib, Samar, 238–39
hadith, 9, 214, 222, 238
Halevy, Judah, 145
Halperin, David, 123, 146
Hammar, Anna Karin, 26
Hanes, Rabbi Meir Baal, 35
Hari-Wonmaly, Azzah, 243
Hashanah, Rosh, 138

Hay, Harry, 144
Hebrew Bible, 17–18, 56, 75, 98,
    102, 110, 112, 115–16; same-
    sex intimacy in, 65
hegemonic masculinity, 237
heterosexuals, 5, 27–28, 30, 55–
    56, 84, 97, 152–54, 169, 171,
    196, 199, 253, 255, 258, 260;
    monogamy, 75
heterosexuality, 70, 114;
    Christianity and, 28, 30
Heyward, Carter, 132, 143
Hijaz, 20
hijra, 146
Hinduism, 6, 8
HIV/AIDS, 157, 191–92, 200;
    and homosexuality in Africa,
    193
homoeroticism, 168, 236, 238
Homophile couples, 198
homophobia, 91, 127, 169, 189,
    192, 199, 214, 234–35, 263
homosexuality, 25–26, 34, 37–39,
    66–67, 70–76, 90–91, 98, 107,
    109, 111–15, 124, 152, 155–56,
    159–70, 169, 174–75, 177, 180,
    184–85, 192–93, 197–98, 249–
    52; among species, 73; in Bible,
    109; condemnation of, 34, 47;
    as crime, 39; in nature, 72–73;
    Quran and, 34; rejection of, 34;
    as 'unnatural,' 38
homosexuals, 41–42, 131, 134,
    165, 167, 169, 174, 176, 184–
    85, 190, 192, 197–98, 246,

249; death penalty for, 178;
    death penalty to, 186; mass
    hatred against, 189; rape,
    110–11; relations, 27
homosociality, 125
honesty, 88–95
honour killings, and Islam, 32
Horner, Tom, 123–24
House of Rainbow Nigeria, 193
human: coupling, 80; dignity, 19,
    43, 83, 215; intimacy, 56, 77,
    86, 130; sexuality, 18–19, 25,
    27, 32, 68, 94, 155, 175, 177,
    196, 198
human rights, 24, 42, 126, 190–
    91, 200, 224
Hume, Cardinal Basil, 83

I am a Woman, 58–62
Ibn Al-Qiyyam, 222
Ibn 'Arabi, 212, 220, 230–33
Ibn Hazm, 221
idolaters, 180, 210
idolatry/idol worship, 102–9,
    113, 180, 184–85, 218;
    Mohammad condemning of,
    218
Ijtihaad, 36, 217–22
Inclusive and Affirming
    Ministries (IAM), 189
infidelity, 7
Initiative for Equal Rights, 190
interfaith dialogue, 18–19, 45
intersex people, 160, 170, 173,
    191

intimacy, 84–85, 94, 130, 197–98
Iqbal, Mohamed/ Muhammad, 36, 51–53, 210
Isaiah **40:26**, 76; **46.5**, 230; **51:1**, 95
Islam, 6–7, 9, 23–25, 27–28, 35–36, 42–43, 49, 51, 207, 211–18, 224–26, 233–35, 237–38, 240, 261; crimes and, 22; followers of, 7; politicisation of, 23; stigmatisation of, 22; sub groups in, 7
Islamic: liberation theologies, 240; marriage, 28; mysticism, 17, 231; queer in traditions of, 8, 25, 27, 31–33, 36, 220, 237; theology of equality and liberation, 233; traditions as anti-women, 32
Islamic State, 23
Islamisation, 19
Islamophobic individuals, 223
Israelites, 91, 96–97, 102–5, 107–8, 116, 118–19

Jainism, 6, 8
Jennings Jr, Theodore W., 118, 123
Jeremiah **1:4–5**, 161; **23:14**, 112
Jesus, *See* Christ, Jesus
Jewish law, 99–101
Jews, sub-groups of Israeli, 7
John **3:16–17**, 153, 195; **20:30–31**, 182
1 John. **4:8**, 83

Johnson, Malcolm, 157
Johnson, Toby, 144
Johnson, William Stacy, 40
John the Baptist, 227
Jonathan, 115–17, 119–25, 180; as armour-bearer, 118; in love with David, 119–20
Joseph, 92–93
Josiah, King, 107
Judaism, 9, 21, 23, 25, 27, 30, 32, 43, 65, 114; idea of jealous God in, 6; followers of, 7
Jude, 114, 164, 178; **1:7**, 178; **7**, 164; **19**, 111–12, 114; **19:22**, 164; **19:25**, 112; **19.54**, 111
Jung, 143
justice, 95–97

Kama Sutra, 'third gender' in, 146
Karim, R.B., 243
karma, 5–9
Kecia Ali, 239
Kennedy, Anthony, 41
Kingdom of God, 28, 180, 184
Kings, Dr, 136
1 Kings 14:24, 107
Kippur, Yom, 138
Knight, Michael Muhammad, 240
Kugle, Scott, 238

laa ilaaha il-Allah, 49, 53, 56
Lamrabet, Asma, 240
Last Day, 46
LaVey, Simon, 73
law of grace, 16

'lesbian continuum,' 69, 124
lesbianism, 99–100; Jewish law
    and, 100
lesbians, 65, 68, 70–71, 97,
    99–100, 102, 135, 137, 139,
    144–45, 161, 164–65, 167;
    children of, 128
Leviticus, 34, 79–80, 92, 94–96,
    98–109, 113, 116, 121, 164,
    178; homosexual temple
    prostitution in, 178; **11:10–13**,
    106; **18**, 103, 121; **18:9–11**,
    116; **18:21**, 107; **18:22**, 34, 79,
    98–102, 105–9, 164; **18:26–
    27**, 103; **18:29**, 103; **19:34**,
    96; **20:10,** 11, 178; **20:13**, 34;
    25:10, 95
Leviticus Rabbah **5**, 114
LGBT, 67, 88, 90, 125–26, 143,
    145, 147, 207, 239–40, 263;
    equality and, 126–27; Jews
    and, 65
LGBTIQs, 160–61, 163–64,
    170, 172, 174, 242, 255–56;
    Africans, 186; asylum seekers,
    185, 187–88; Christians,
    154–55, 173; clergy, 153;
    community, 153–54, 156–58,
    172, 187, 189–93, 196,
    199–200
LGBTIs, 154–55, 157, 173, 190–
    91, 194, 196, 200
liberation/kaivalya /moksha/
    nirvana, 8, 24, 95, 207, 233,
    237, 242

licentiousness, 114
loneliness, 66, 81, 85
Lot, 110–11
Louima, Abner, 112
love, 55, 83–88; between men in
    the Bible, 115–26
Luke **6:36**, 18; **7:1–10**, 181;
    14:25–26, 28
lusts, 84, 179
Luther, Martin, 29

Mahabharata, 'third gender' in
    146
Maimonides, 212
Makdisi, George, 221
Malachi 2:11, 105
Malala, 22
male: anal sex, 104, 106–7, 109,
    113; homosexuality, 74–75,
    103; prostitutes, 180
Mark **12:30–31**, 55
marriage, 27–29, 40–41, 120,
    124, 127–29, 174–77,
    197–98, 216, 219–20, 223,
    264; arranged, 75, 129, 264;
    Calvin and, 29; and coming
    out in Islam, 28, 219–23;
    countries of redefining, 175;
    definition of, 175; gay, 41,
    164; heterosexual, 27–28,
    30, 33, 55; interracial, 129;
    interreligious, 129; in Judaism,
    28; of opposite-sex, 41, 130;
    same-sex, 41, 128, 130, 164,
    176; of same-sex unions in

Islam, 216–23; sanctity of, 30; Tertullian and, 29; voluntary, 129; to young children, 75

Marriage (Same Sex Couples) Act, of Church of England, 174

masculine, 9, 142–44

Massad, Joseph, 239

Mataka, Elizabeth, 192

meditation, 6, 151

Melanesian model, 168

Men who sex with men (MSM), 193

Mephibosheth, 122

Mernissi, Fatima, 238

Micah **6:8**, 95, 170, 194

Michal, 120

Miner, Jeff, 170–71

Mishna Avot 5:1, 122

Mohammed/Muhammad, Prophet, 7, 9, 16, 21, 213, 218–19, 223, 225, 229, 233

Molech worship, 106

Mollenkott, Virginia Ramey, 143–44

monogamy, 129; heterosexual, 75

monotheism, 212

Monroe, Irene, 143

Moroccan Islamic feminism, 240

Moses, 103, 126, 183, 231

Murdoch, Iris, 134

Muslims: definition of, 22; foundation of, 22

Muslim women, 20, 23–25, 35, 42, 243; characteristics of, 24

myths, 4, 6, 10, 65, 87, 96, 109, 141, 162

Naomi, 115, 180

Nardelli, Jean-Fabrice, 123

Nathan, Rabbi, 114

Native Americans: traditions of, 144; tribes as third-gender, 74

'natural family,' 72

'natural law,' 75

Nelson, James B., 131, 143

New Testament, 17–18, 28, 55–56, 100, 129

Nissinen, Martti, 123

Noah's story, 174, 182–83

nuclear families, 129

Numbers Rabbah 9, 114

one God, idea of, 5, 8

Ottoman Empire, 9, 225, 234

Oubrou, Tarek, 222

Pakistan, 13, 42, 51–53, 155; terror attacks in, 22

Paramahamsa, Ramakrishna, 213

Parents and Friends of Lesbians and Gays (PFLAG), 138

Pastor, I Am Gay, 156

patriarchal culture, 30, 33

Pentateuch, 55

persecution, 54, 154, 187

Philip II and Richard, 123

Philistines, 118–20, 122

Philo, 76

platonic love, 123

'Political Islam,' 23

polyandry, 175

polygamy, 75, 129, 175

polytheism, 211

prejudices, 55, 134–36, 152, 166, 200, 216, 222, 226, 232, 241

procreation, 81, 130, 168, 197; sex and, 30

prostitution, 75, 105, 129, *see also under* cultic; Leviticus

Proverbs, Book of, 105–6

Psalm **19:1**, 76; **101:7–8**, 89; **103**, 18; **139:13–14**, 161

punishment, 178, 184, 191

Queen of Sheba, 228–29

queer, 3–5, 8, 72, 142, 145, 161, 193; dis-identification, 239; in karmic faiths, 8; theology, 141, 143

Quinet, Edgar, 213

Qur'an, 9, 14, 20, 43, 208, 216; **2.30–32**, 235; **6.103**, 230; **7.143**, 231; **17.110**, 233; **21.7**, 222; **29.41**, 217; **31.21**, 223; **38.69**, 235; **42.11**, 230; **43.22**, 223; **49.13**, 235; **53.14,** 229; **53.23**, 223; **61.4**, 235; 'Adam' in, 20; in Arabic, 20; as ehsaan, 15; God's justice in, 15; God's mercy in, 17; marriage in, 28; Surah with Bismil-laah ir Rahmaan ir Raheem, 16; ummah in, 15; as 'the Word of God,' 21

Rabbis, 88, 91, 101, 122

racism, 49, 135, 165

Rahman, Fazlur, 221

rape, 99–100, 110–12, 114, 129, 176, 247, 255

Rashi, 100

religions, 4, 9–14, 189; as cultural system, 152; as source of stories, 4

religious: communities, 66, 68, 91, 131, 135–38, 140–41, 163, 166, 193; consciousness, 127, 139; fundamentalism, 160, 189; homophobia, 188–90; negation of lesbian/gay voices, 68; rights, 72, 169; traditions, 27, 30, 33, 67, 70–71, 77–78, 84, 89, 91, 96, 138, 143, 261

remarriage, 105

Rich, Adrienne, 69

Richard, 123

ritual purity law, 104

Rogers, E.F., 176–77

Romans, 34, 79, 94, 107, 164, 183–84; **1:18–32**, 34; **1:21–28**, 164; **1: 21–32**, 179; **1:26–27**, 100; **1:27**, 79; **1:28–32**, 184; **5:12–15**, 183; **9:19–20**, 193; **9:25–26**, 196

Rowson, Everett, 238

Rumi, Jalaluddin, 36, 57, 145, 215, 217, 226–27, 231

Ruth 1:16–17, 115, 180

same-gender behaviour, 160, 189

same-sex: behaviour, 70, 72, 98; intimacy, 65, 86, 133, 146; marriage rights in US, 41; partners, 73, 219, 223; relationships, 80, 86, 154, 162–63, 166–68, 175, 177, 183, 185, 187, 191, 197, 199–200; romantic love, 125; unions, 101, 151, 200; van Wijk-Bos on, 34

1 Samuel **1:23**, 26–27, 180; **16**, 117–18; **16:7**, 118; **16:12**, 117; **18:1–3**, 119; **19:1**, 120; **20:30–31**, 121; **20:41–42**, 122; **31:5**, 118

2 Samuel **1:18–27**, 122; **1:26**, 176; **9:1–13**, 122; **11:2**–5, 114

Sarah, 111, 116

Saul, King, 117–23

Schimmel, A.M., 50

Scripture, 5, 9, 35, 48, 79, 87, 94, 141, 147, 193, 198

Secret Garden, 246, 250–51, 253

Secret Garden activities, 251

Segesvary, Victor, 224

Semitic language, 20

sex, 83, 85, 89, 100–101, 124, 129, 131, 133, 176–77, 193, 196, 262; Heyward on, 132; legitimacy of, 30; nature of, 198

sexual: ethics, 131, 239; identity, 39, 46, 56, 69–70, 91, 137,

254, 260; minorities, 96–97, 136, 140, 142, 145–46, 151–52, 186, 190, 194, 207, 211, 237; orientation, 39, 91–92, 127–28, 139, 141–42, 151–52, 175, 177, 252, 254, 256–57, 259, 262; violence, 99, 112; Williams on union of, 177

sexual diversity, 68, 71–72, 76–77, 79, 84, 126–34, 136, 140, 143, 160; as God's plan, 72; Jewish perspective on, 73–74

sexuality, 9, 27, 55–56, 68, 70–71, 73–75, 82–84, 125–26, 130–32, 134, 151–53, 161, 185, 191–92, 197

Sexual Orientation and Gender Identity (SOGI), 160, 186–88

Shaitan, 209

Sharia law, 9

Shariati, Ali, 240

Sharpe, Keith, 154, 164

Shir Hashirim Rabbah 1:9, 89

sin, 18, 22, 29, 44, 106–7, 109, 113, 133, 135, 180, 183, (*see also* abomination; fornication); non-heterosexual as, 5; of Sodomites, 110

Soderblom, Nathan, 50

Sodom and Gomorrah, 109–15, 176, 178, 238

Sodomites, 110, 112, 114, 180

sodomy, 70, 109, 113

Solomon, King, 107, 116, 129
Song of Songs, 82, 84–85
Spencer, Daniel, 143
spirituality, 27, 78, 90, 151, 161, 179, 191, 196, 199, 218, 226
Ssemp, Martin, 155
St Ambrose of Milan, 29
St Augustine, 29
St Jerome, 29
St Paul, 28, 75, 129, 138, 158, 184–85; and celibacy, 28; doctrine, 75; indictment of, 184
St Theresa, 134
strange flesh, 178–79
Sullivan, Andrew, 92
Sunna, 216, 218, 221, 235
Surah 2: *Al-Baqarah*: **62**, 45–46; **185**, 16–17; **186**, 17
Surah 3: *Al-'Imraan*: 79, 49
Surah 4: *An-Nisa'* 25–28, 17; **14–15**, 34; **21**, 28; **148–149**, 45
Surah 5: *Al-Maa'idah*: 7, **17**; **32**, 13; **69**, 46
Surah 6: *Al-An'am*: **147**, 17
Surah 7: *Al-'A'raf*: **80–81**, 34
Surah 11: *Hud*: **77–79**, 34
Surah 12: *Yusuf*: **40**, 53
Surah 15: *Al-Hijr*: **67–72**, 34
Surah 16: *An-Nahl*: **120–122**, 50
Surah 17: *Al-'Israa'*: **70**, 31
Surah 21: *Al-Anbiyaa'*: **71**, 74, 34
Surah 24: *An-Nur*: **16–19**, 45
Surah 26: *Ash-Shu'araa'*: **165–168**, 34

Surah 27: *An-Naml*: **54–55**, 34; 62, 17
Surah 29: *Al-'Ankabut*: **1–3**, 54; **28–29**, 34
Surah 30: *Ar-Rum*: **21**, 27
Surah 33: *Al-Ahzab*: **35**, 46
Surah 40: *Ghafir*: **60**, 17
Surah 42: *Ash-Shura'*: **21**, 49
Surah 49: *Al-Hujurat*: **13**, 43
Surah 50: *Qaf*: **16**, 17
Surah 53: *An-Najm*: **43**, 14
Surah 95: *At-Tin*: **3**, 14

Talmud, 9, 122
Tanis, Justin, 144
Tawheed, 49–56, 207–13, 215, 229, 231–32, 234, 240–41
Tehranian, Majid, 233
Tehrike-Taliban, 23
Tertullian, 29
1 Timothy **1:10**, 164
toevah, 99, 101–8, 113
Tolbert, Mary, 182
Torah, 101, 105, 108, 141
Toynbee, Arnold, 45
traditional values, 94, 126–27
transgender, 3, 42, 56, 146, 170, 191, 209, 235, 238, 246
transgress, 76, 220
truth, 4, 10

ummah (ideal society), 15, 262
Unitarian Universalist church, 260

United Nations Assembly,
  decriminalizing
  homosexuality, 187
United States, gays in, 66

van Wijk-Bos, Johanna W.H.,
  34
Vasey, Paul, 73
Vines, Matthew, 151
violence, 13, 45, 69, 104, 114,
  136–37, 141, 155, 191–92,
  232, 236
virginity, 29
vulgar, 127, 131

Wadud, Amina, 240
Williams, Rowan, 177, 197–98
Wilson, Alan, 157
wisdom (pragnya), 8
Wisdom of Solomon, 107
women, 3, 7, 19–20, 24–25, 30–
  34, 44, 46, 68–69, 75–76, 81–
  82, 98–101, 115–16, 135, 141,
  178–79, 237, 239–40; honour
  killing of, 32; as inferior, 31;
  lower status of, 33; Paul on,
  75; Quran and, 30

Yogyakarta Principles, 190, 191